The 1960s
Ireland in Pictures

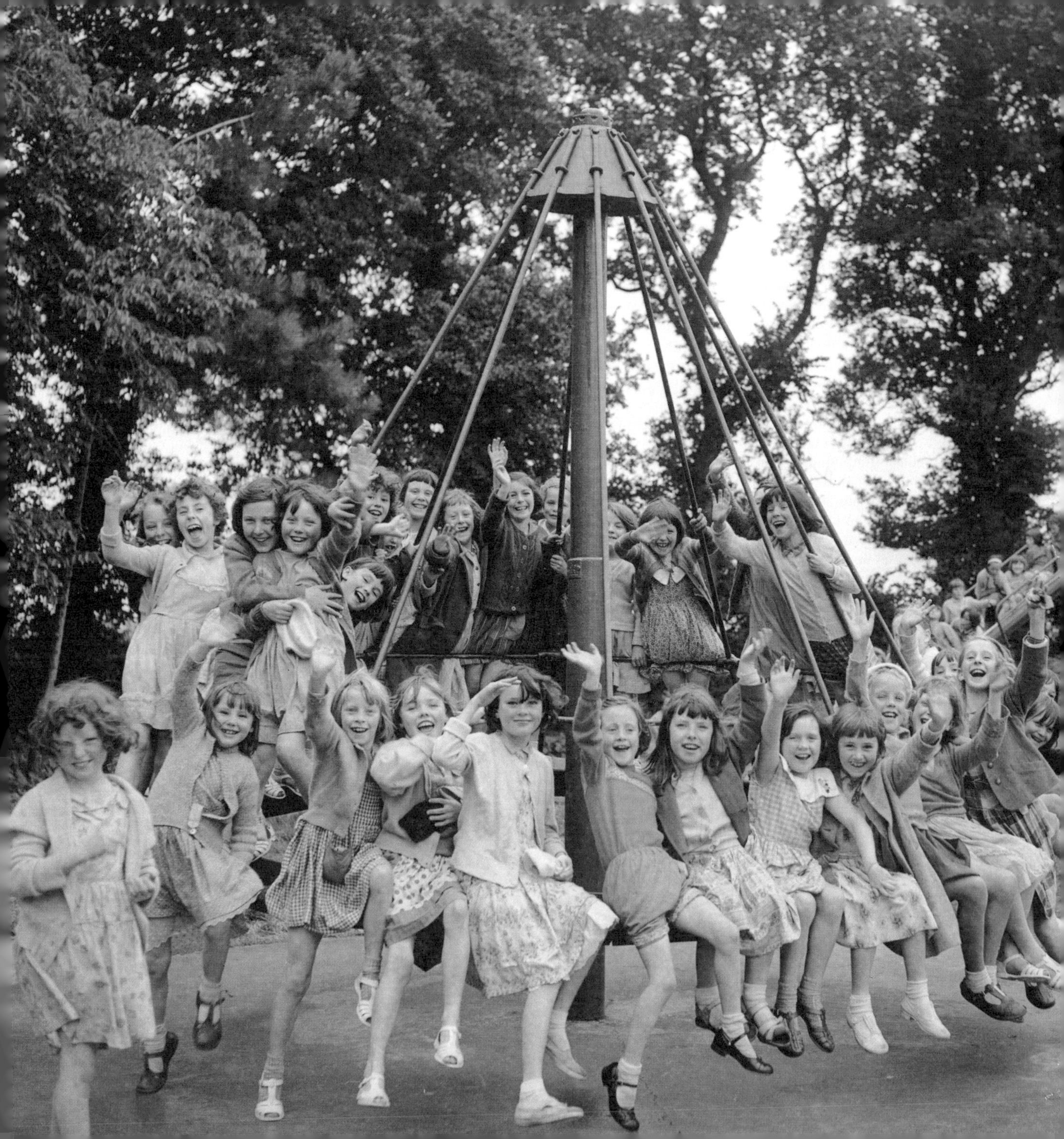

The 1960s
Ireland in Pictures

Lensmen Photographic Archive

THE O'BRIEN PRESS
DUBLIN

City children enjoying the roundabout on a day out.
27 August 1961

First published 2011 by The O'Brien Press Ltd.,
12 Terenure Road East, Rathgar,
Dublin 6, Ireland.
Tel: +353 1 4923333; Fax: +353 1 4922777
E-mail: books@obrien.ie
Website: www.obrien.ie

ISBN: 978-1-84717-303-4

17 Nottingham St., North Strand, Dublin 3, Ireland. Tel: +353 1 8197738
Email: info@lensmen.ie Website: www.lensmen.ie

British Library Cataloguing-in-Publication Data
A catalogue reference for this title is available from the British Library.

1 2 3 4 5 6
11 12 13 14 15 16

Editing: The O'Brien Press Ltd
Design: Sin é design
Printed and bound by GraphyCEMS

Acknowledgements: It would not have been possible to put this book together without the help of the following: Susan Kennedy,
Tara Keown, Jill Quigley, Lydia Diaz Navarro, Eleanor Keegan,
Sarah Knopp, Johanna Korbik, Judith Lutz, Michael O'Neill.
Special thanks to PJ Maxwell for advice on GAA photographs.

Kathleen Watkins waits for the cameras to roll on opening night. Marie O'Sullivan, Nuala Donnelly and Kathleen Watkins were the first women to appear on Teilifís Éireann.
© RTÉ Stills Library.

31 December 1961

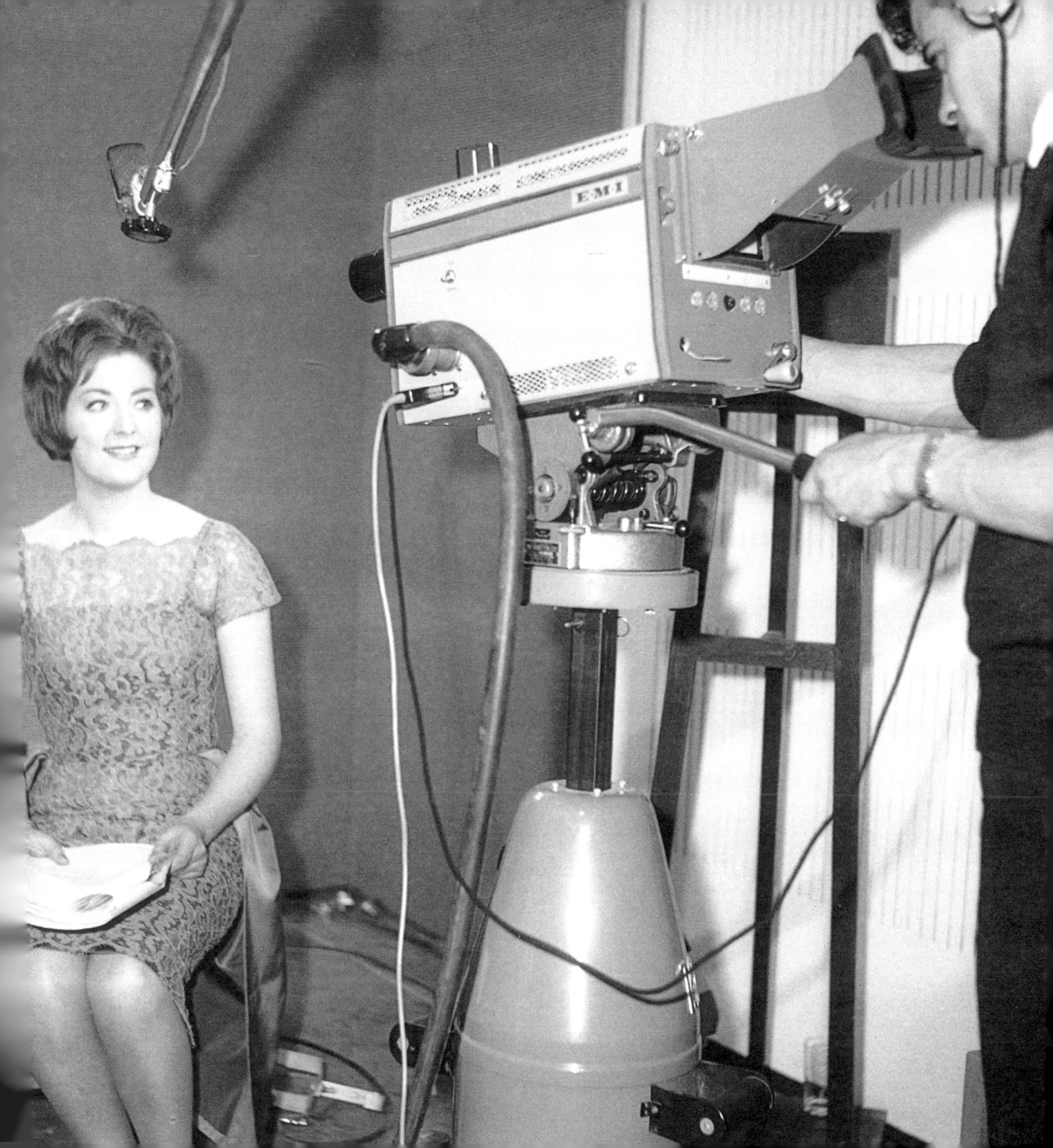
E·M·I

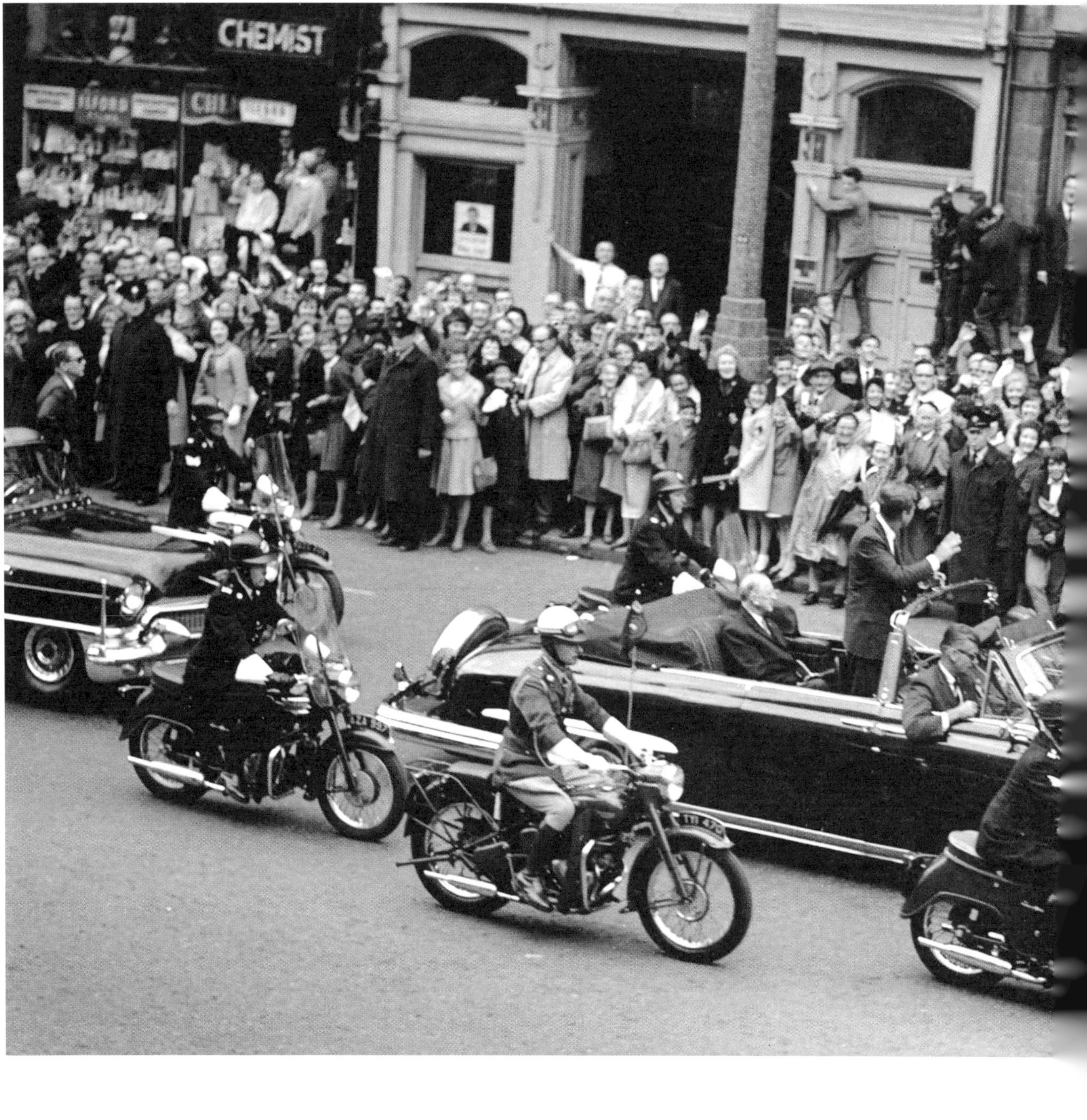
CHEMIST

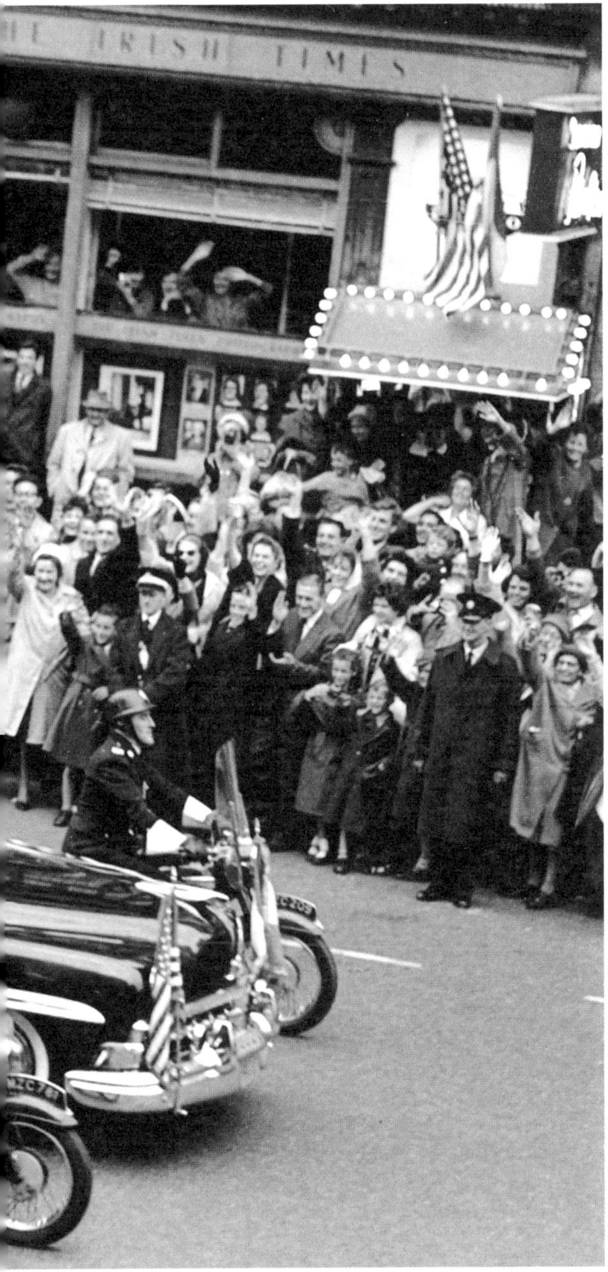

President John Fitzgerald Kennedy is welcomed by thousands as his motorcade travels through Dublin.

26 June 1963

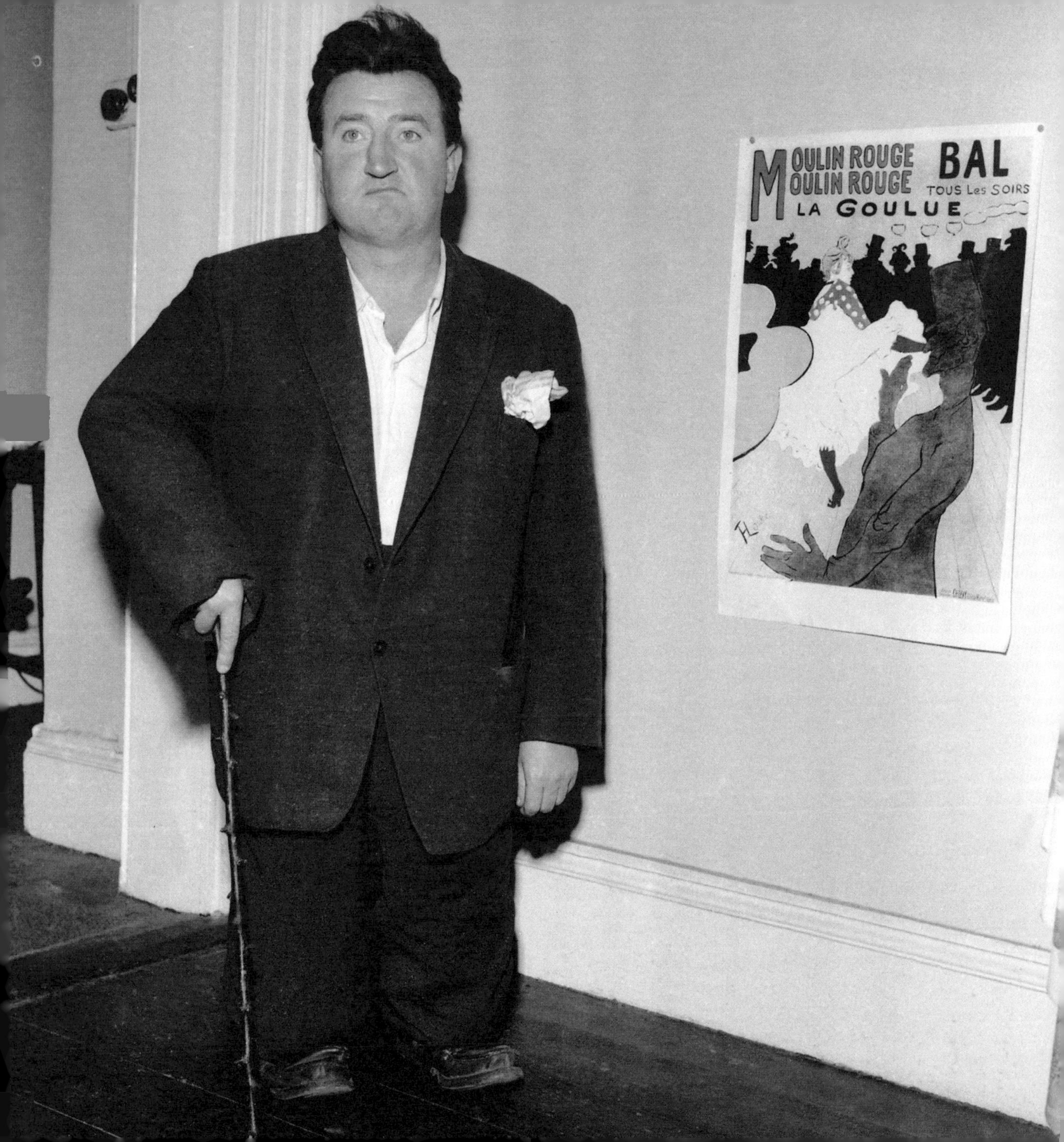
MOULIN ROUGE
MOULIN ROUGE
LA GOULUE
BAL
TOUS Les SOIRS

The Sixties

The 1960s in Ireland was a decade of change. On the one hand there was high unemployment, and the majority of rural school-leavers had no choice but to come to Dublin or emigrate in search of work. Women were forced to leave public service and other jobs when they married. The Rural Electrification Scheme had made great headway but there were pockets of the country still not connected to the grid. Cars, foreign holidays, telephones, and in some cases indoor plumbing were considered luxuries.

But there were signs of progress, and hope for better things was in the air. Taoiseach Sean Lemass brought a modernising influence to Government and with Dr T K Whitaker introduced the revolutionary Programmes for Economic Expansion, the effects of which would be felt for decades to come. The first high-rise blocks at Ballymun were built. The arrival of television in 1961 brought international events and foreign programming, much of it American, into our homes. The iconic 'Late Late Show' arrived in 1962, and our first rural soap, 'The Riordans', followed in 1965.

Dancehalls around the country reverberated to the sounds of the showbands, and while we could not lay claim to being part of the 'Swinging Sixties', the Beatles came, as did the Rolling Stones; hemlines and hairdos rose dramatically, and those big transistor radios were more likely to be switched to Radio Luxembourg or Alan Freeman's 'Top Twenty' than to the Waltons-sponsored Irish music programmes.

The Patrician Year of 1961 was celebrated with great ceremony, although vocations to the priesthood had already begun to plummet. The election of John Fitzgerald Kennedy as first Catholic President of the US was a cause of much rejoicing and his 1963 visit could be described as the highlight of the decade. His assassination threw the country into grief, but we were proud of the young Irish Army cadets who performed the honours at his graveside.

Rising expectations in terms of wages and conditions resulted in strikes by bus drivers, bank clerks, teachers, ESB workers, and the huge farmers' march on Dublin in 1966, to highlight how that sector was being disadvantaged. The Irish army took up UN peacekeeping duties in the Congo and in Cyprus and the subsequent deaths of nine soldiers in the Niemba ambush shocked the country.

In 1966, the year of the 50th Anniversary of the Easter Rising, Nelson's Pillar was blown skyward by an IRA bomb. The Civil Rights movement in Northern Ireland gained momentum and the shadow of 'The Troubles' was felt everywhere from the late Sixties onwards.

As the decade closed, negotiations were ongoing to join the then EEC and we were about to adopt decimal currency.

The pictures in this book are glimpses into Ireland in the 1960s: home life, city, rural and sporting pursuits, political changes, big events; the personalities who entertained us; visits that delighted us and losses that devastated us. For those who remember the Sixties, we hope they bring many moments of recognition; for those who don't, perhaps they will give a feel for what that decade was all about.

Mary Webb, Editor.

Brendan Behan in the guise of Toulouse Lautrec.

1 August 1960

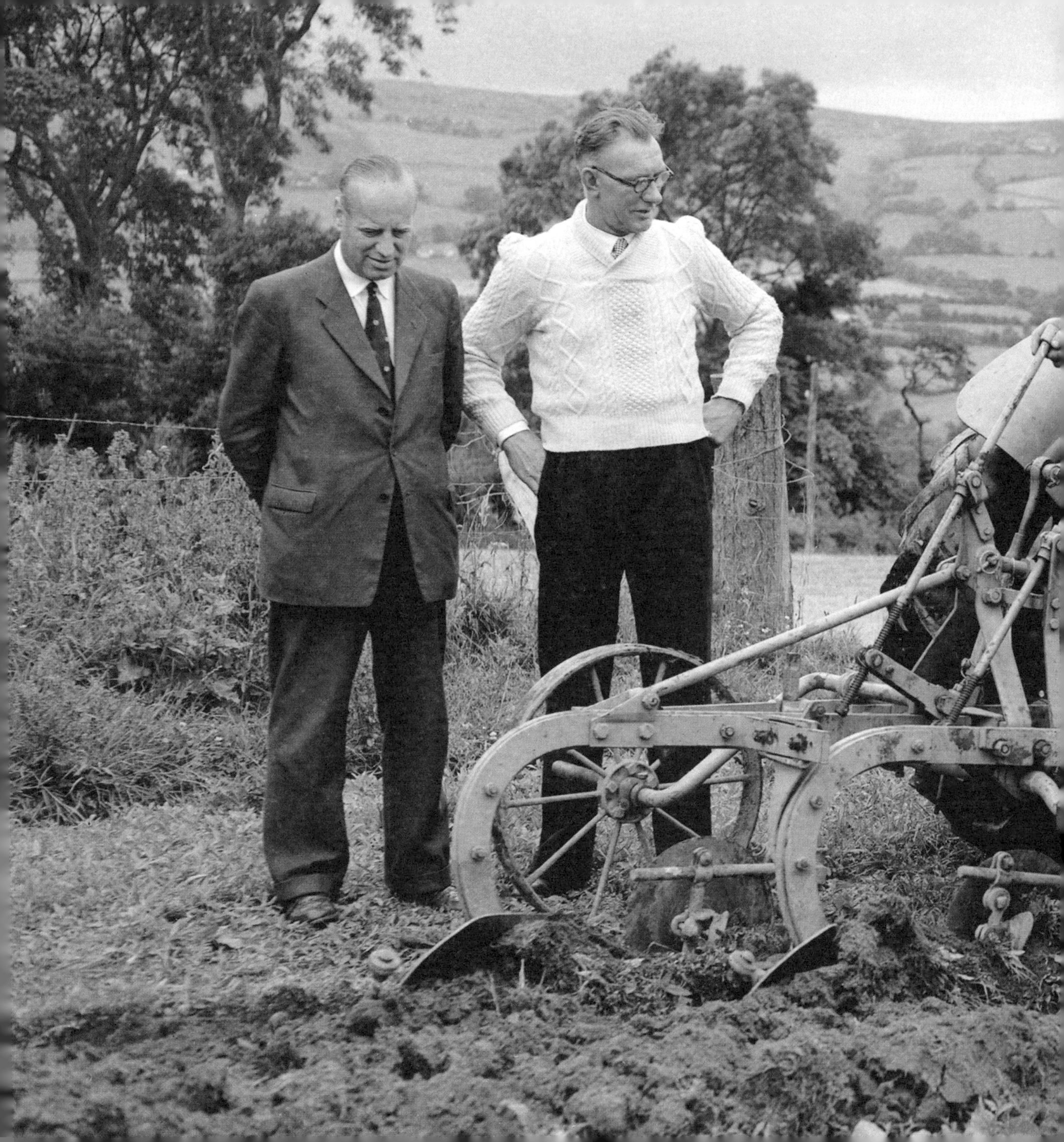

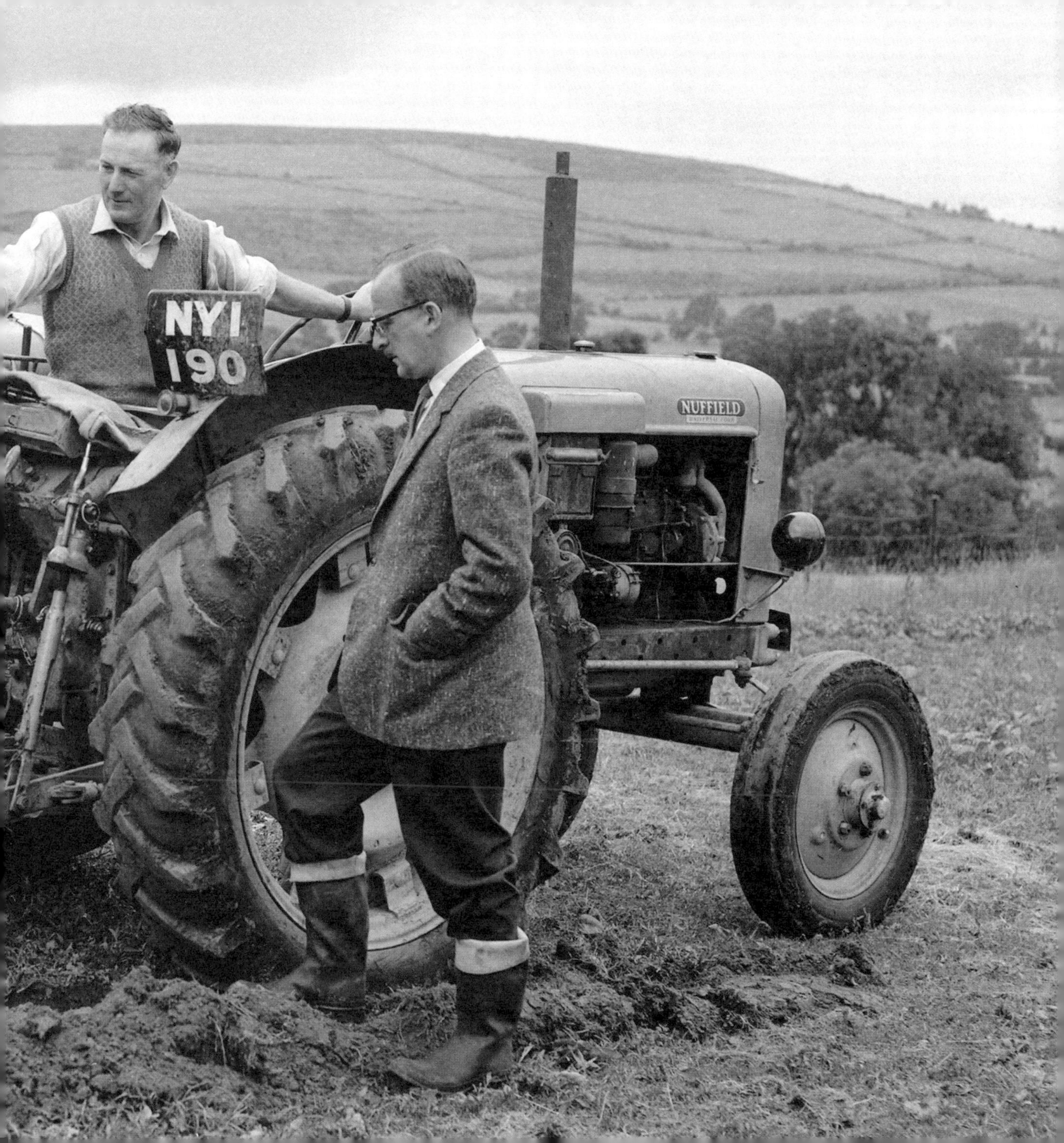
NYI
190
NUFFIELD

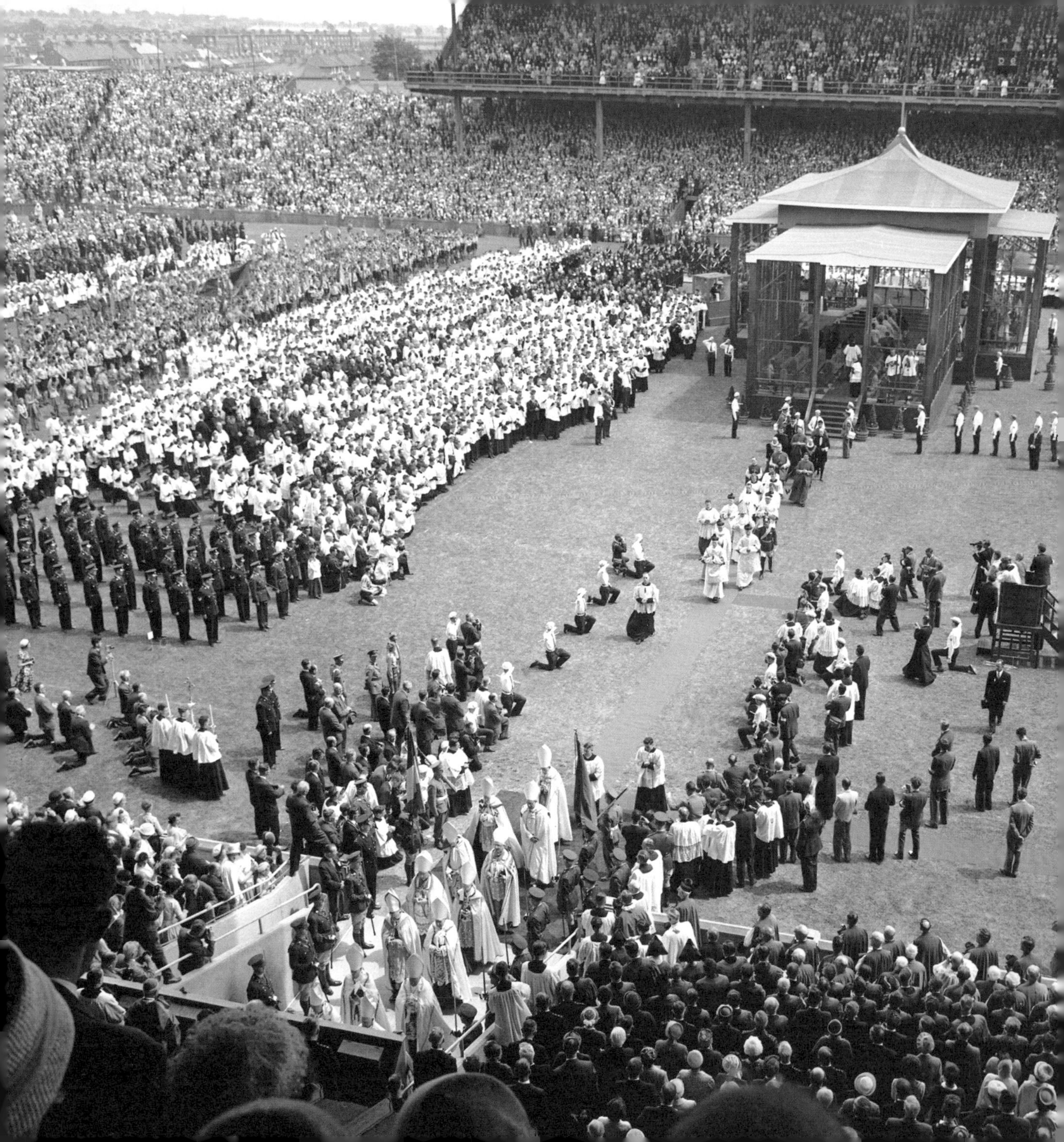

The photographers: Lensmen

Andrew Farren and Pádraig MacBrian were both staff photographers in the Irish Press. Pádraig recalls that his first press photo was of cattle being loaded onto a ship on Dublin's South Wall. At the time, his wages were £1 a week!

In 1952, still only in their twenties, the pair set up Lensmen as a commercial news photographic service, initially in rented offices in Westmoreland Street, Dublin. They covered major news stories for British national newspapers and for the Cork Examiner. In the early 1960s business had expanded substantially, with Lensmen having the agency for all major Irish government departments, as well as working for PR companies and commercial businesses. They bought Nos. 10 and 11 Essex Street, and called it Lensmen House. This developed into a major agency, employing fifteen people, including five photographers. Interestingly, one of their jobs was to take photos of Irish life and events for the Irish editions of British newspapers to replace their 'Page 3 Girl' pictures, which were not considered suitable for Irish readers!

Among the stand-out events they covered were the visits of the Beatles, Princess Grace and President Kennedy. Andy can remember the excitement of being on board one of the US press helicopters going to the Kennedy ancestral home in Dunganstown in 1963.

A key development for the business was the purchase of a wire machine that could transmit photos over the telephone. This was used extensively during the period of Jack Lynch's government, including the fallout from the Northern Troubles.

In the early days they used Linhof cameras with glass plates, both 9x12cm and the US standard 5x4ins. These plates survive in today's Lensmen, run by photographer Susan Kennedy, who bought the business in 1995. The meticulously recorded Lensmen archive includes a record of each day's photographic assignment as well as details of the shoot, making it a valuable visual history resource.

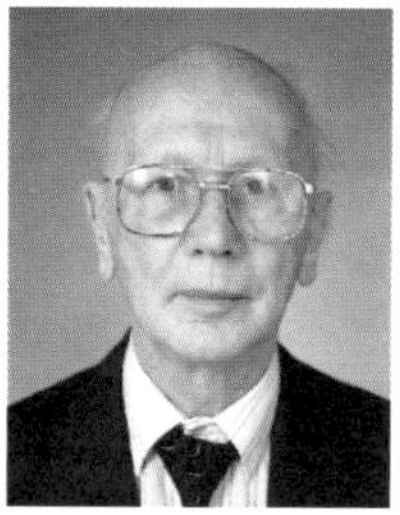

Andrew Farren

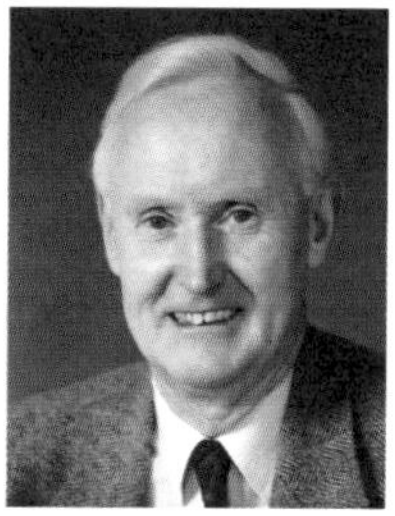

Padraig MacBrian

This book is dedicated to Andrew Farren and Pádraig MacBrian, photographers and founders of Lensmen, for the excellence and accuracy of their work.

Previous page
Contestants in the Esso Ploughing Championships, Kilkenny.

11 July 1961

Opposite
One of the closing ceremonies of the Patrician Year was this open-air Mass at Croke Park.

25 June 1961

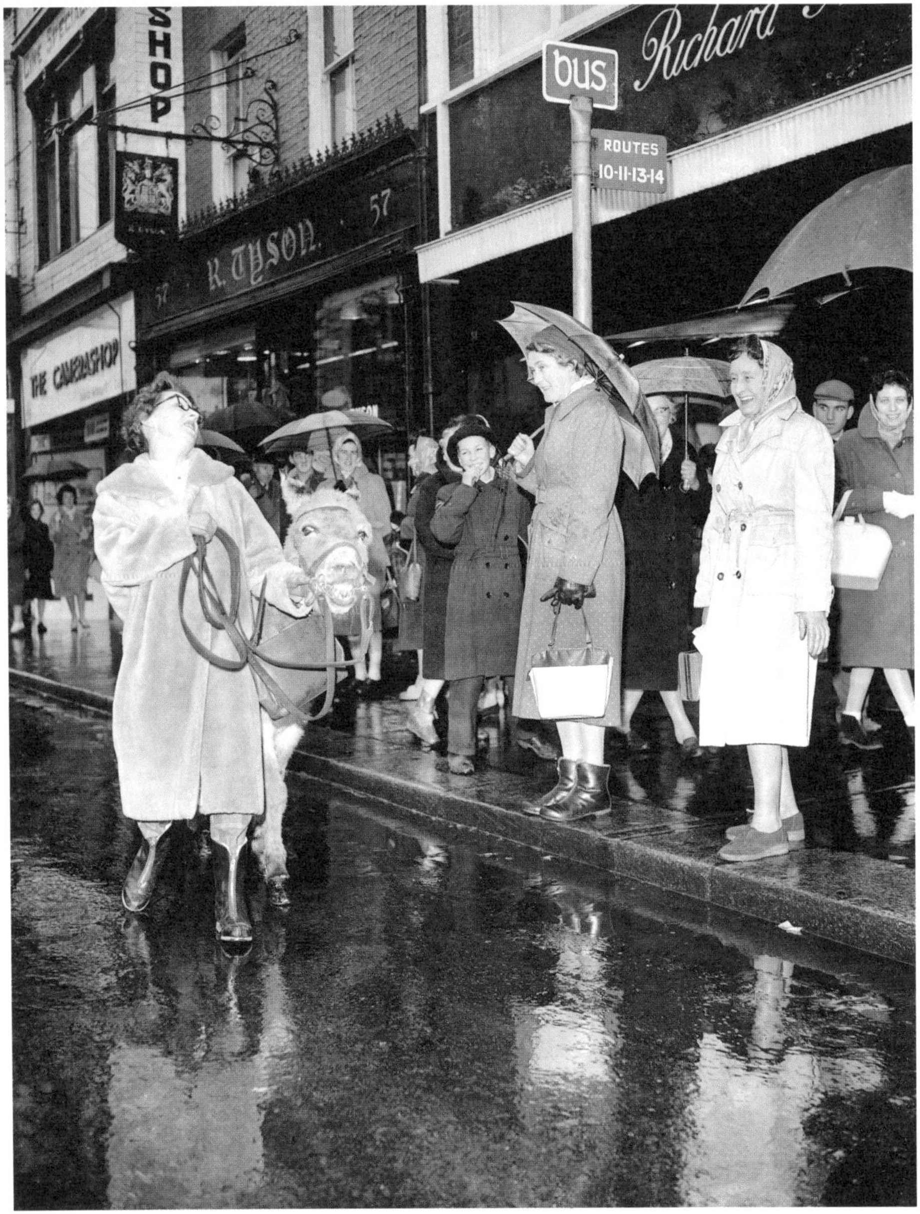

'Bus Fares Up' Maureen Potter finds an alternative mode of travel as a protest about an imminent increase in bus fares.

15 January 1960

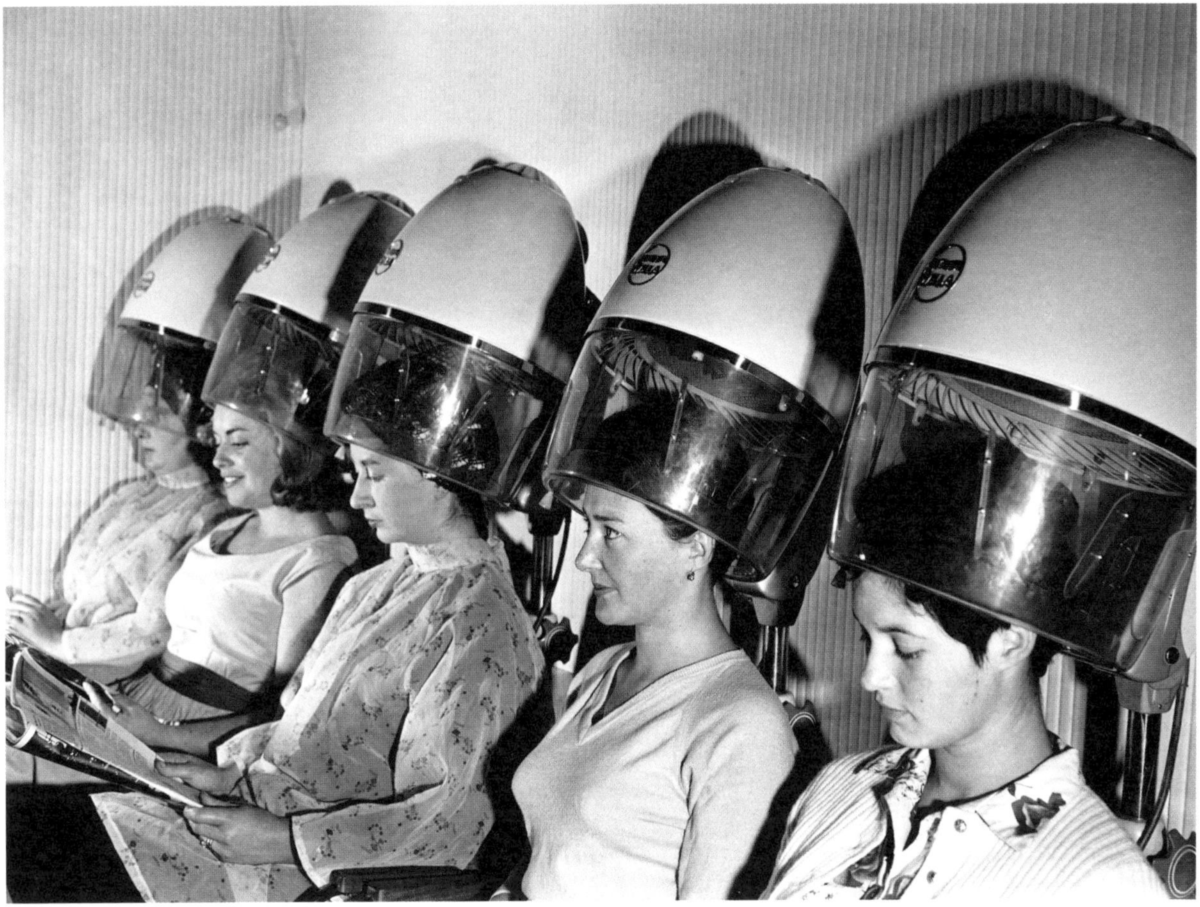

Being 'beautified' at the Jewel Hair Salon. Before the days of the 'blow-dry', ladies stoically endured the heat and noise of these contraptions.

5 February 1960

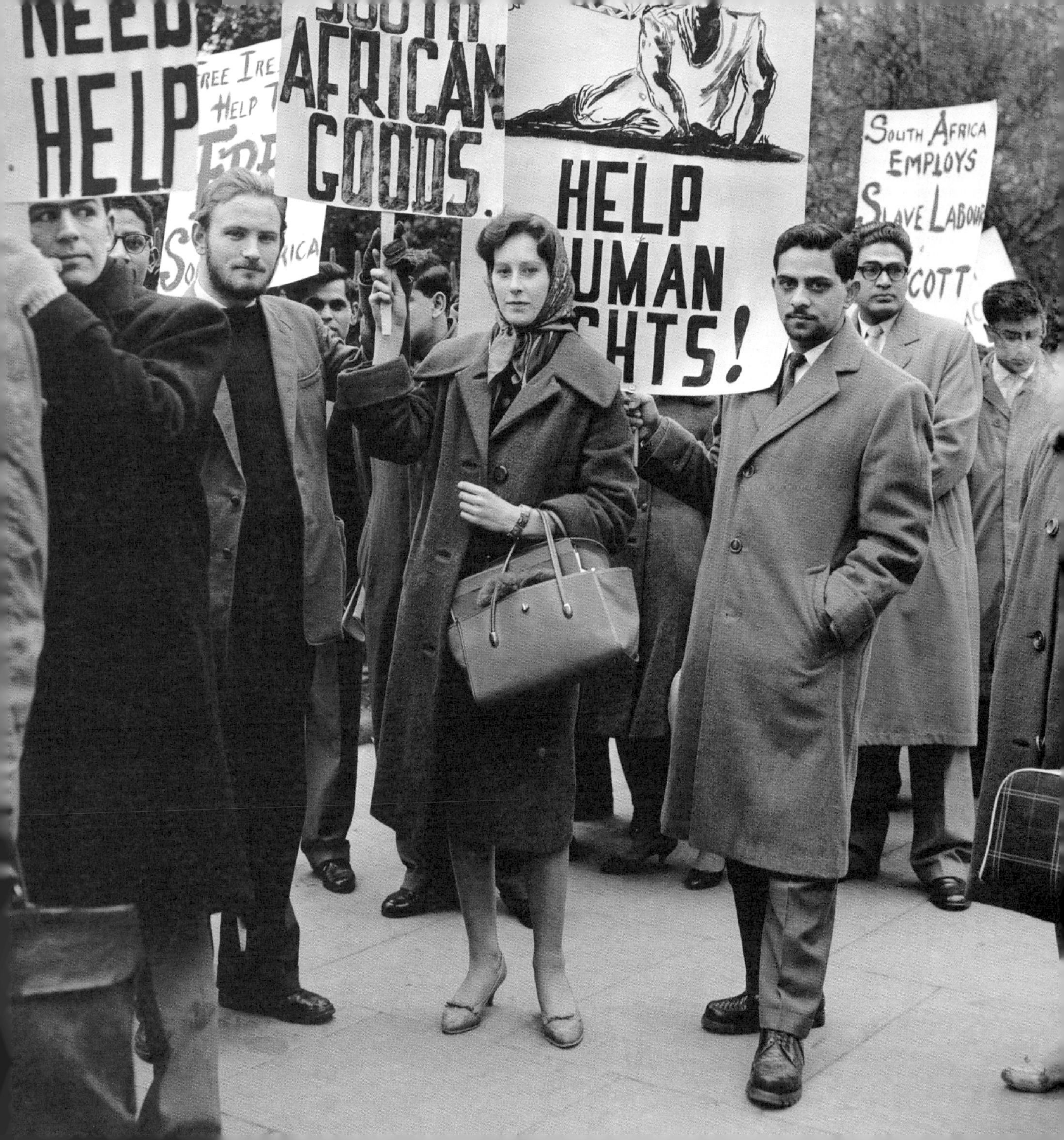
HELP
AFRICAN
GOODS.
HELP
SOUTH AFRICA
EMPLOYS

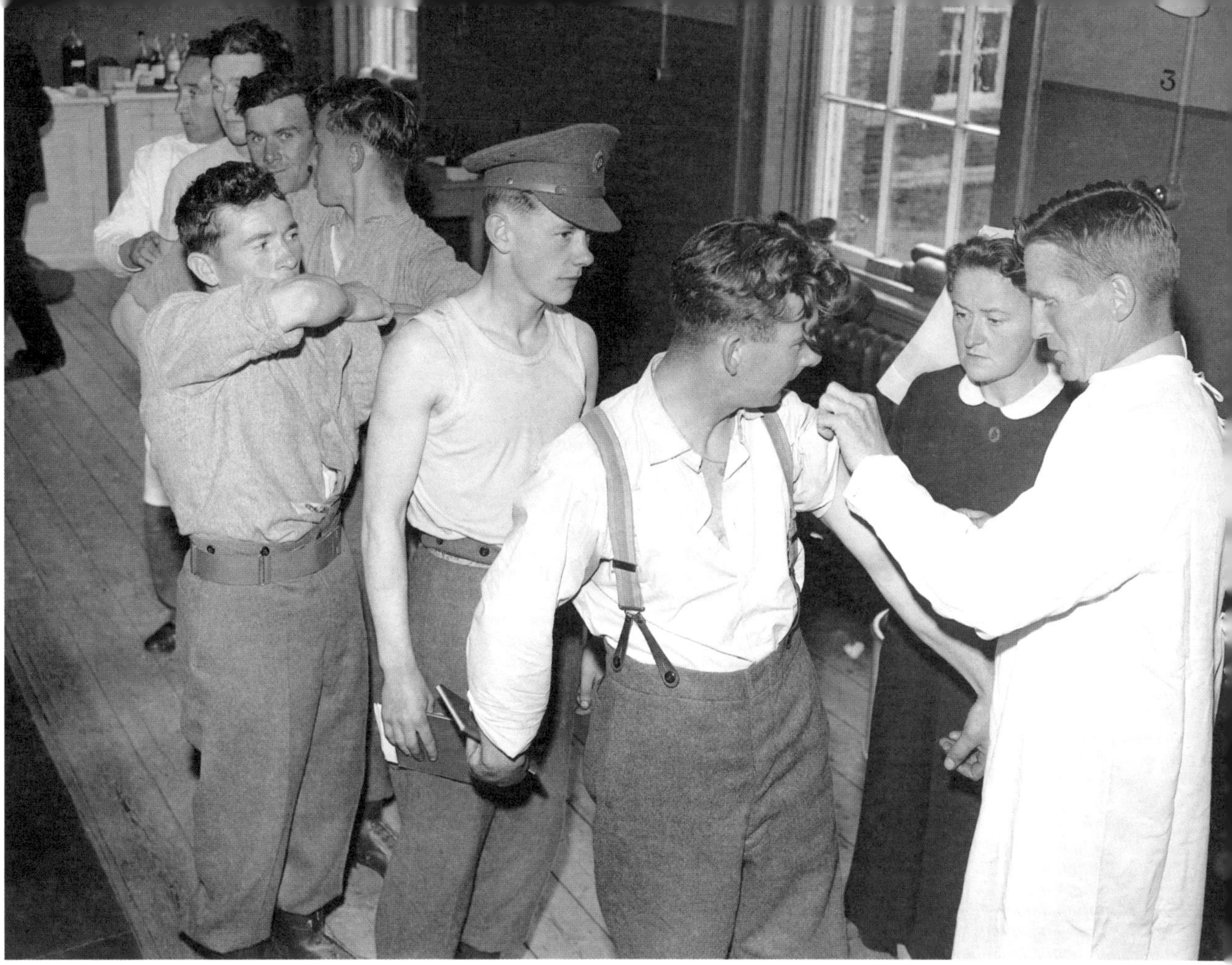

Pte. K O'Sullivan and men from the 6th Battalion line up to be vaccinated against yellow fever by Comdt Laurence O'Toole, Army Medical Corps. The troops were on their way to the Congo.

22 July 1960

Students and members of the public join in a 'Boycott South African Goods' march in Dublin. The Dublin campaign, part of an international effort to highlight the injustices of the apartheid system, was initiated by the Irish branch of the Afro-Asia Society.

10 February 1960

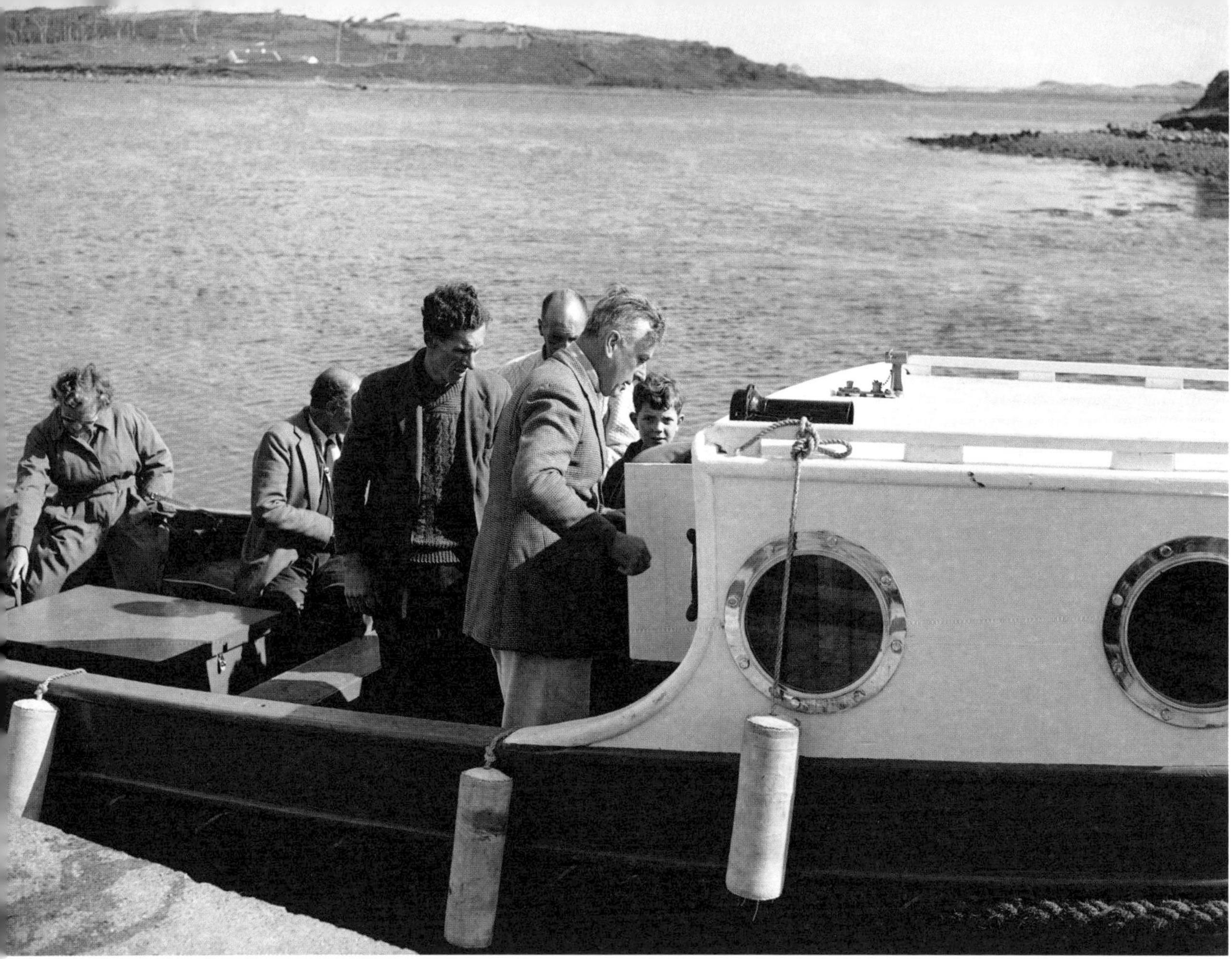

Lord Mountbatten inspects his new boat, the Shadow V at Mullaghmore, Co Sligo. Mountbatten, along with members of his family, and a local boy, died when the IRA blew up this boat in Mullaghmore in 1979.

29 July 1960

Irish athletes and officials depart for the Rome Olympics. In the front row is Maeve Kyle, a noted track athlete who also gained 58 caps for Ireland in hockey. Melbourne gold medallist Ronnie Delany is fourth from top, right.

20 August 1960

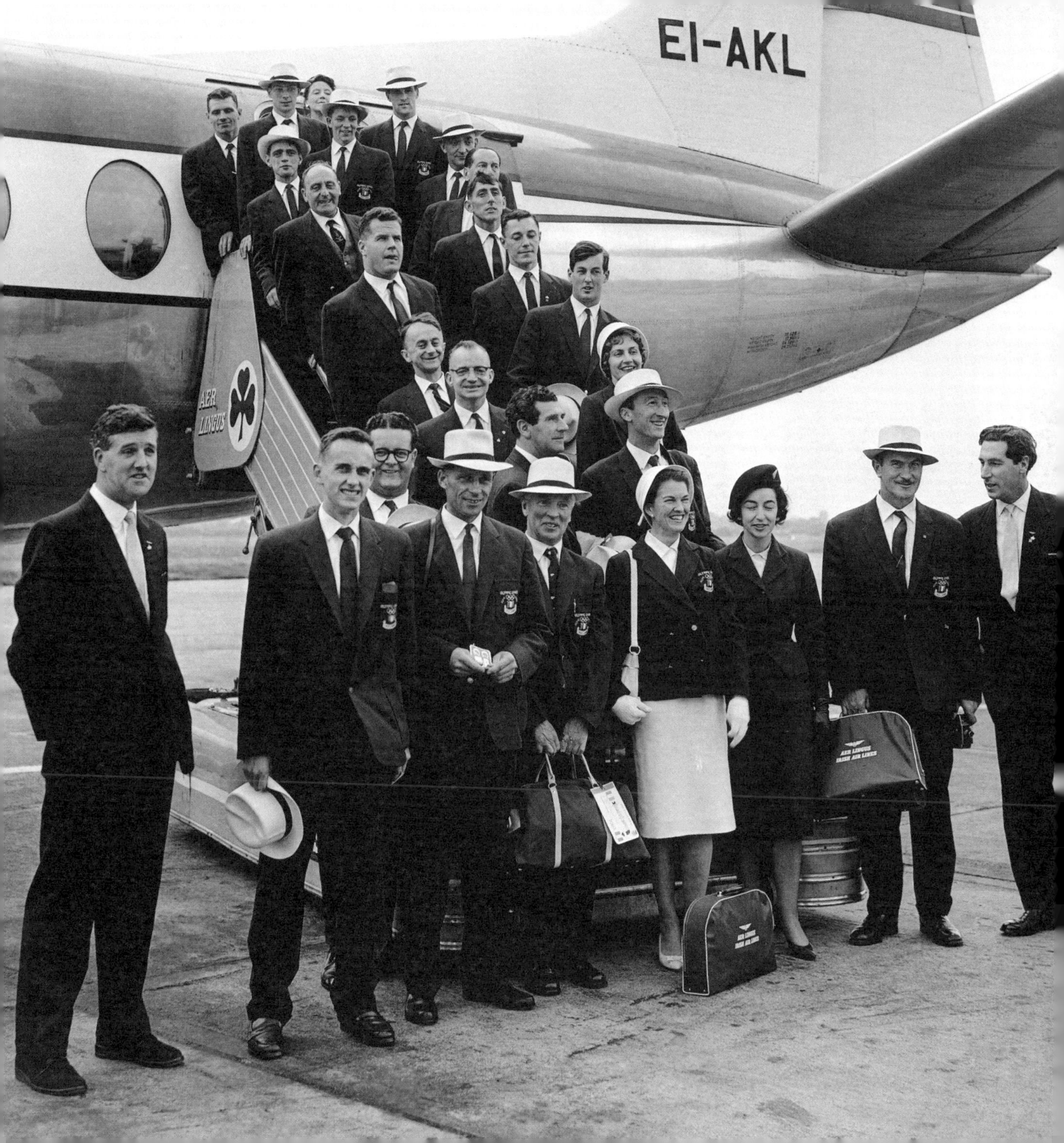
EI-AKL
AER LINGUS
AER LINGUS
IRISH AIR LINES

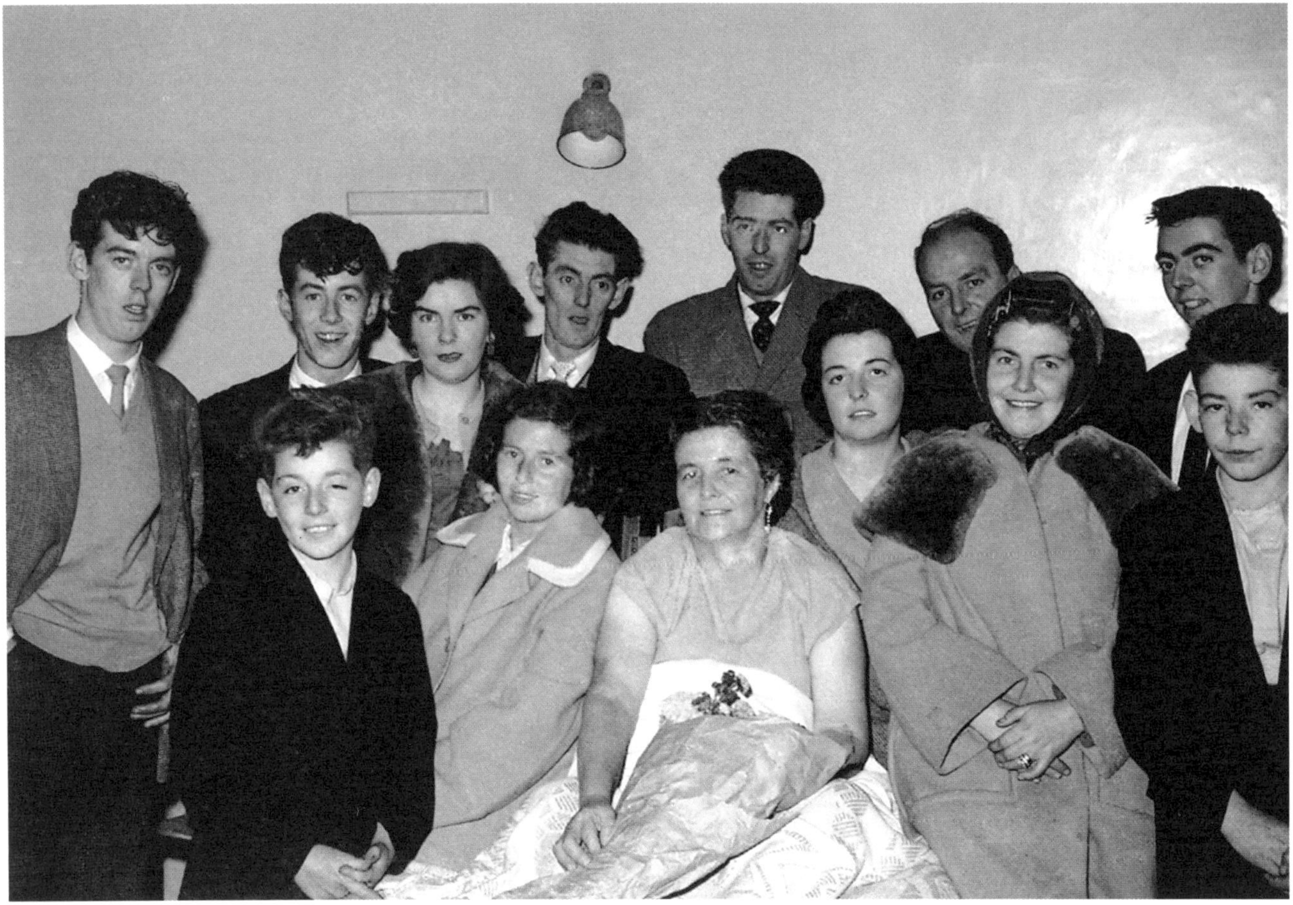

Mrs Maguire, (with bouquet), surrounded by other members of her family, celebrates the arrival of her 20th baby at the Rotunda Hospital. Even for its time, this was an unusually large family, and the event made the British as well as the Irish papers.

9 October 1960

Irene Ruth Kane, winner of the Miss Ireland contest, 1960, pictured with other finalists at the Four Provinces Ballroom (later the Television Club). She came in the Top Ten in the Miss World competition.

9 October 1960

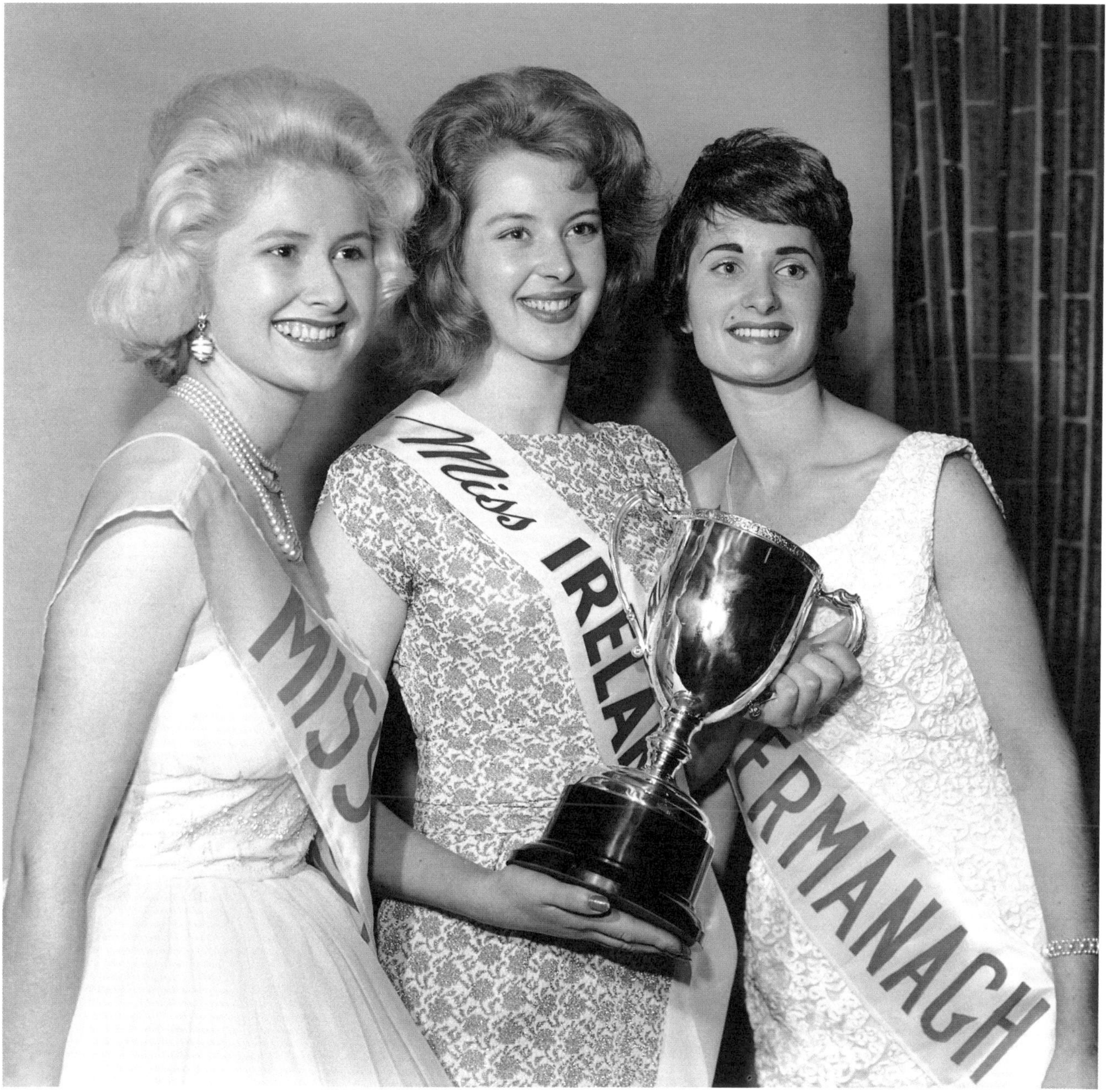
Miss

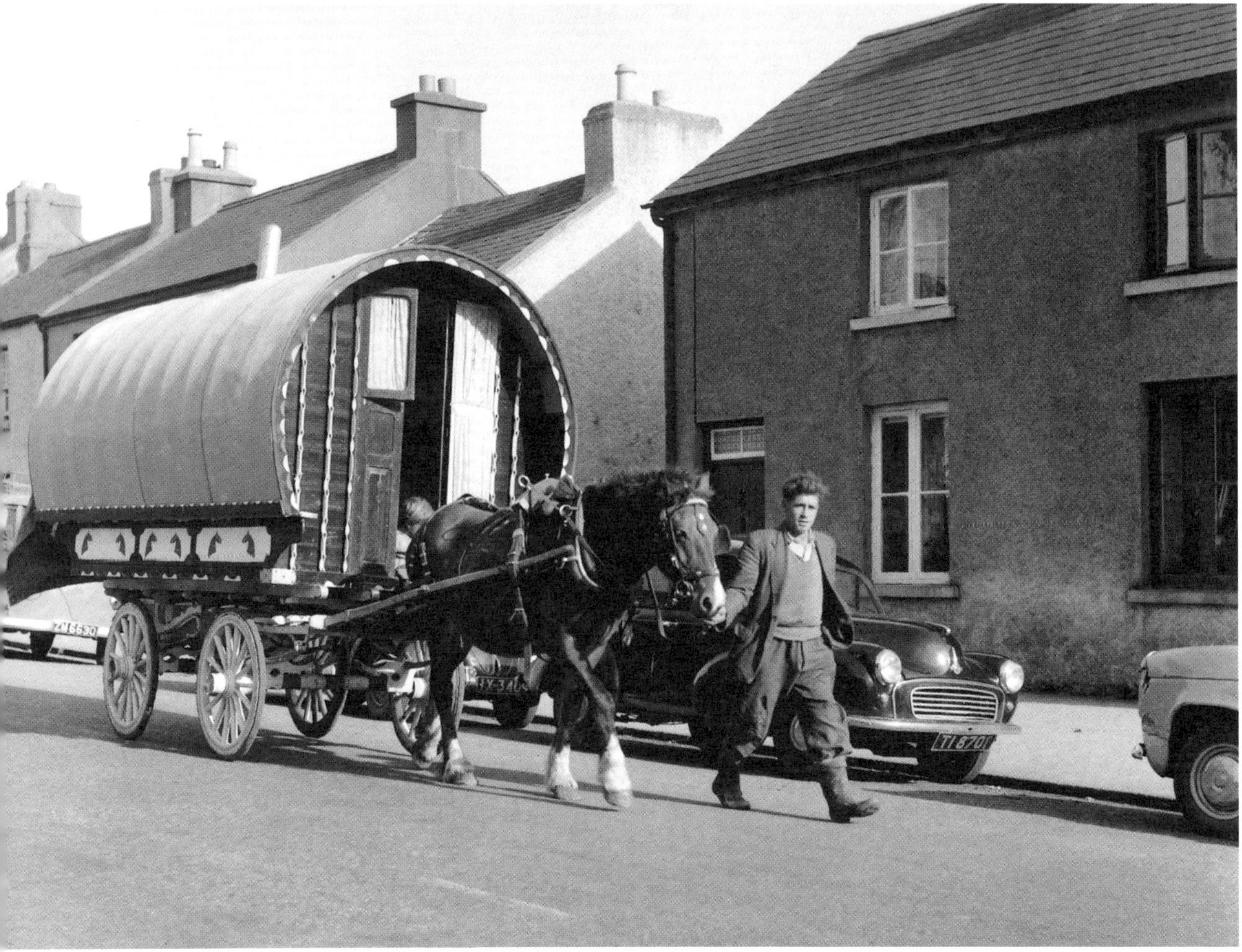

The Ballinasloe Horse Fair Tinker King.

15 October 1960

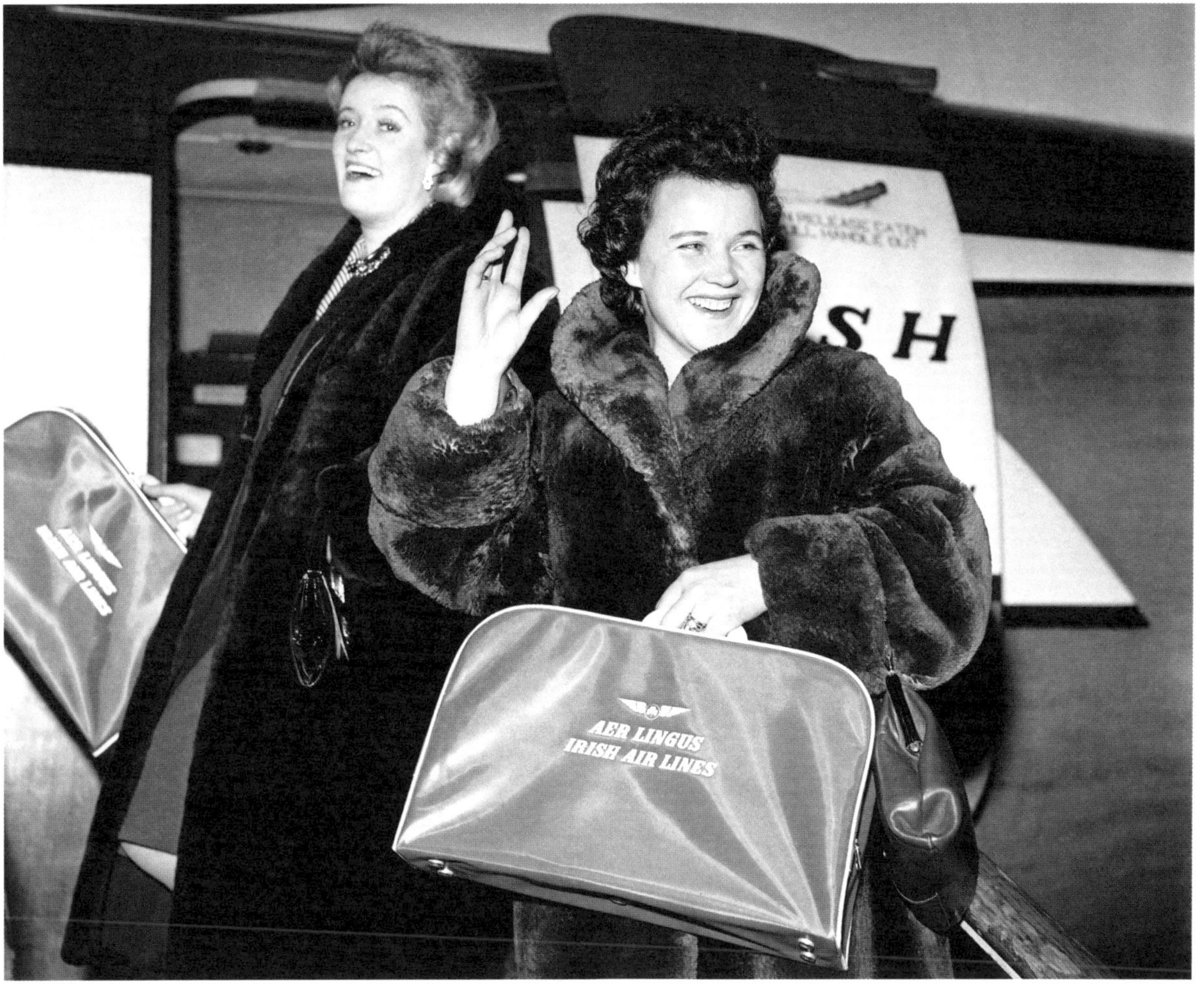

Singer Bridie Gallagher waves goodbye as she departs for New York where she performed at Carnegie Hall. The Donegal-born performer was hugely popular and had a string of hits, including the one for which she is most famous, 'The Boys From the County Armagh'.

29 October 1960

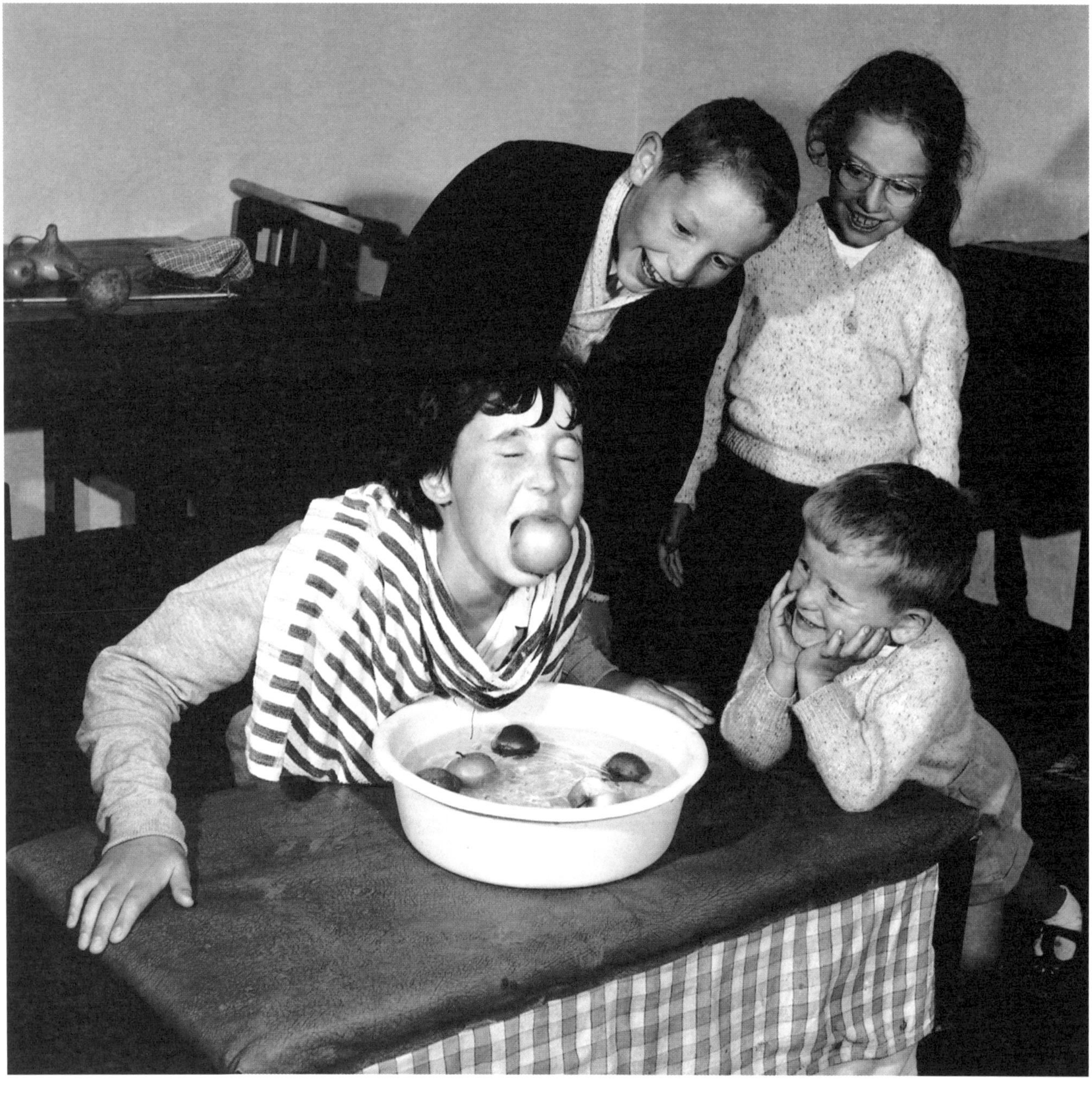

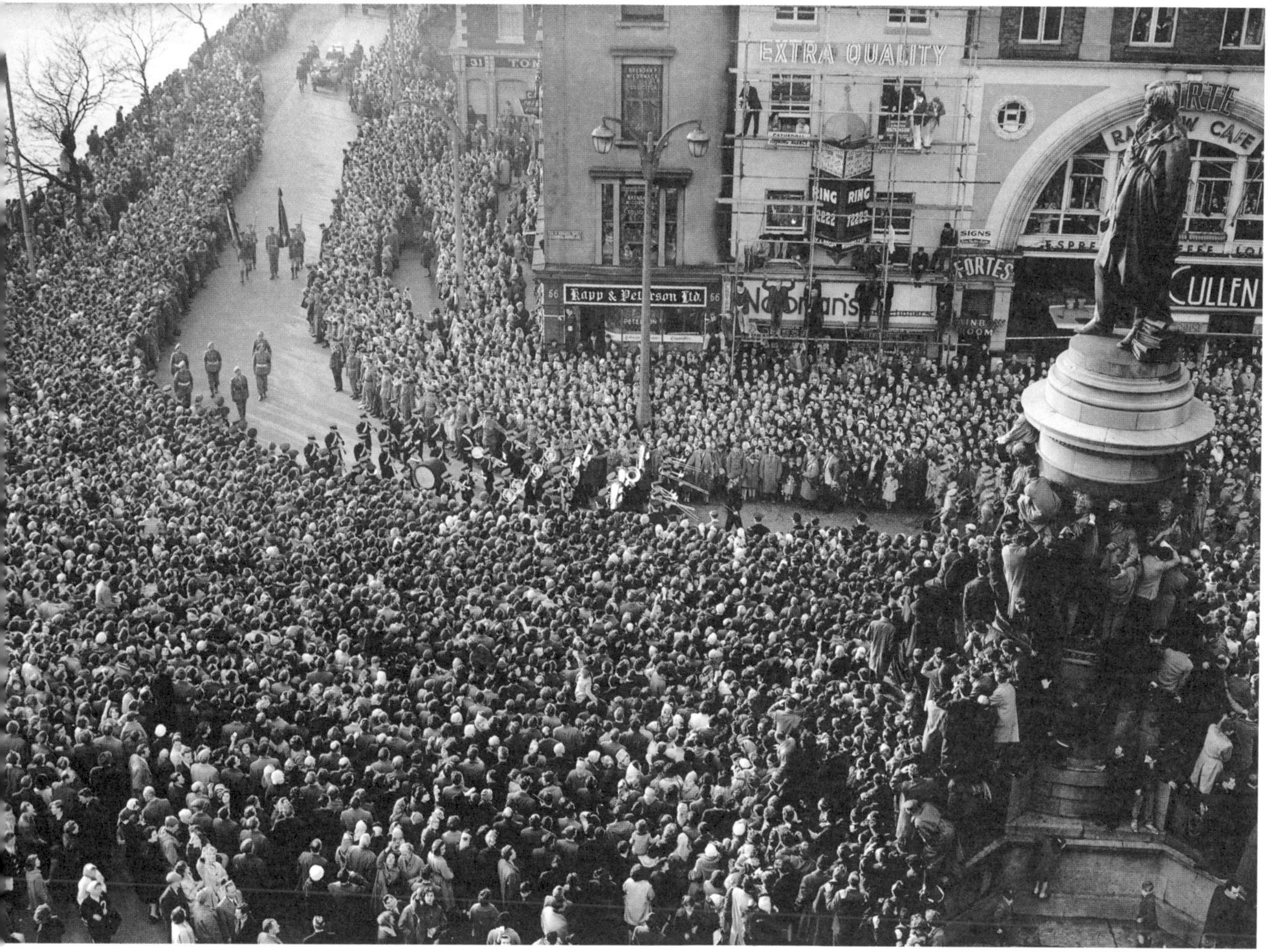

The Stephens children bob for apples at Hallowe'en.

31 October 1960

Huge crowds lined the route of the funerals of the Irish soldiers killed in the Niemba ambush while on UN duty in the Congo. On 8 November an 11-man Irish platoon on patrol in Niemba were ambushed by Baluba tribesmen. Nine were killed: Lieut. Kevin Gleeson, Sgt. H Gaynor, Cpl. P Kelly, Cpl. L Dougan, Pte. M Farrell, Tpr. T Fennel, Tpr. Anthony Browne, Pte. M McGuinn and Pte. G Killeen.

19 November 1960

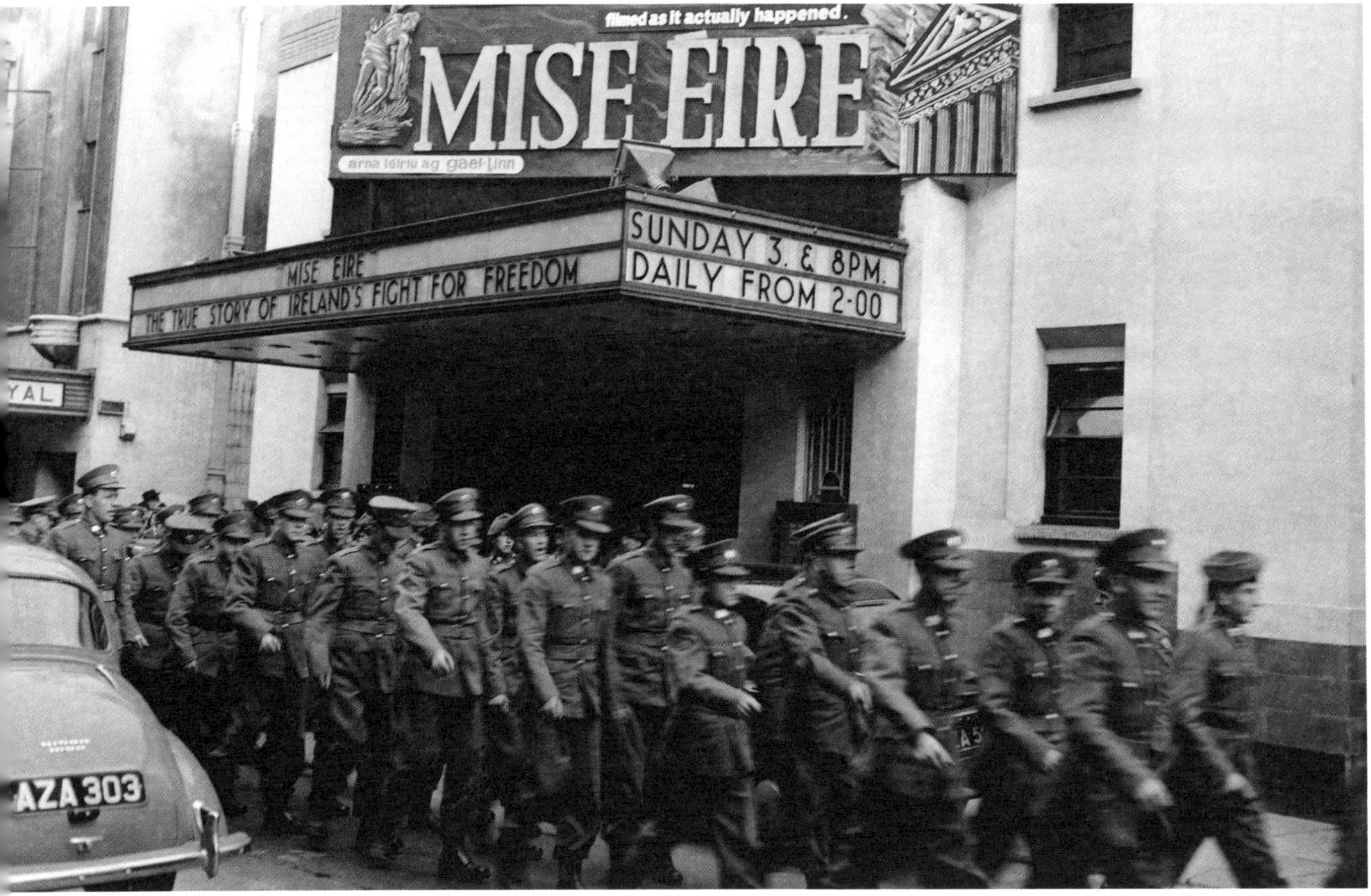

Soldiers attend 'Mise Eire'. George Morrison's film showed over twenty years of Irish history, from the 1890s to 1918, through existing archive material. Its soundtrack, an orchestral score by Sean O Riada, became hugely popular and is still available on CD.

30 November 1960

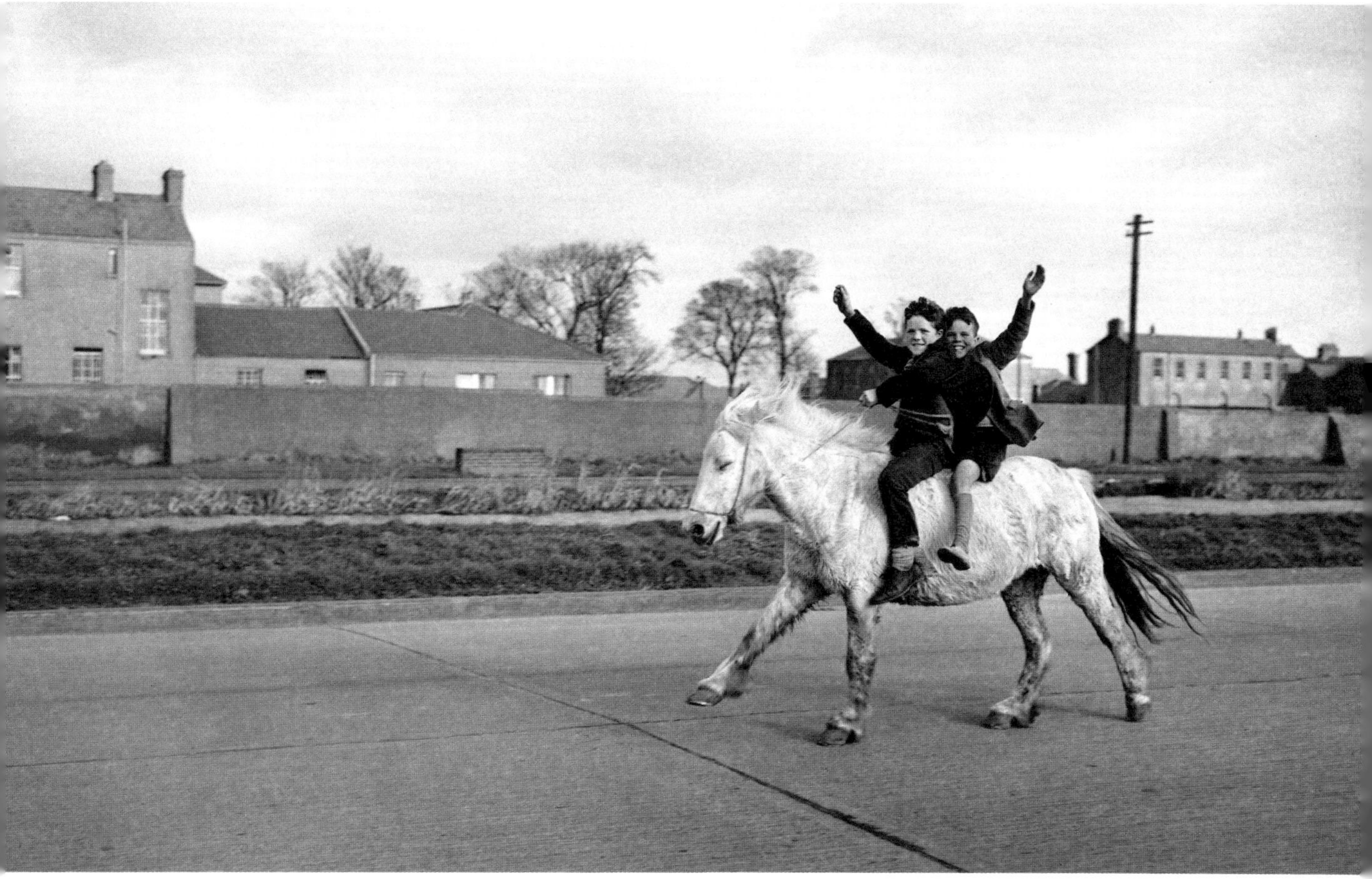

These aspiring cowboys and their steed enjoy the freedom of the roads.

18 February 1961

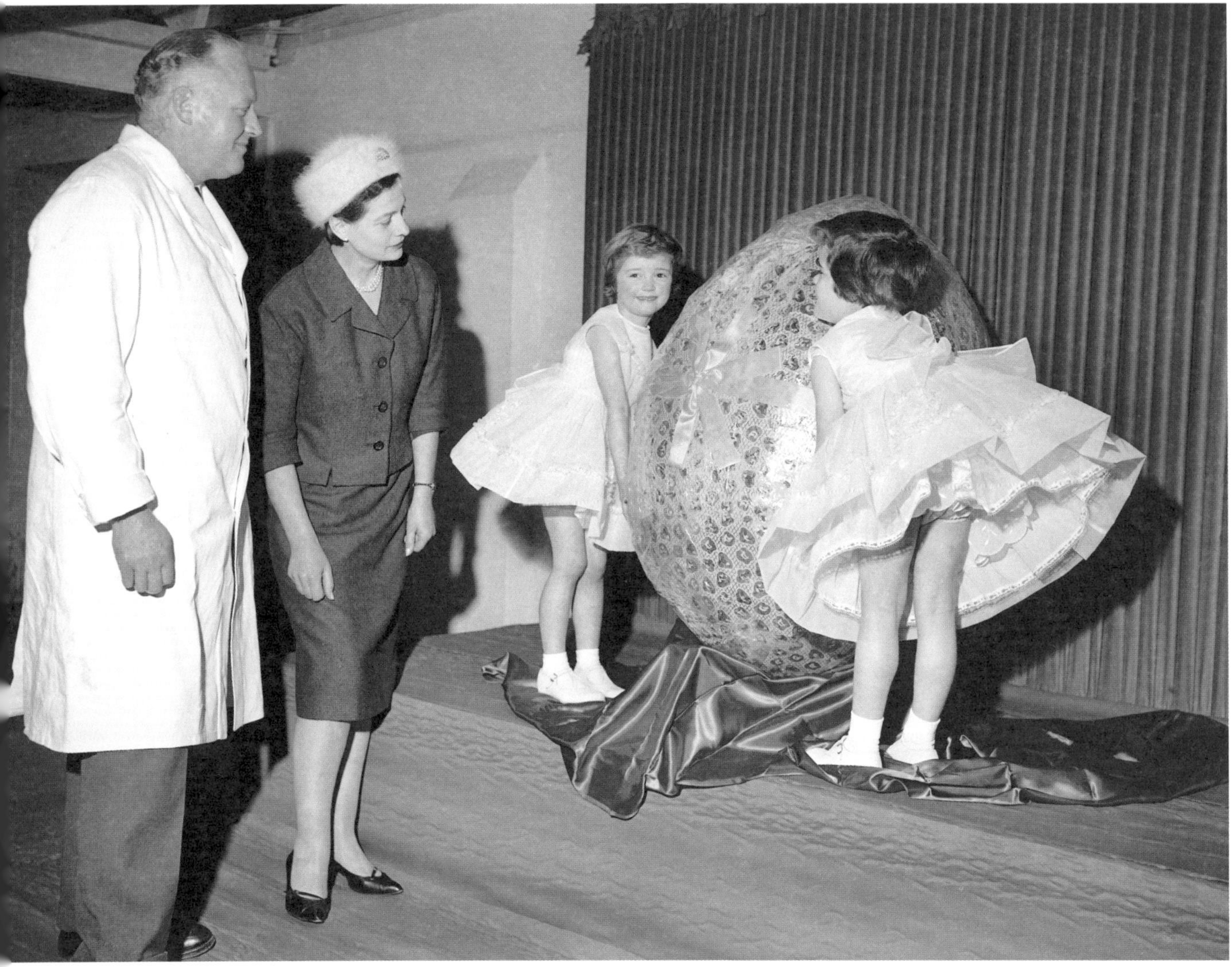

Chocolate manufacturers Urney present a giant Easter Egg to the ISPCC.

23 February 1961

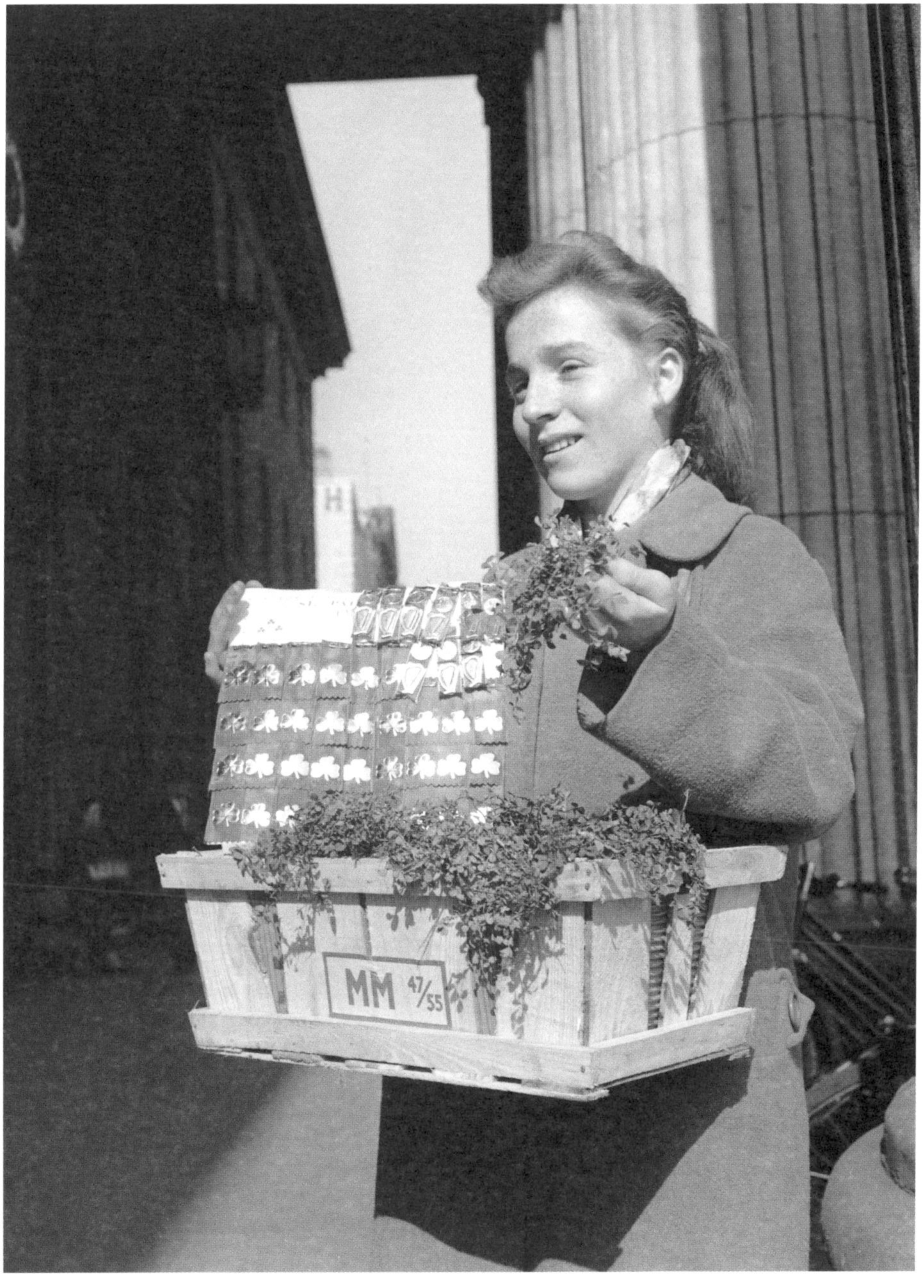

Anyone for a badge or a spray of shamrock?

17 March 1961

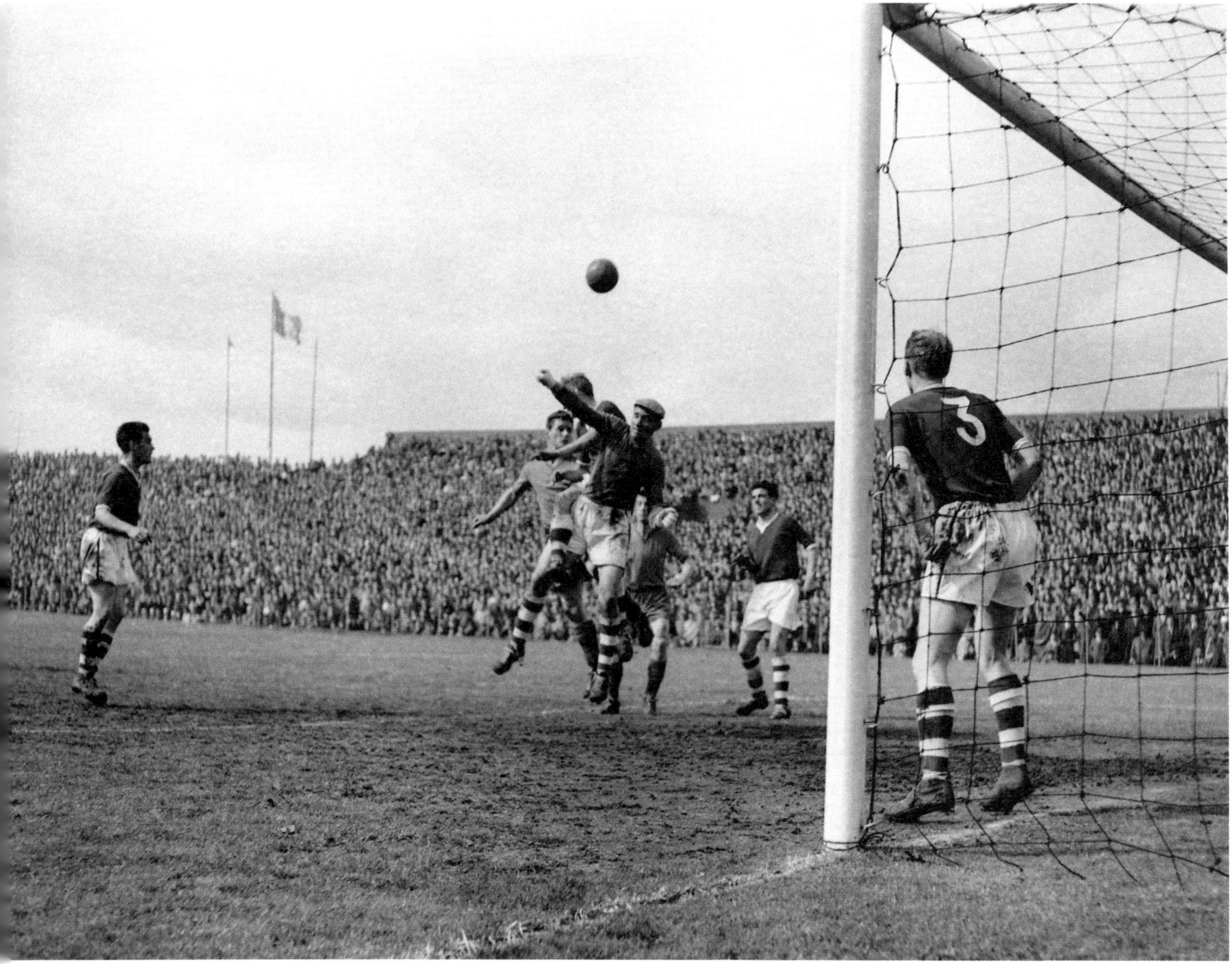

Action during the FAI Cup Final, Dalymount Park.
St Patrick's Athletic beat Drumcondra 2-1.

23 April 1961

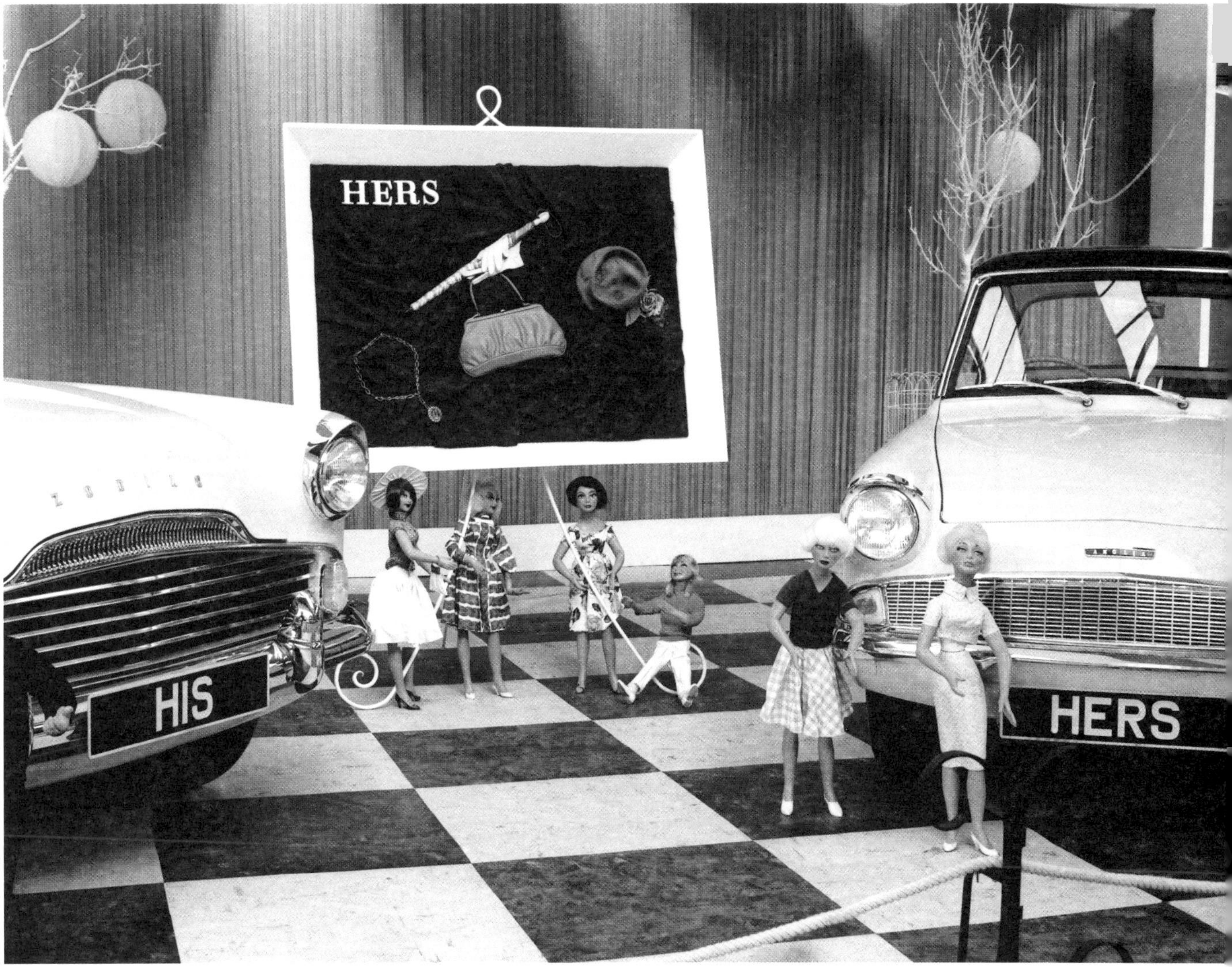

The must-have 'His' and 'Hers' cars of 1961 at the Henry Ford stand at the RDS: a Zodiac for him; an Anglia for her.

2 May 1961

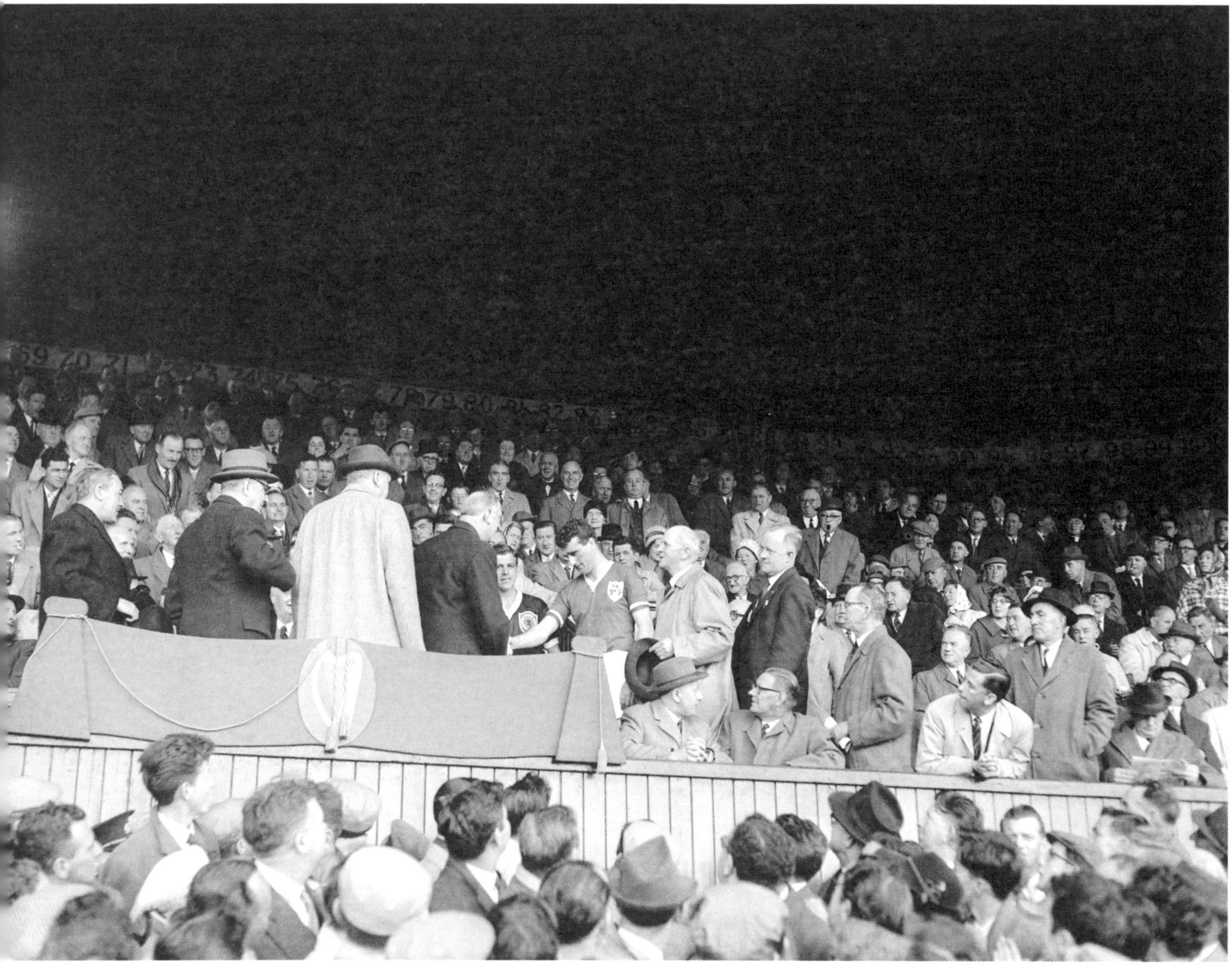

World Cup. Ireland v Scotland, Dalymount Park. Noel Cantwell, captain of the Irish side, shakes hands with Eamon de Valera. Scotland won the match 3-0.

7 May 1961

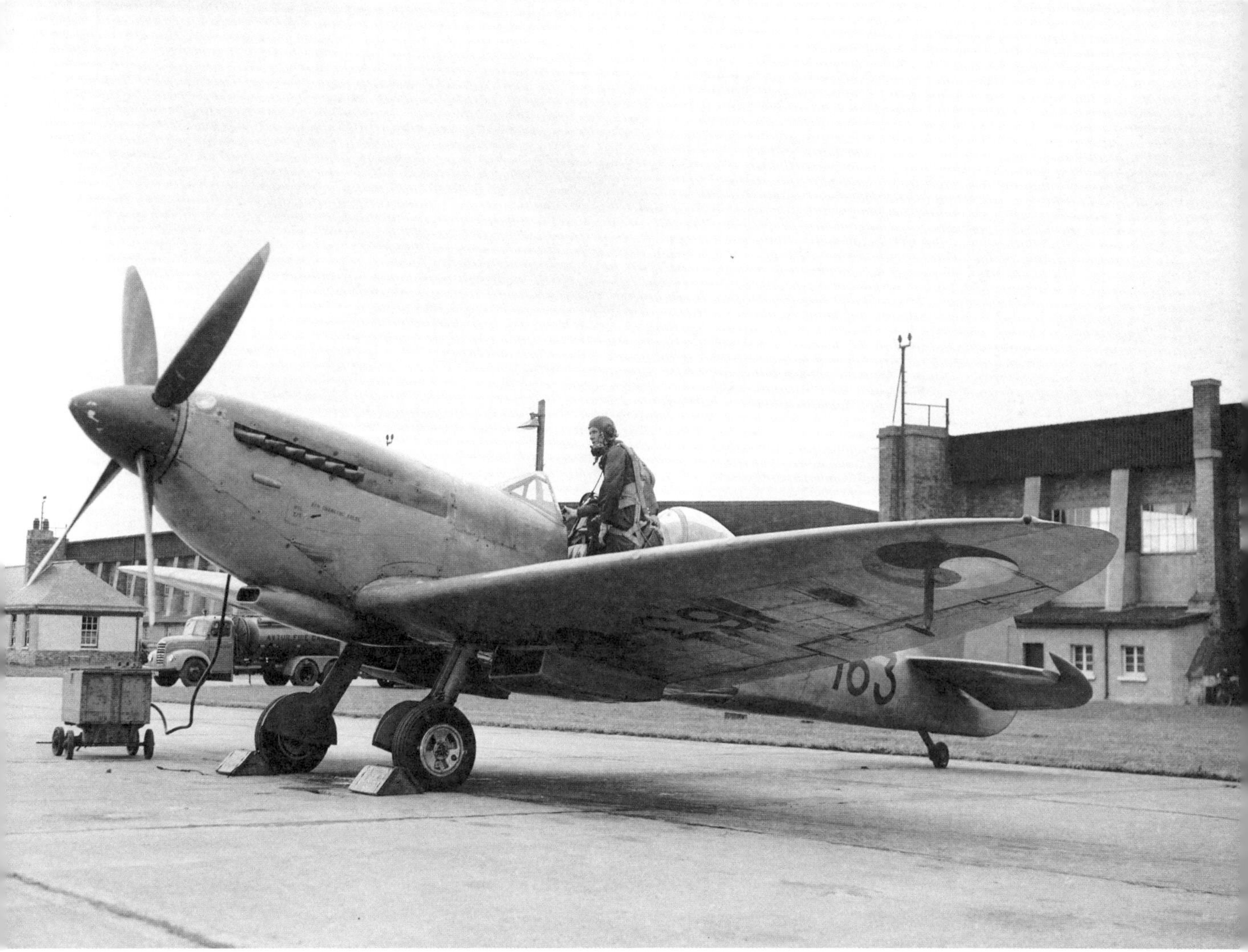

The last Spitfire used by the Air Corps departs Baldonnel. The Spitfire TR9 '163' was in use from 1951 as a training aircraft.

19 May 1961

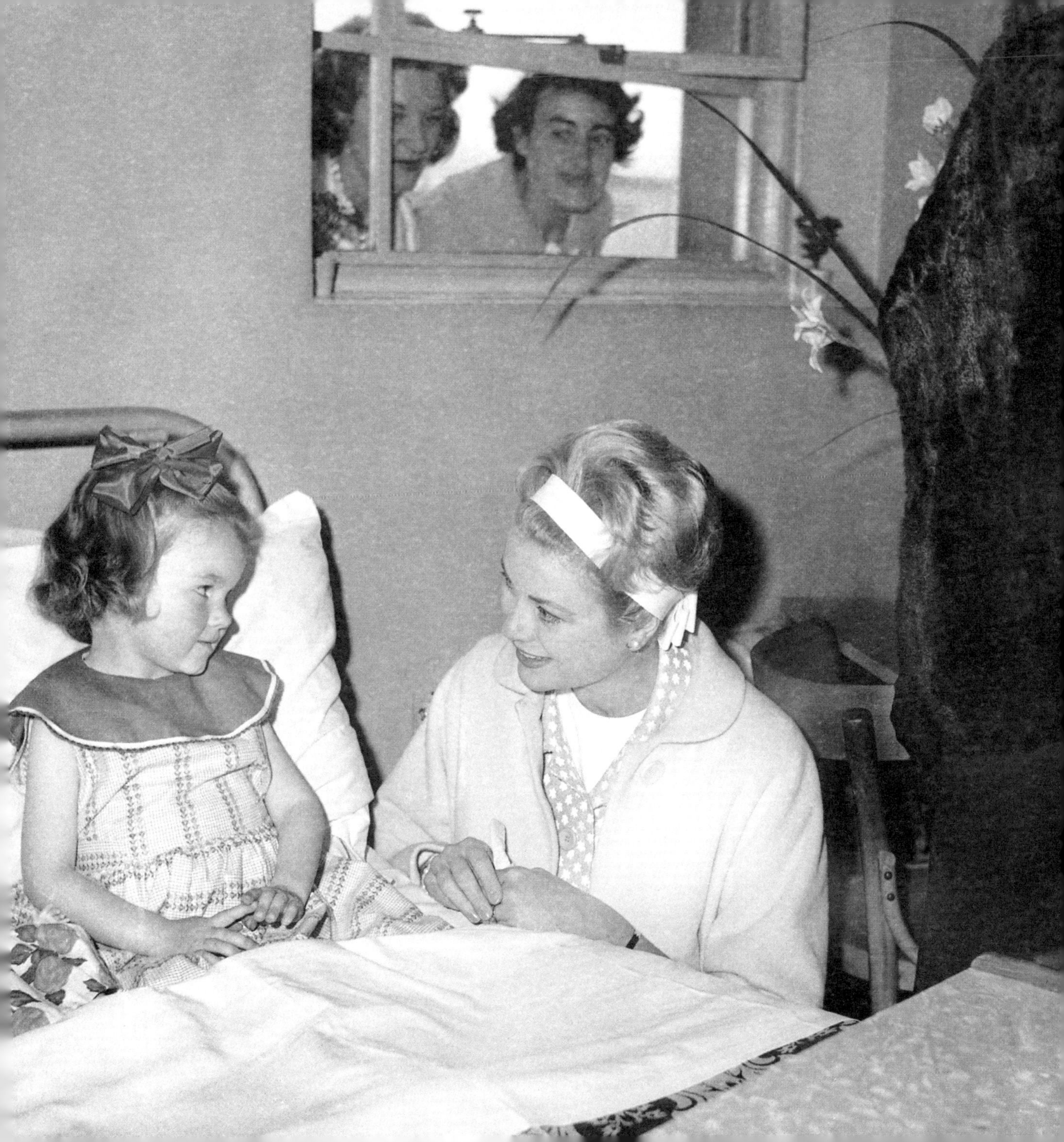

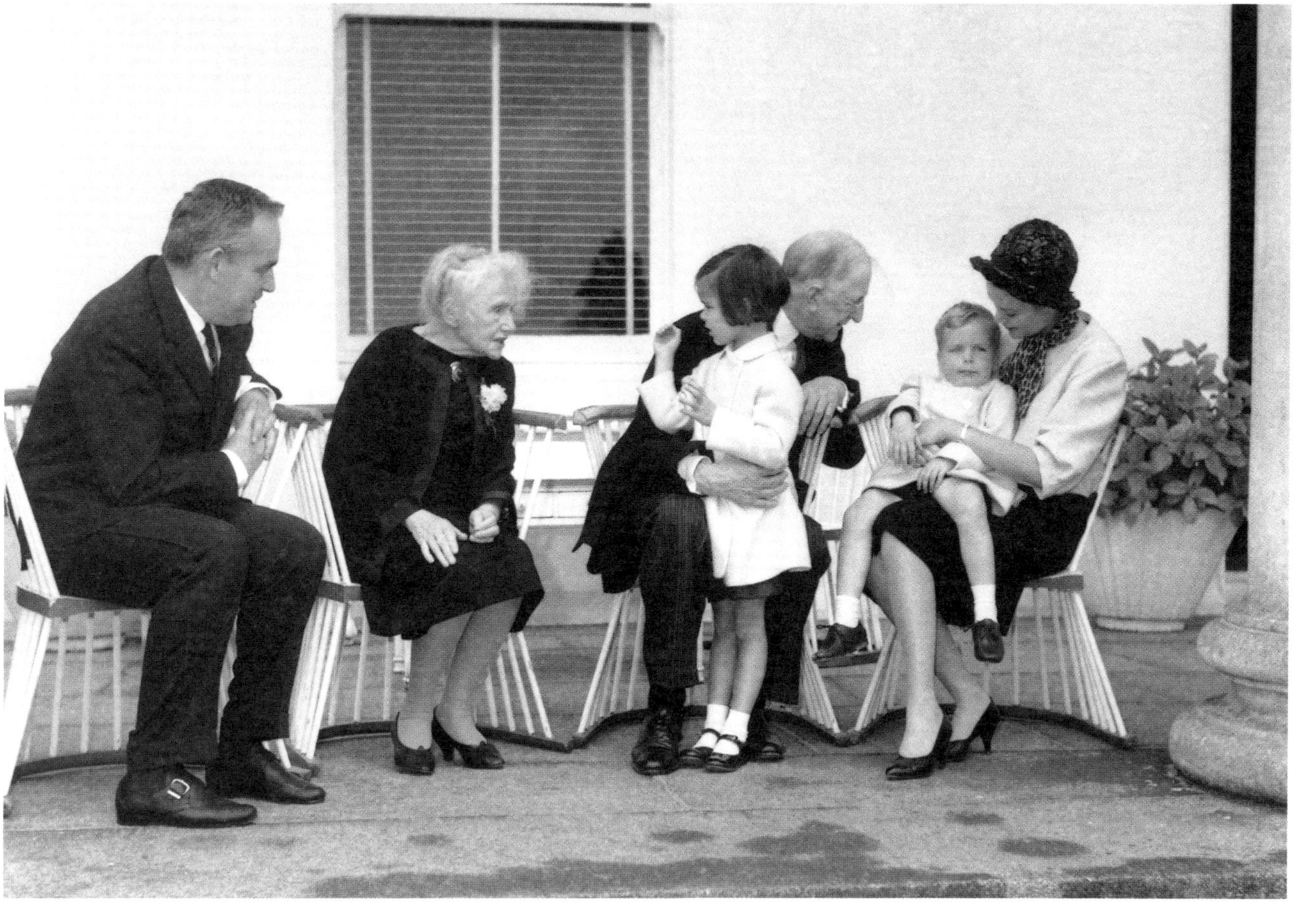

At Aras an Uachtaráin, Sinéad Bean de Valera and President de Valera help Prince Rainier and Princess Grace with looking after Prince Albert and Princess Caroline.

15 June 1961

One of the most popular visitors to Ireland was Her Serene Highness, Princess Grace of Monaco, formerly Grace Kelly. Here she chats with a young patient in Our Lady's Hospital, Crumlin.

12 June 1961

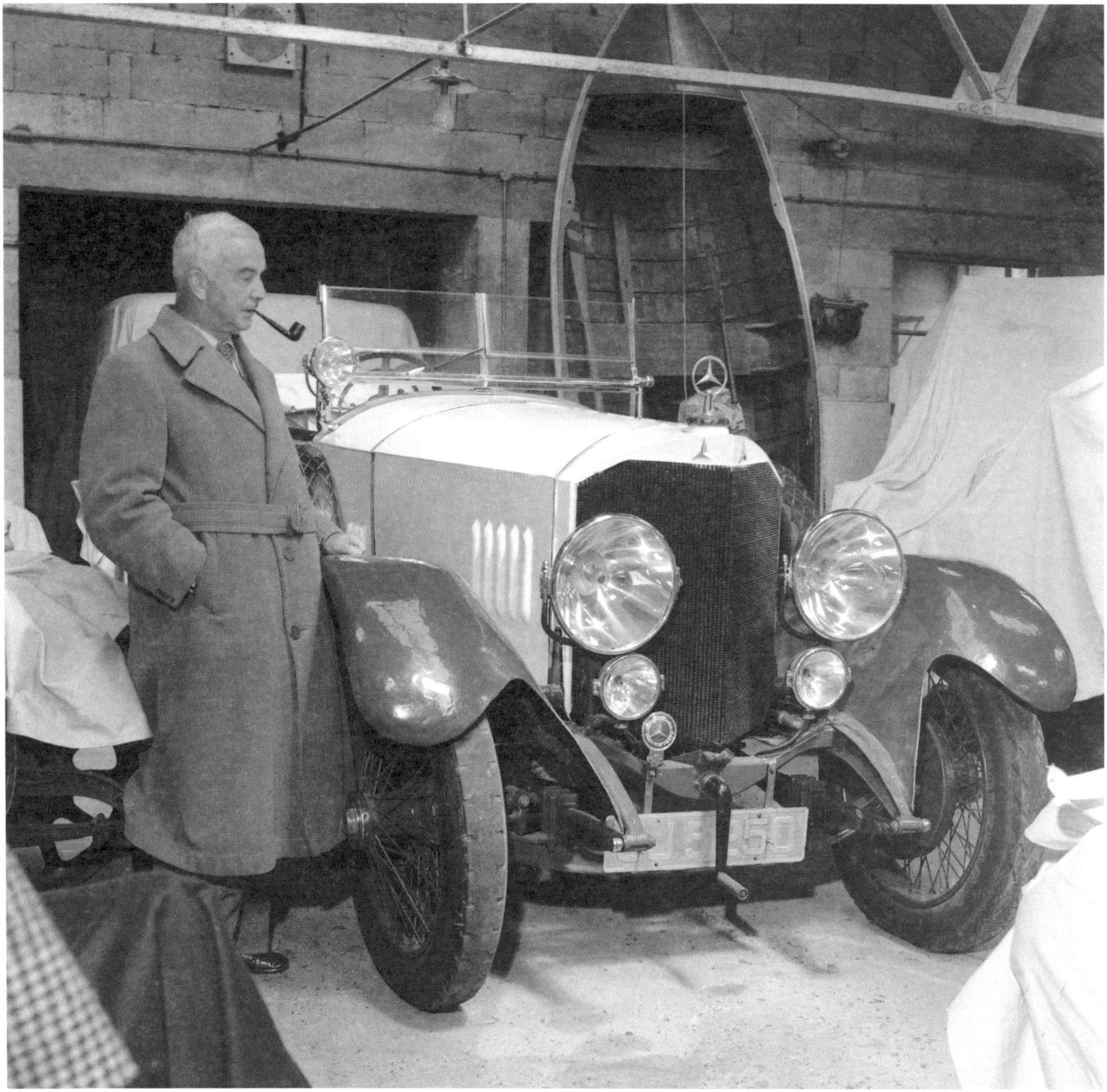

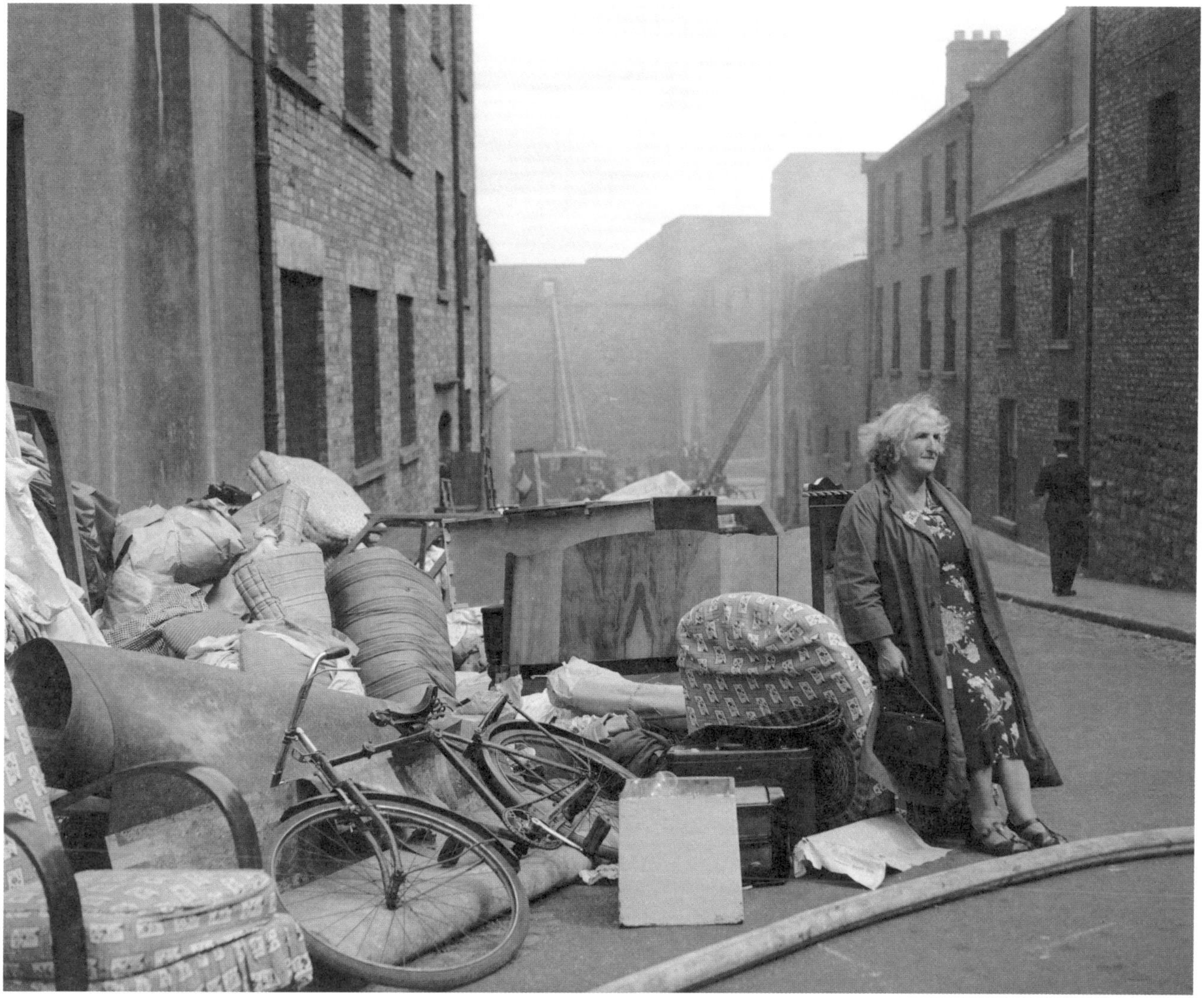

Motorcycle manufacturer John Ellis with one of his veteran cars at Straffan House.

23 May 1961

A fire in a warehouse containing 4,000 hogsheads of maturing whiskey at Powers Distillery on John's Lane in Dublin caused the evacuation of local factories, the John's Lane school and residents of Oliver Bond Flats. This lady, surrounded by her belongings, awaits the 'all-clear'.

5 July 1961

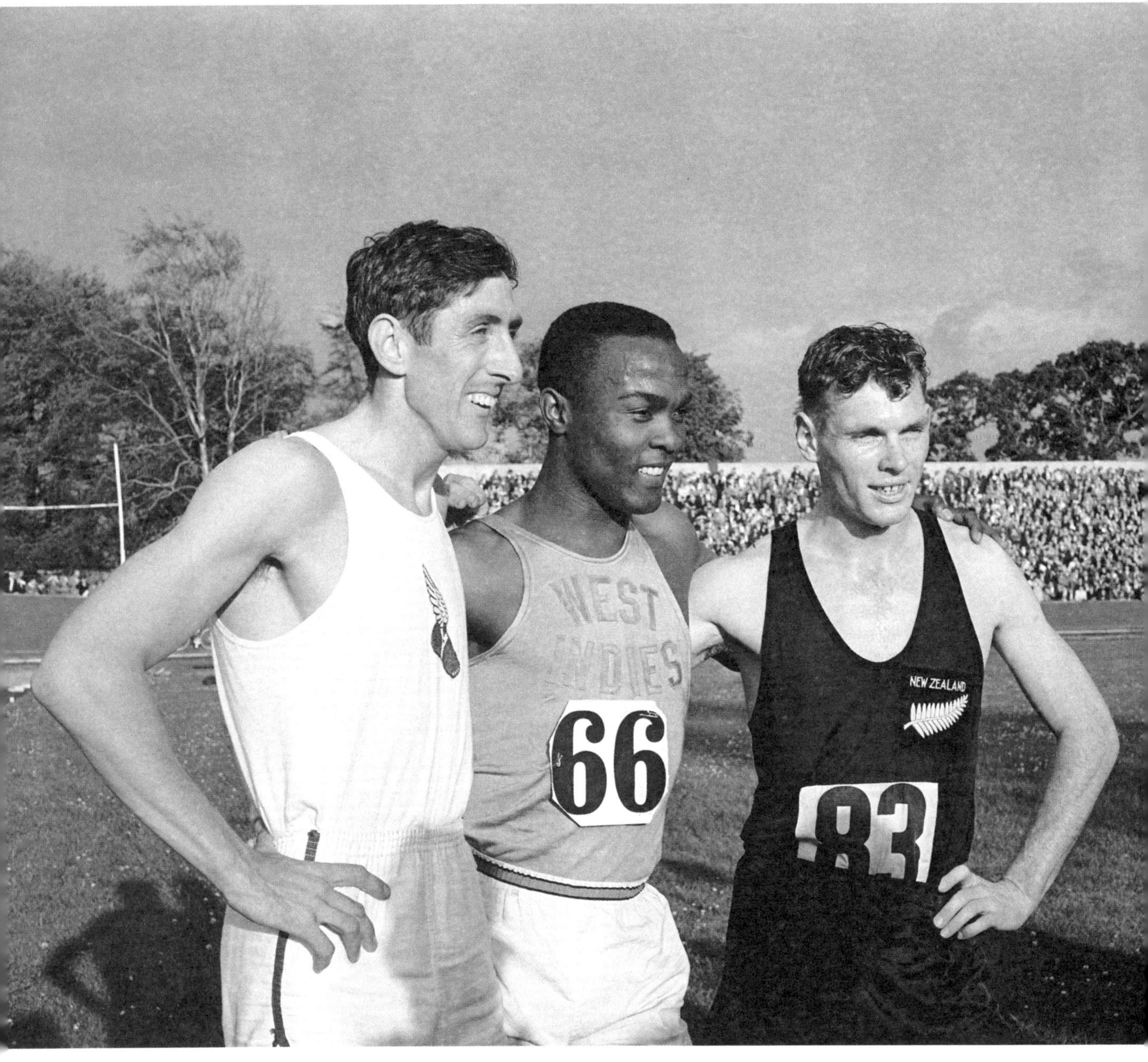
WEST
INDIES
66
NEW ZEALAND
83

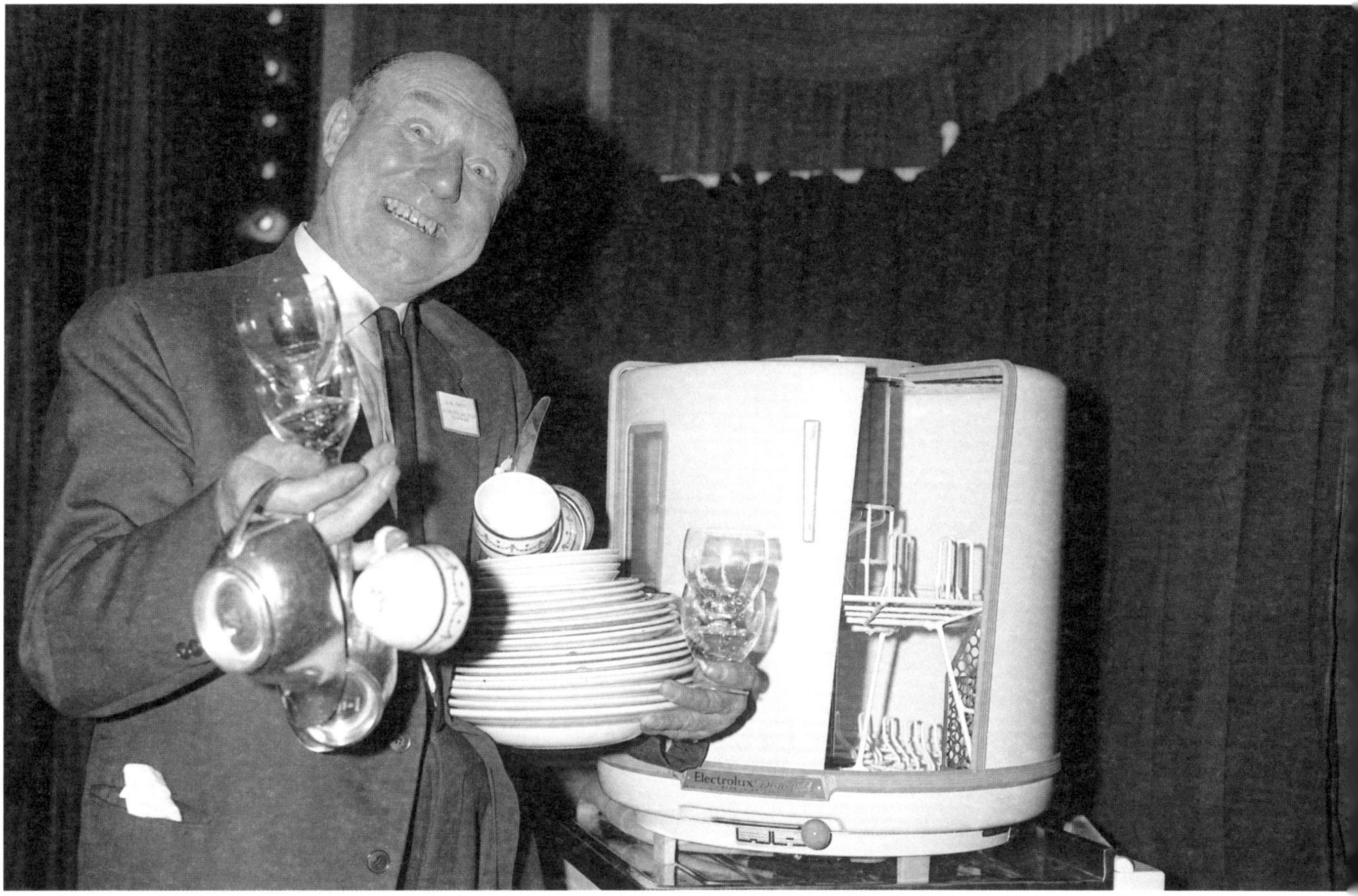

Electrolux introduced the 'Dishmaid', promising that 'with its powerful jets and rotating action, it will cope with the washing-up for 4-5 people while you enjoy leisure or get on with other work about the home.'

19 July 1961

Olympic Gold medallists Ronnie Delany and Peter Snell (New Zealand) flank bronze medallist George Kerr (Jamaica) at Santry stadium. The three competed in the ½ mile at Santry, which was won by Snell. Delany's time of 1m 47.1s set a new Irish national record.

17 July 1961

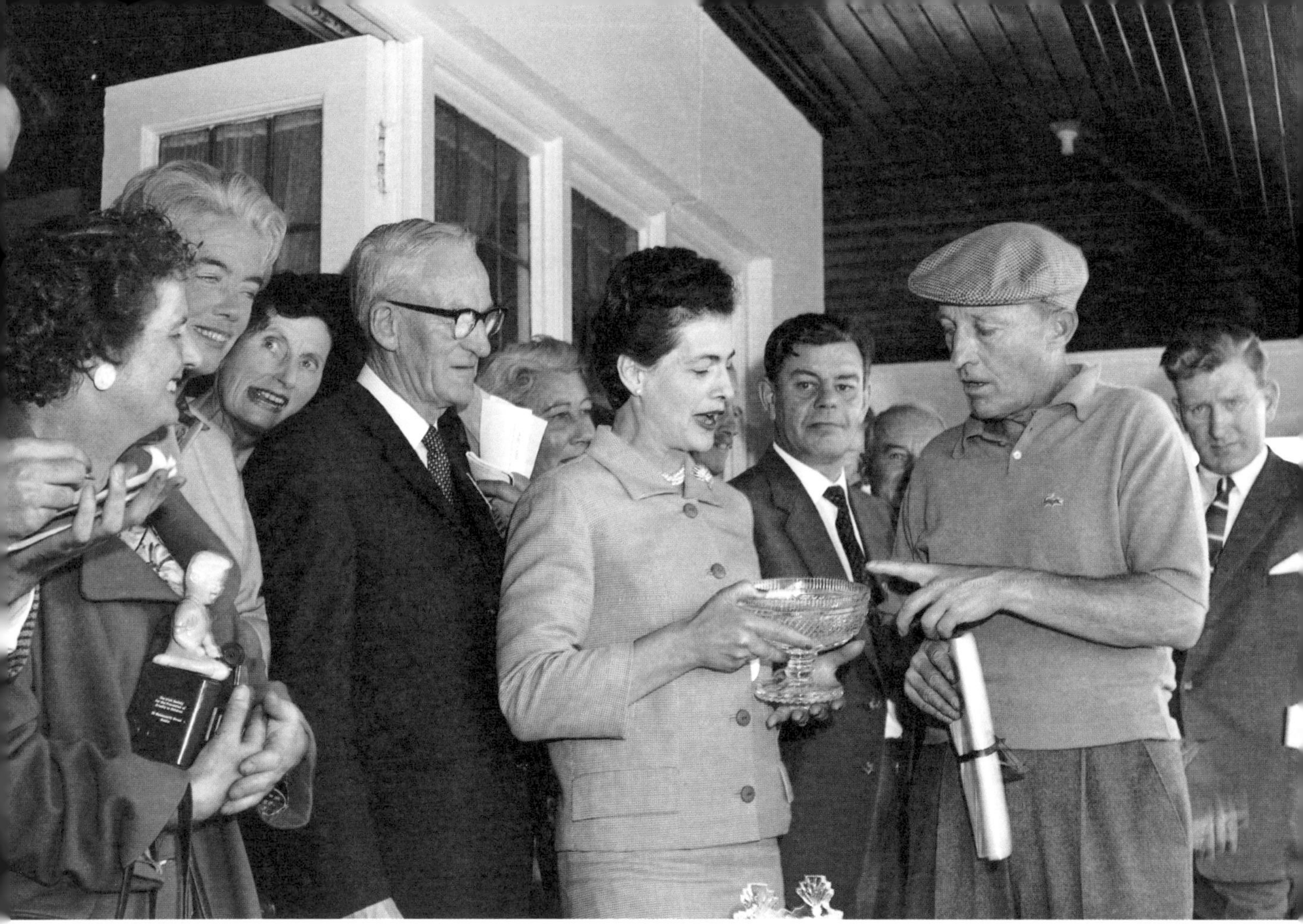

Bing Crosby was a regular visitor to Ireland. An avid golfer, he is pictured here at Woodbrook.

15 September 1961

The Irish Rowan under construction at Verolme Cork Dockyard. It was the first vessel built by the newly-formed dockyard and was operated by Irish Shipping.

30 November 1961

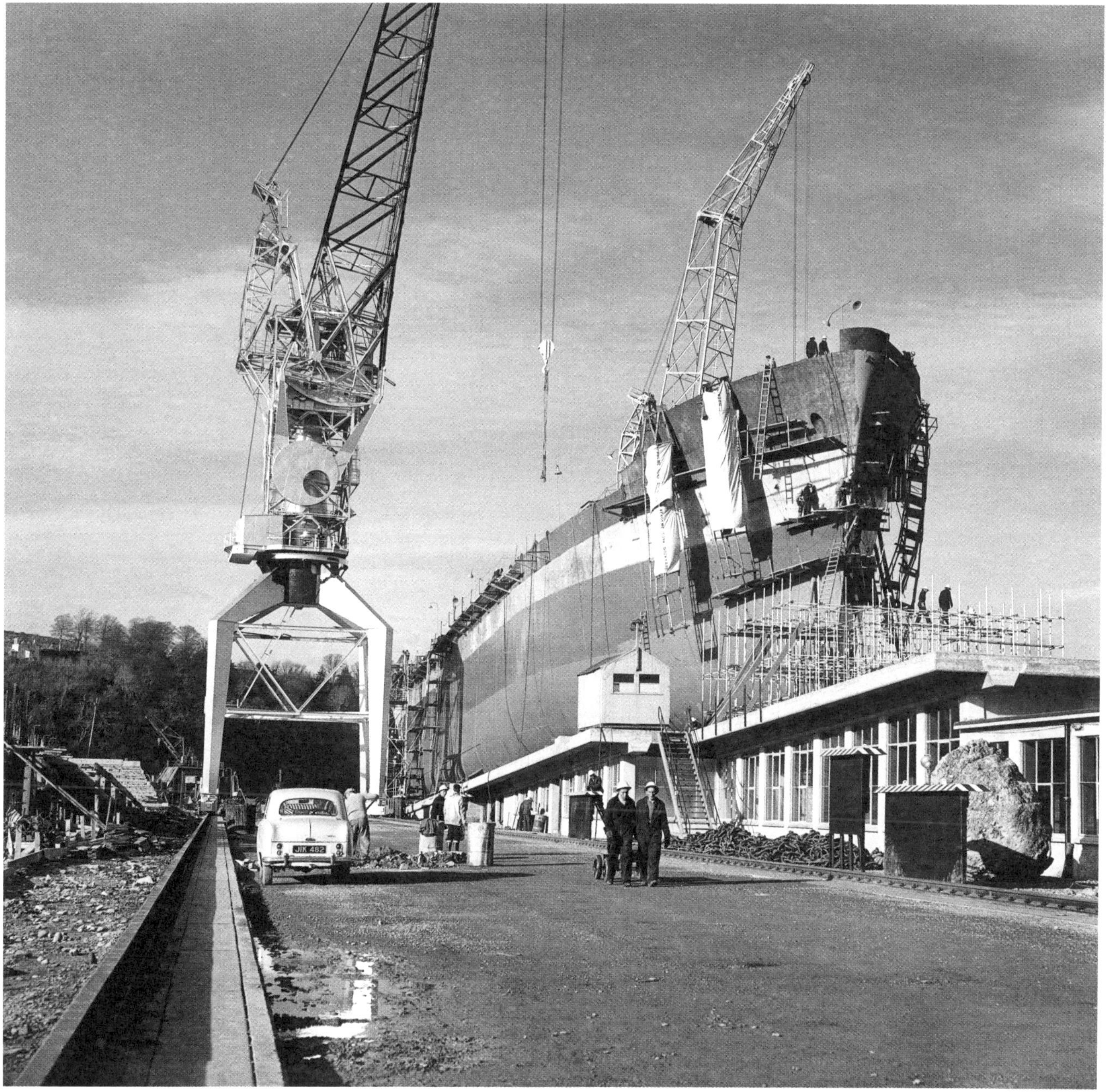
JIK 482

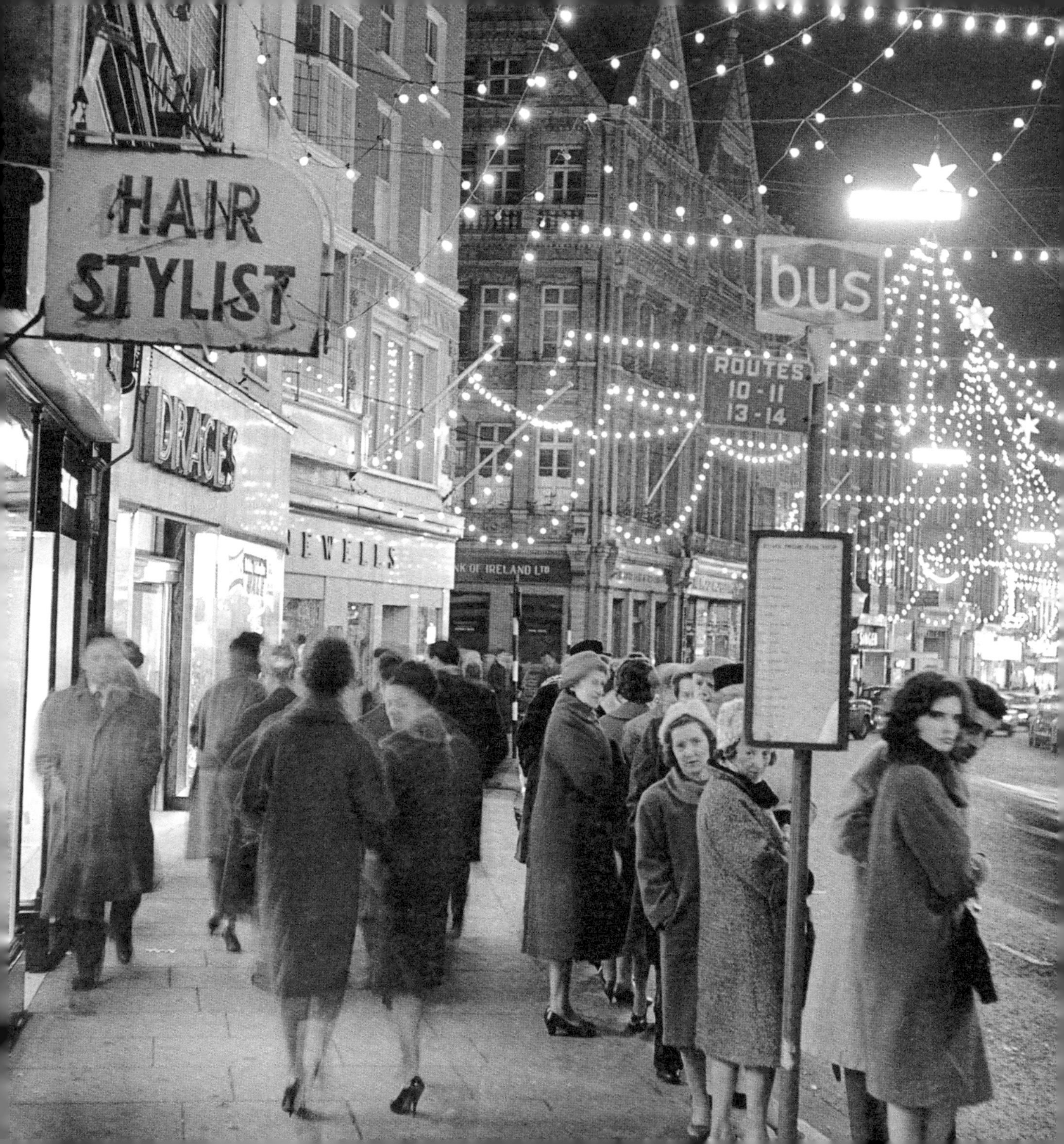
HAIR
STYLIST
DRAGES
bus
ROUTES
10 - 11
13 - 14

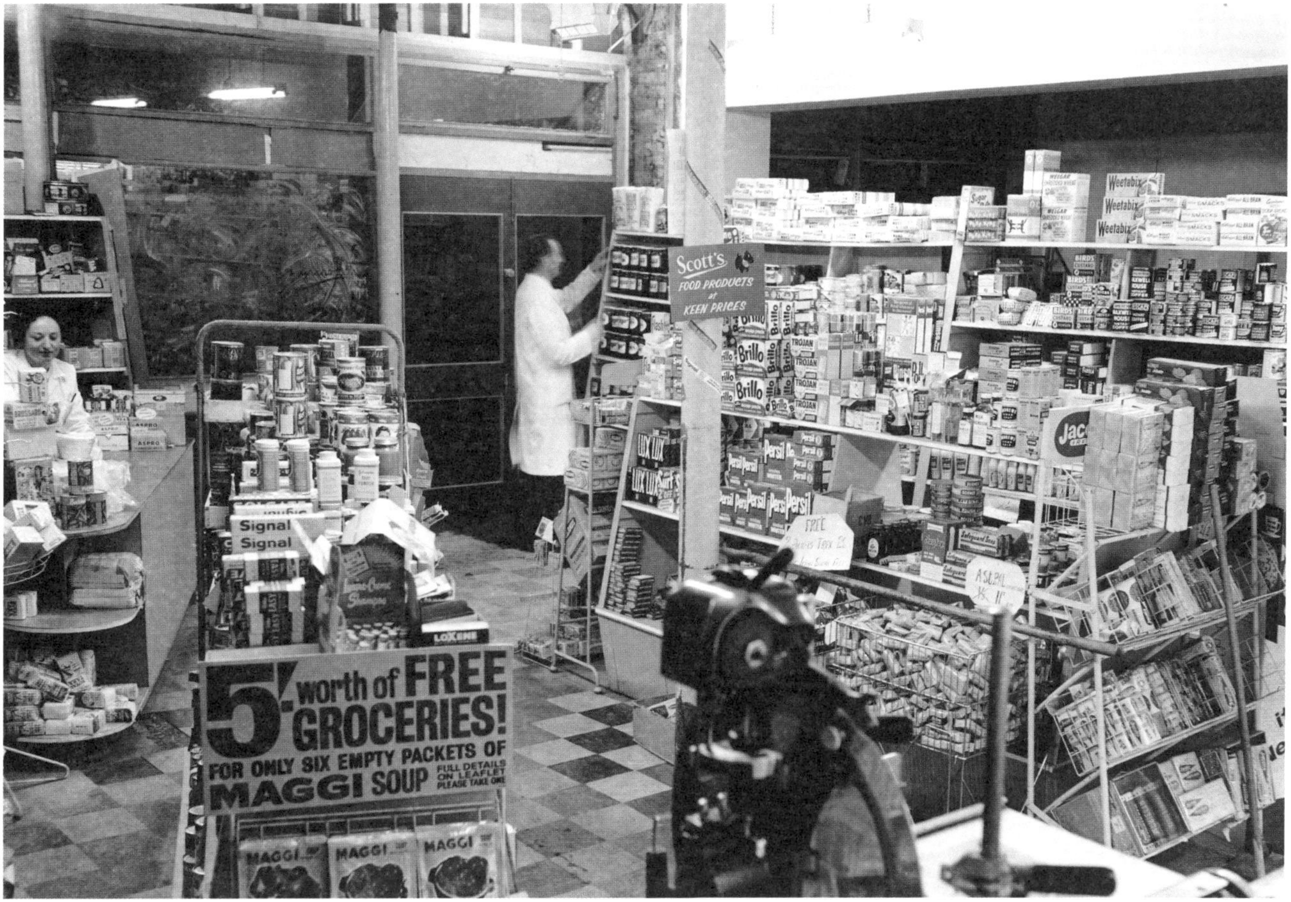

Feeneys of Dundrum, a modern grocery store, complete with white-coated shop assistants and all the essentials, from Brillo Pads to Milk of Magnesia.

16 December 1961

Waiting for the bus under the Christmas lights, Grafton Street.

9 December 1961

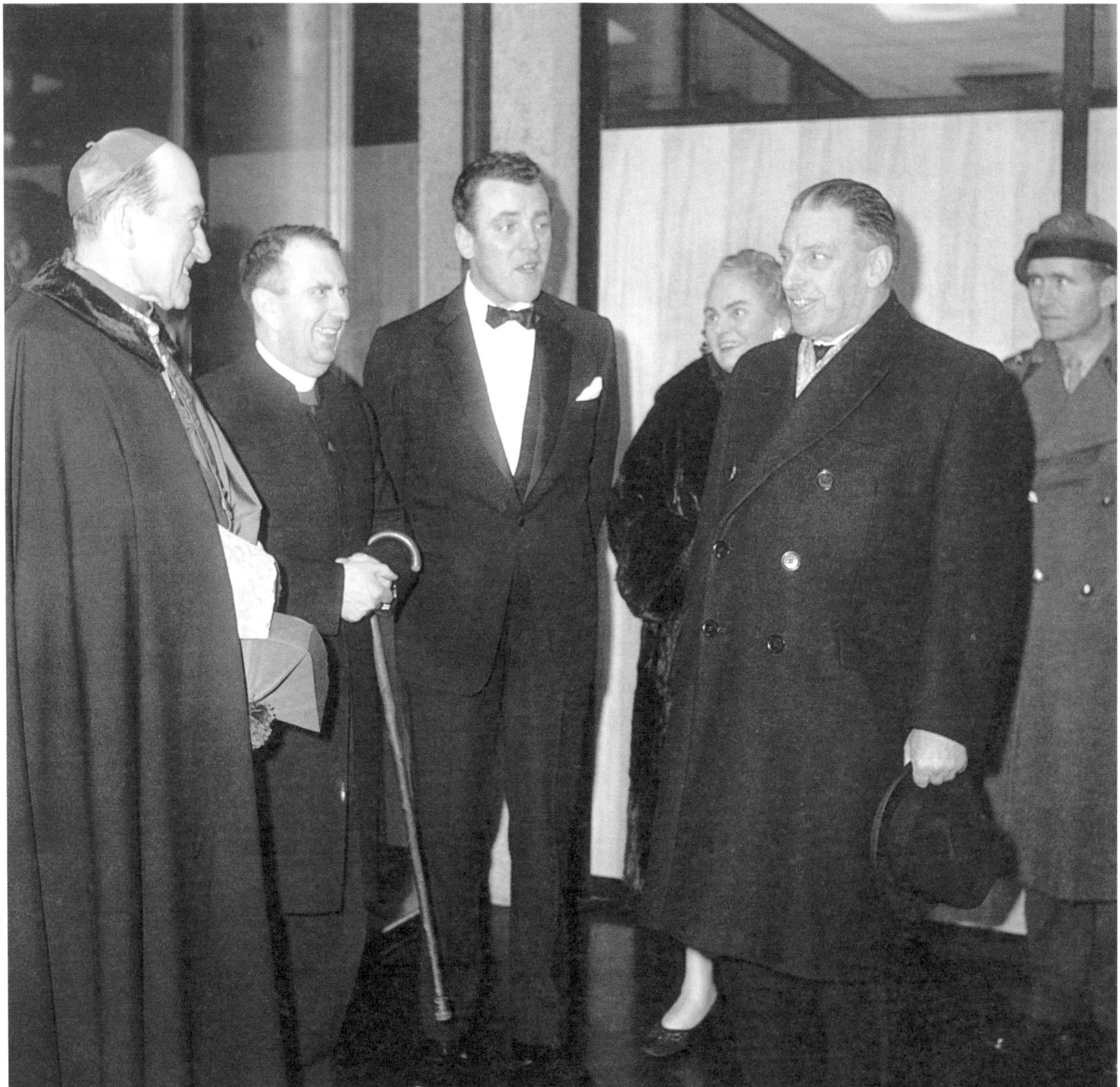

© RTÉ Stills Library.

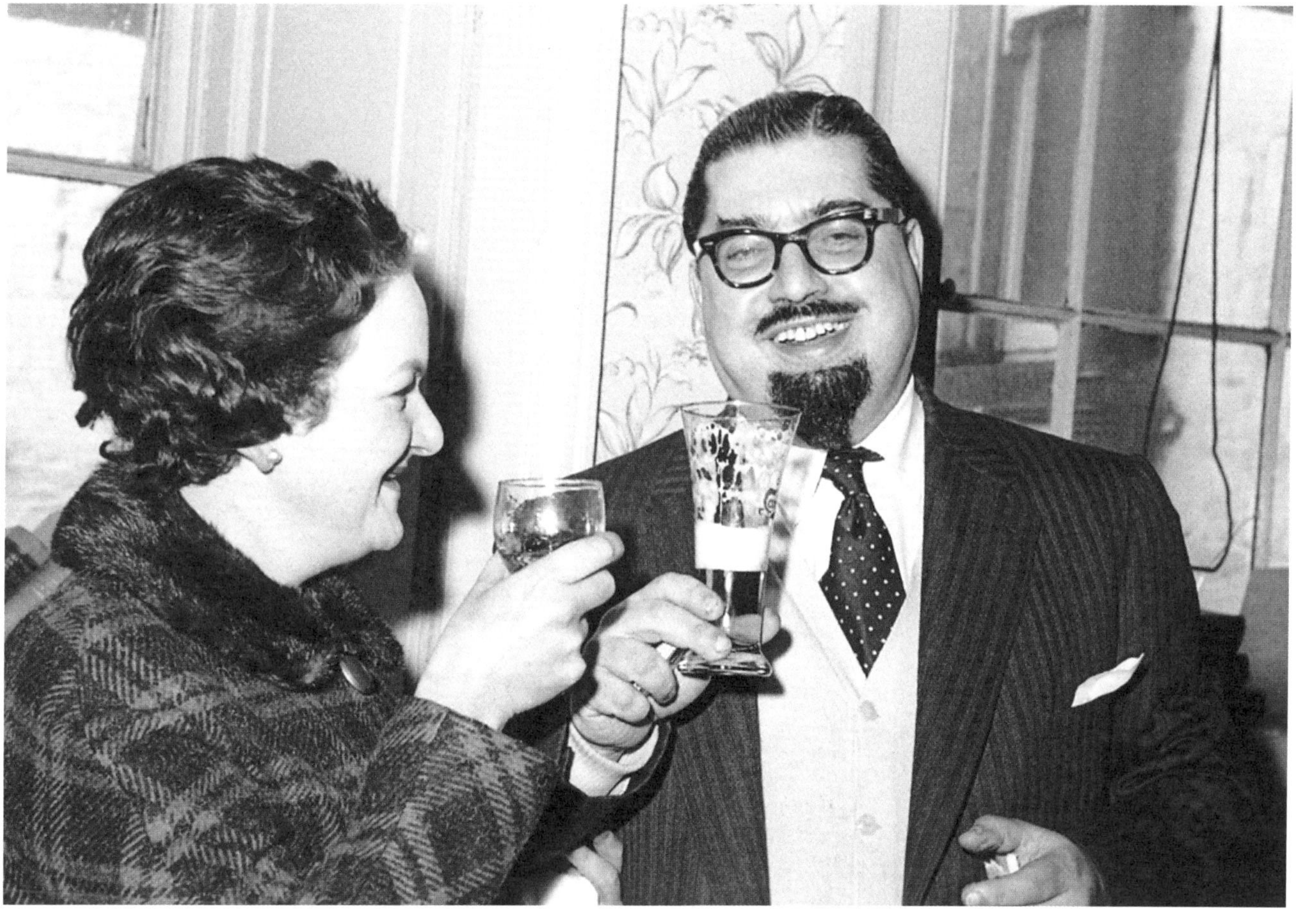

Dr Paul Singer celebrates his acquittal by the Criminal Court. He had previously been tried for fraud and sentenced to 14 years in connection with the Shanahans Stamp Auctions affair.

24 January 1962

The arrival of television was a huge event in the life of the country. The first broadcast from Teilifís Éireann was on New Year's Eve, 1961. Included in the opening night picture are Archbishop John Charles McQuaid, Eamon Andrews, Mrs Lemass and Taoiseach Sean Lemass.

31 December 1961

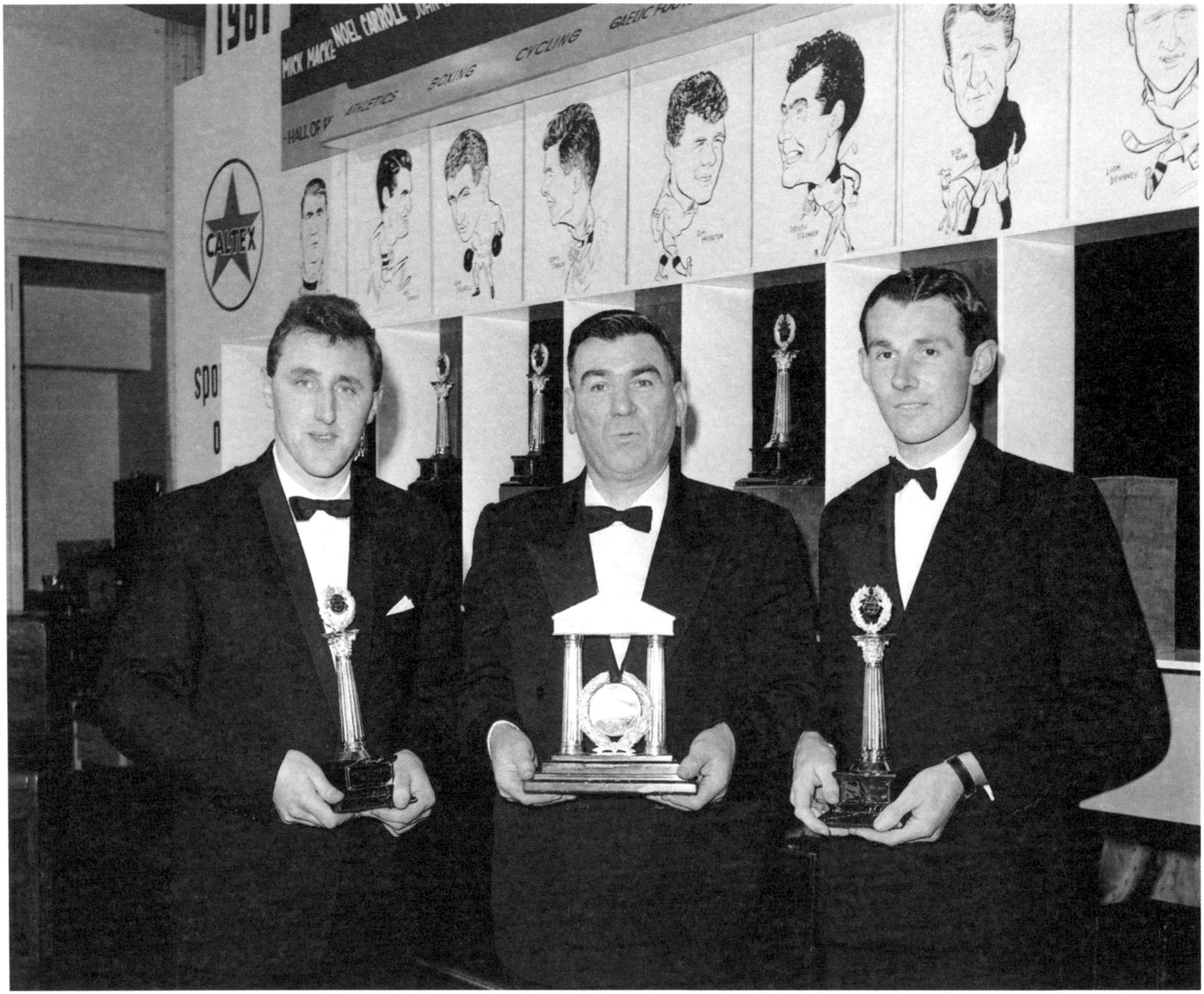

Caltex sports stars award-winners: Liam Devaney, Tipperary, (Hurling); Mick Mackey, Limerick (Hall of Fame), Tommy Wade, Tipperary (Show Jumping).

1 February 1962

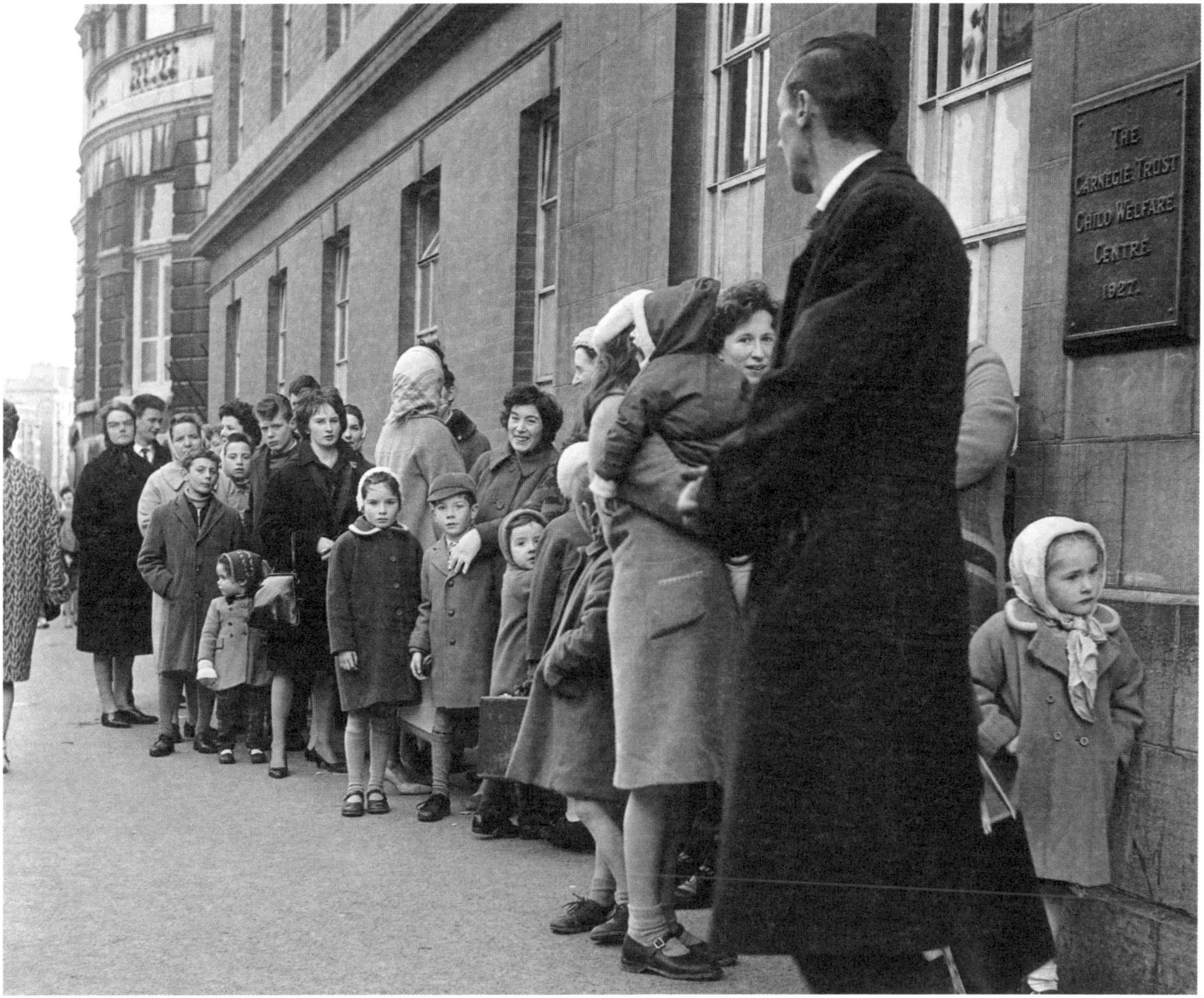

Mothers and children queue outside the Carnegie Trust Child Welfare Centre on Lord Edward Street to get vaccinated against smallpox.

5 February 1962

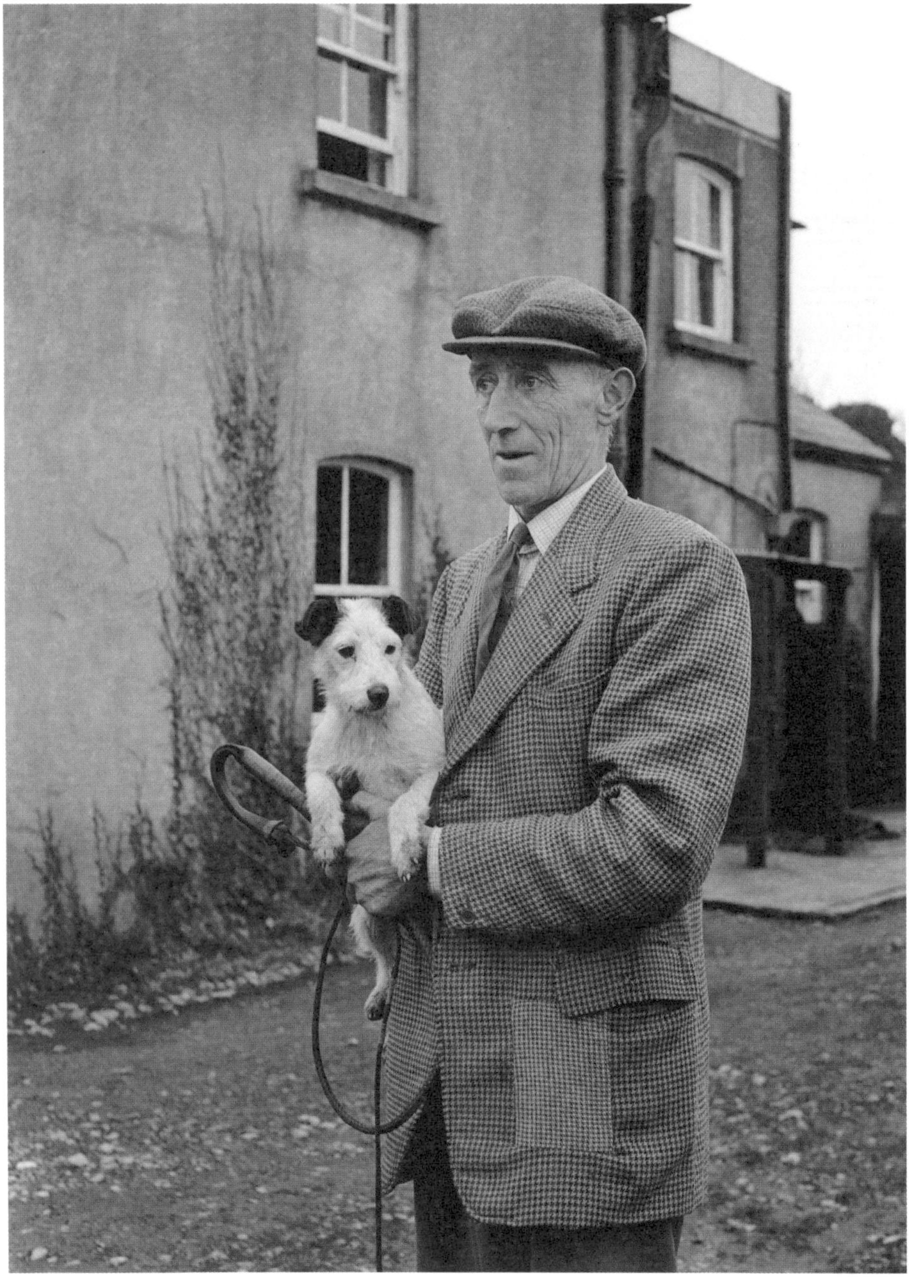

Harry Walker, Kennelman, Westmeath Hounds, Mullingar, with his dog, Judy, at the Kennels, Knockdrin, Mullingar.

5 February 1962

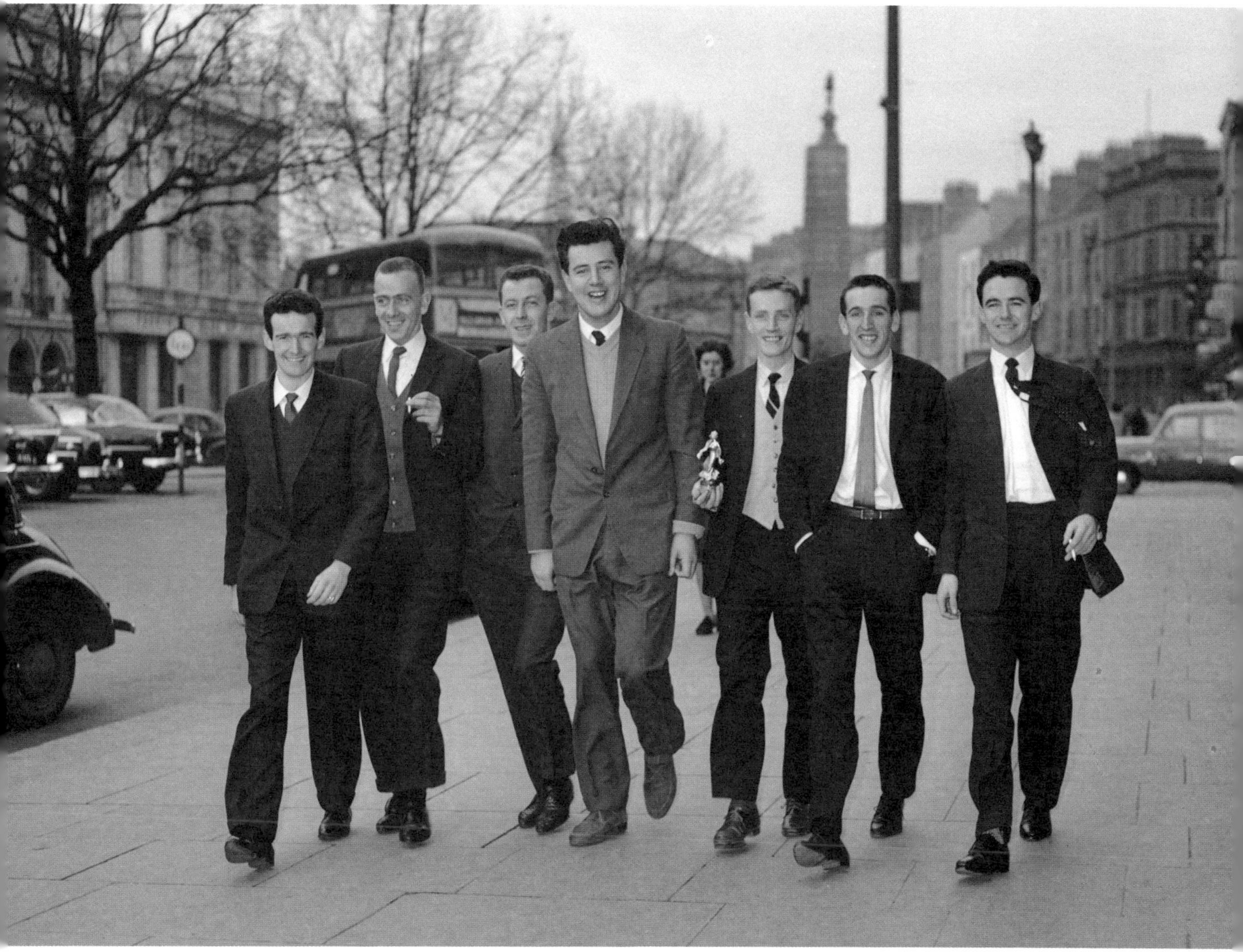

Members of the Royal Showband, Waterford, pictured with the Carl Alan award, which they received in London the previous night. From left: Tom Dunphy, Gerry Cullen, Eddie Sullivan, Brendan Bowyer, Michael Coppinger, Charlie Matthews, Jim Conlon.

6 February 1962

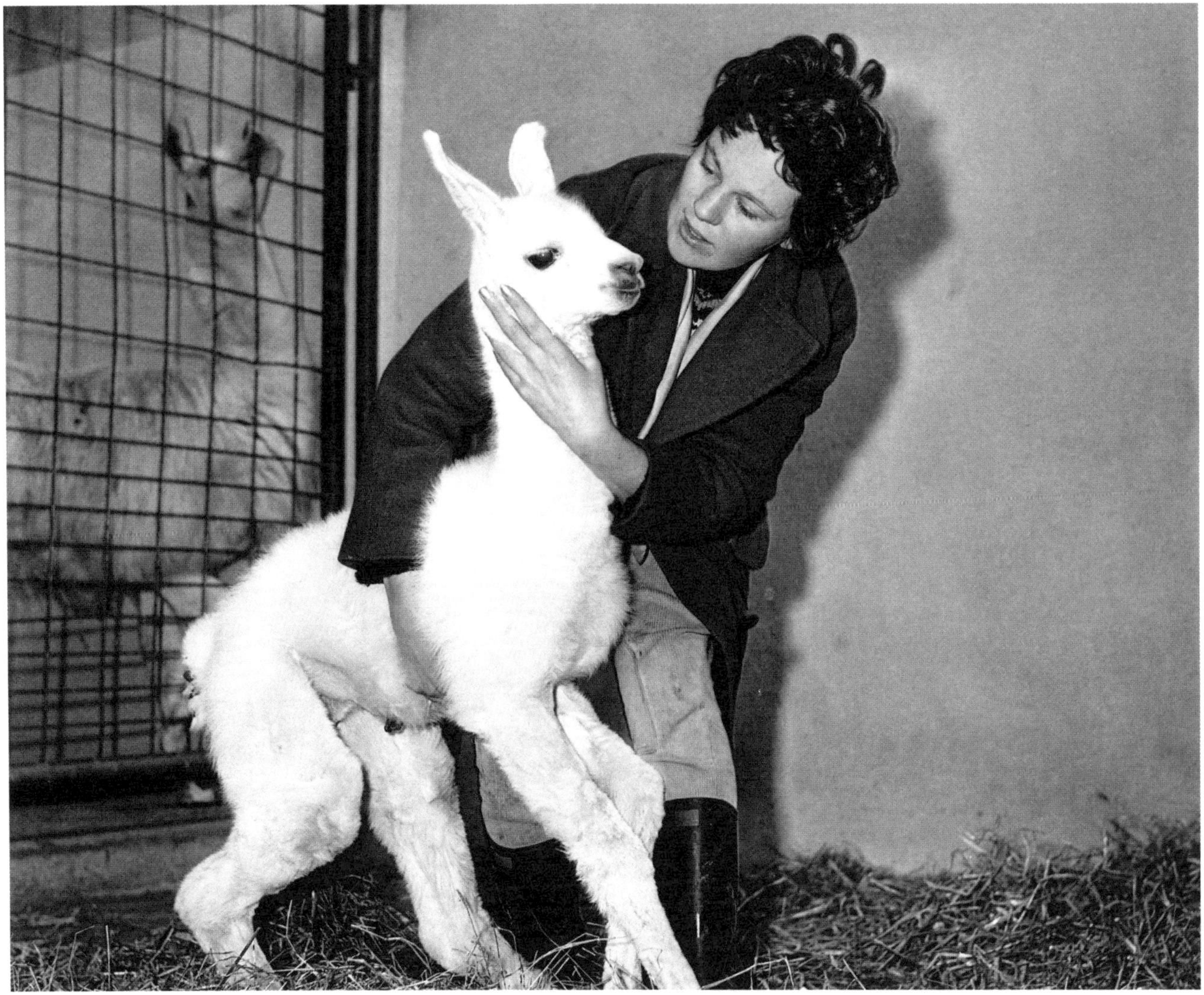

Miss Maeve Allen, with five-day-old llama 'Snowdrop' at Dublin Zoo.

7 March 1962

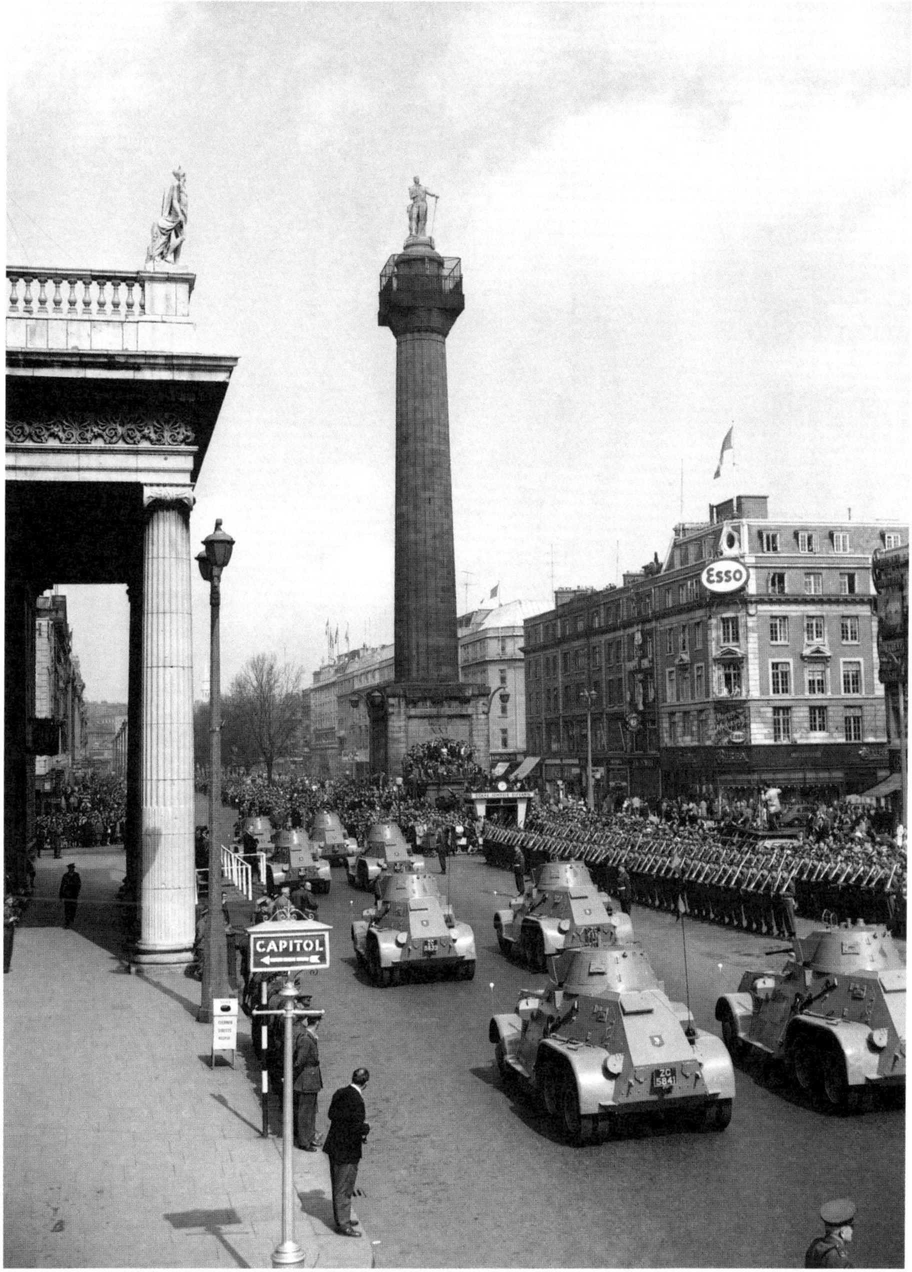

The army's armoured car division passes by the GPO and Nelson's Pillar during the Easter Sunday Military Parade.

22 April 1962

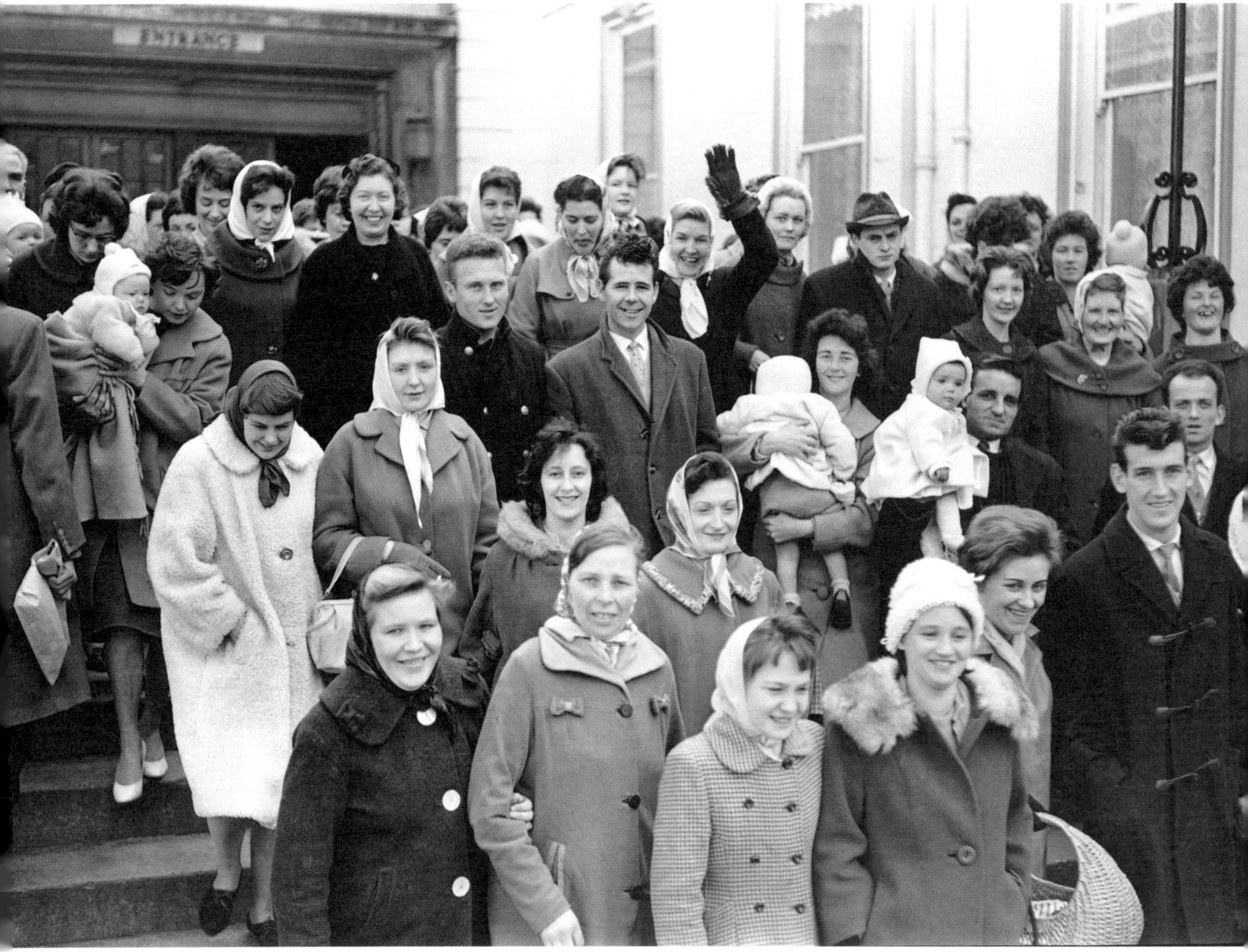

Some of the hundreds who turned up at the Mansion House for the annual draw for houses for newly-weds.

6 April 1962

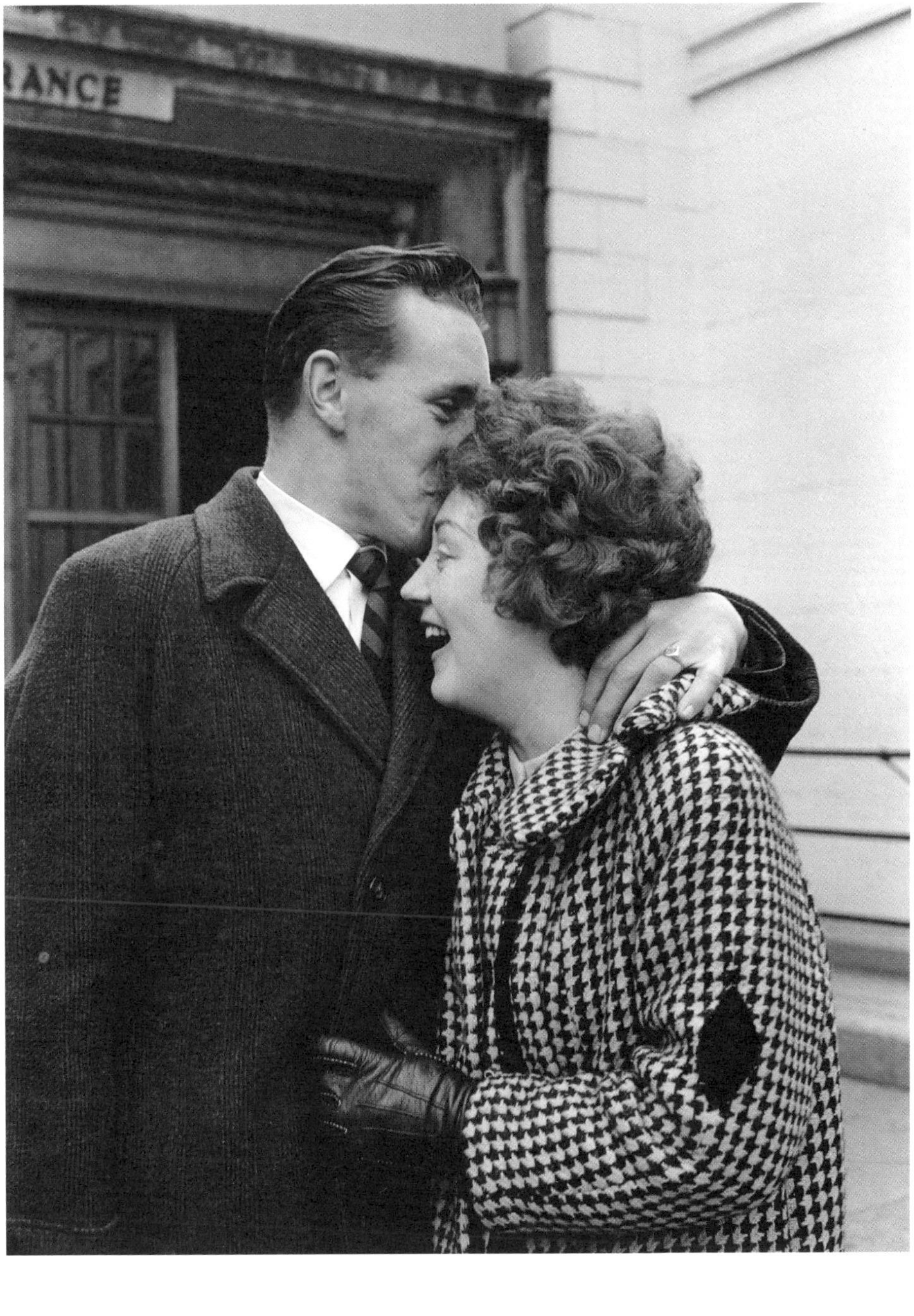

Bus conductor Liam Alfred and his wife of 8 months, Mary, were one of the lucky couples to get a house. (Note the diamond patch on Mary's coat sleeve. It was commonplace at the time for family members to wear a black patch at the time of bereavement.)

6 April 1962

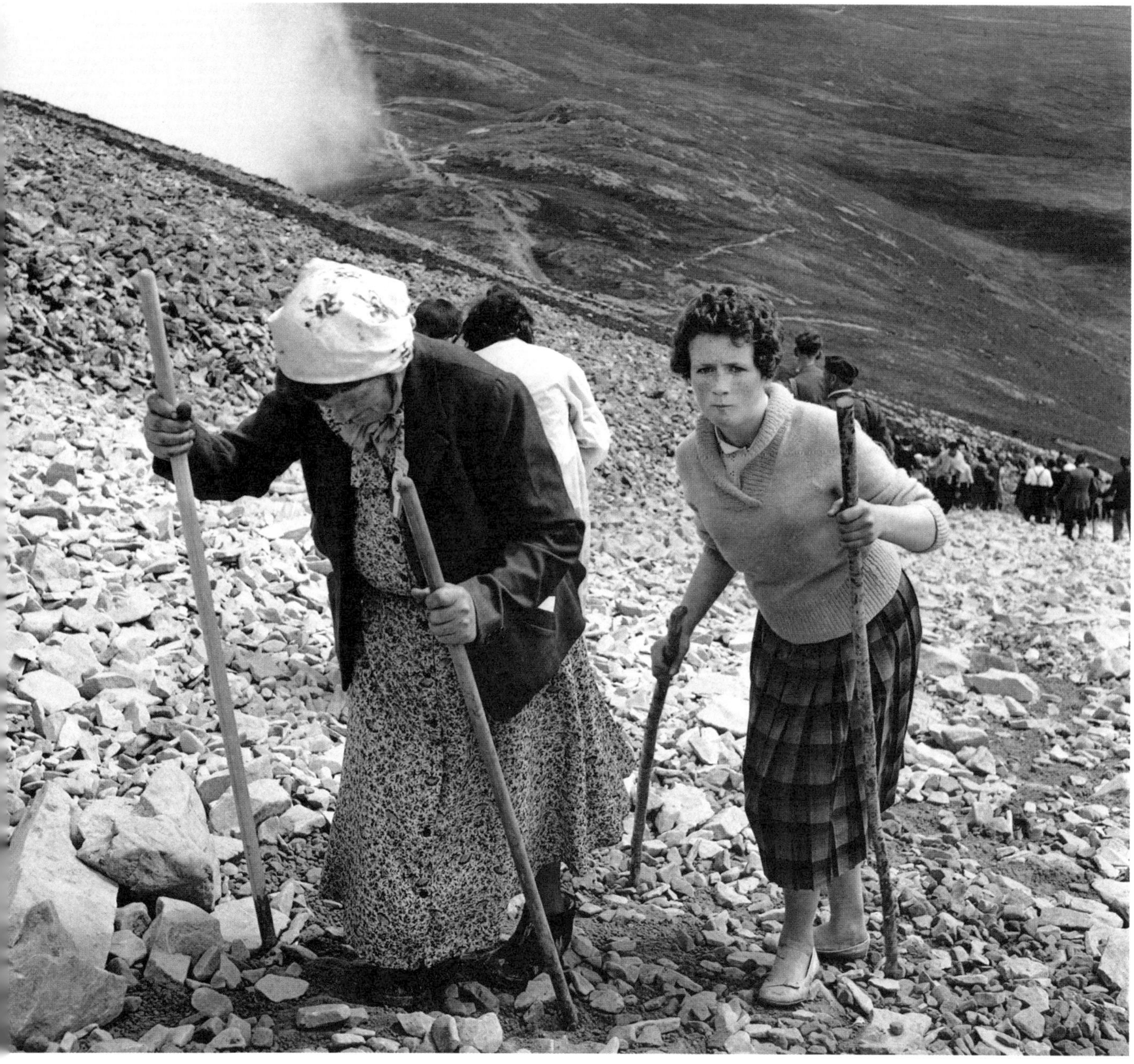

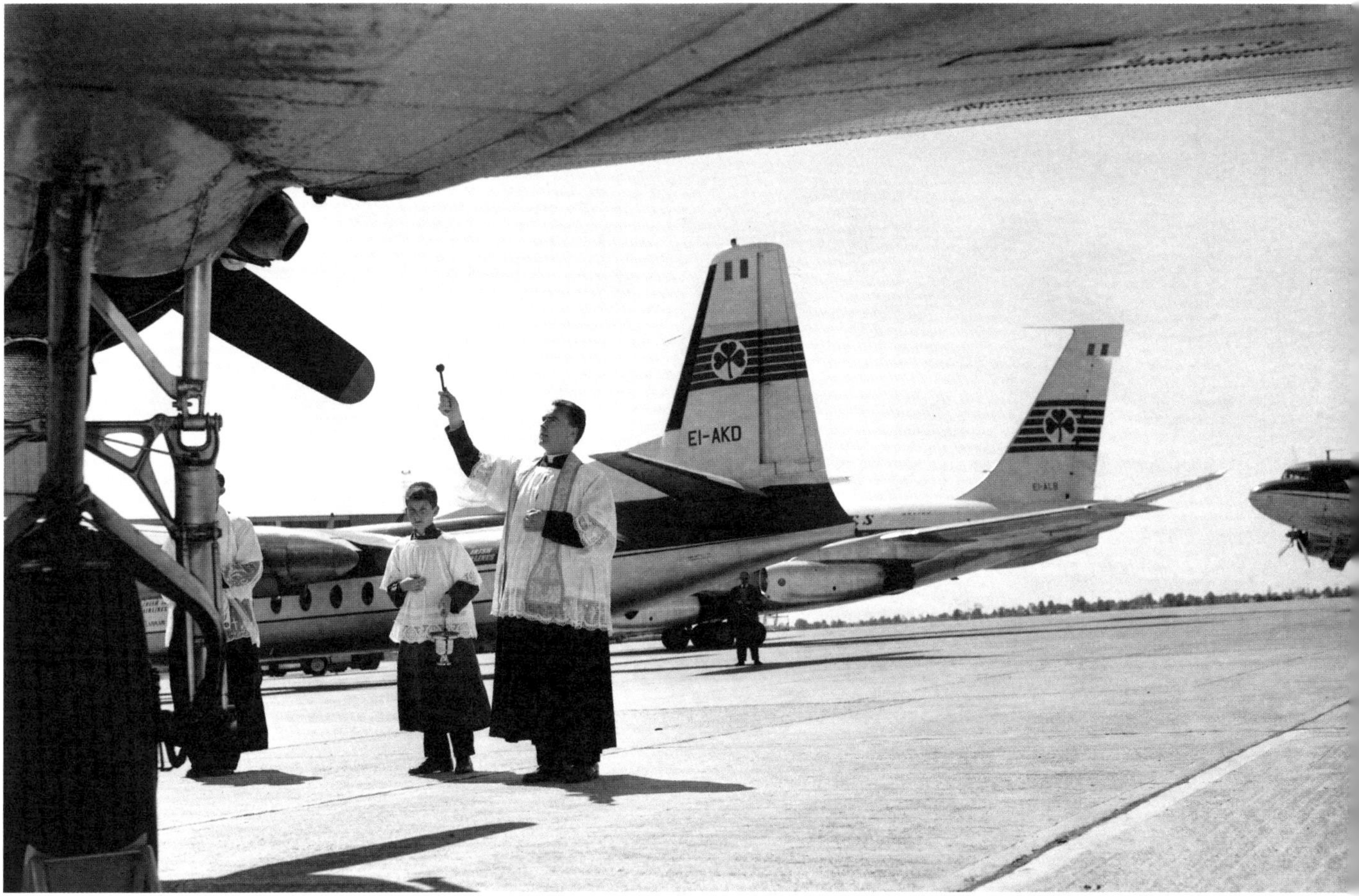

Fr. Donal O'Leary, C.C. Swords, carries out the annual ceremony of the Blessing of the Fleet at Dublin Airport.

3 June1962

Pilgrims make the arduous climb up to the top of Croagh Patrick, Westport, Co. Mayo. A place of pilgrimage since St Patrick's time, and some say before that, on 'Reek Sunday', the last Sunday in July, thousands make the treacherous ascent.

16 May 1962

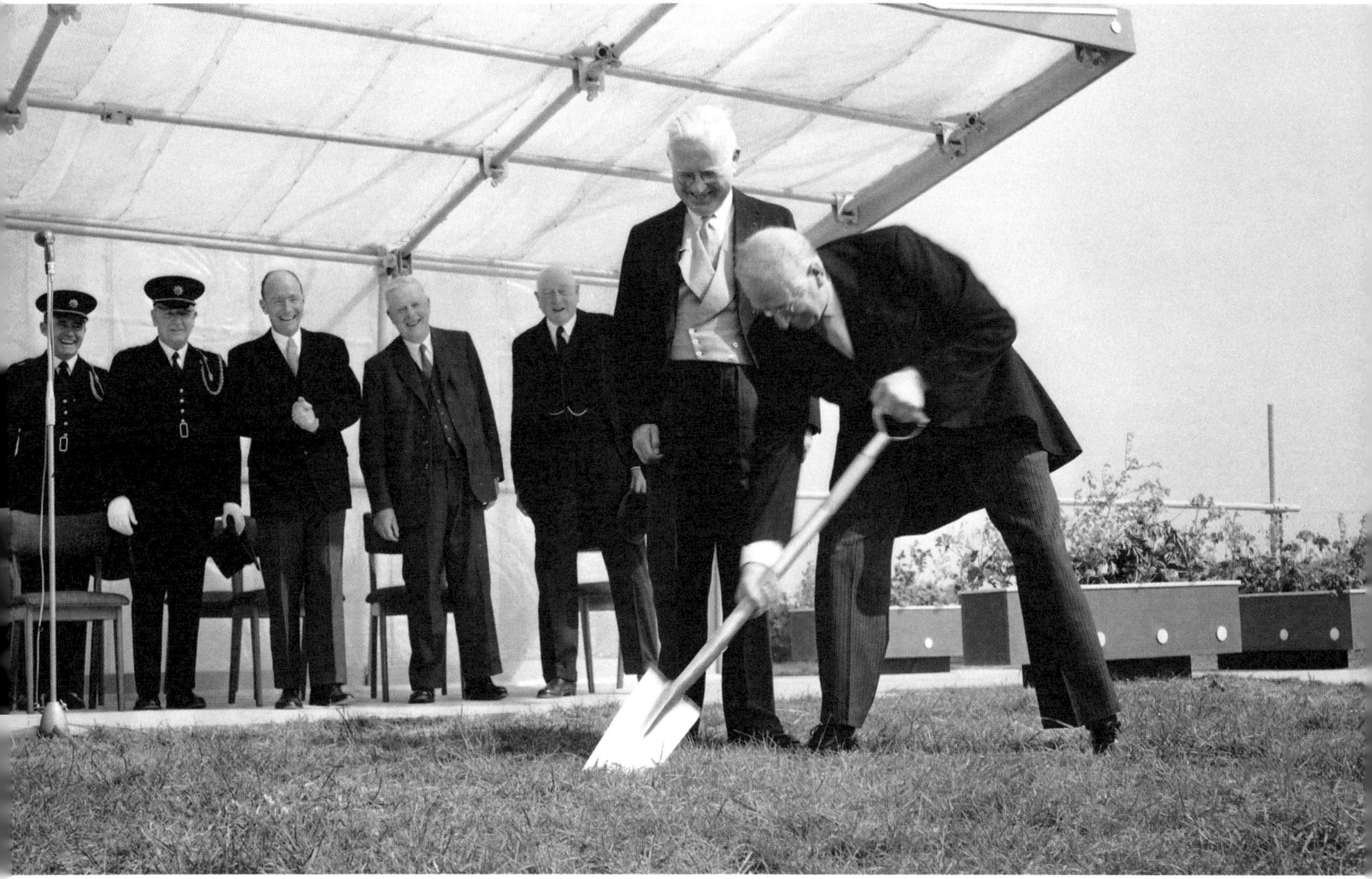

President de Valera cuts the first sod for the Faculty of Science building of University College Dublin, at Belfield. This was the first building of the new university campus. Behind the President is Professor Michael Tierney, President of the college, and among those in the background are Dr Patrick Hillery, Minister for Education, and Dr Ryan, Minister for Finance.

7 June 1962

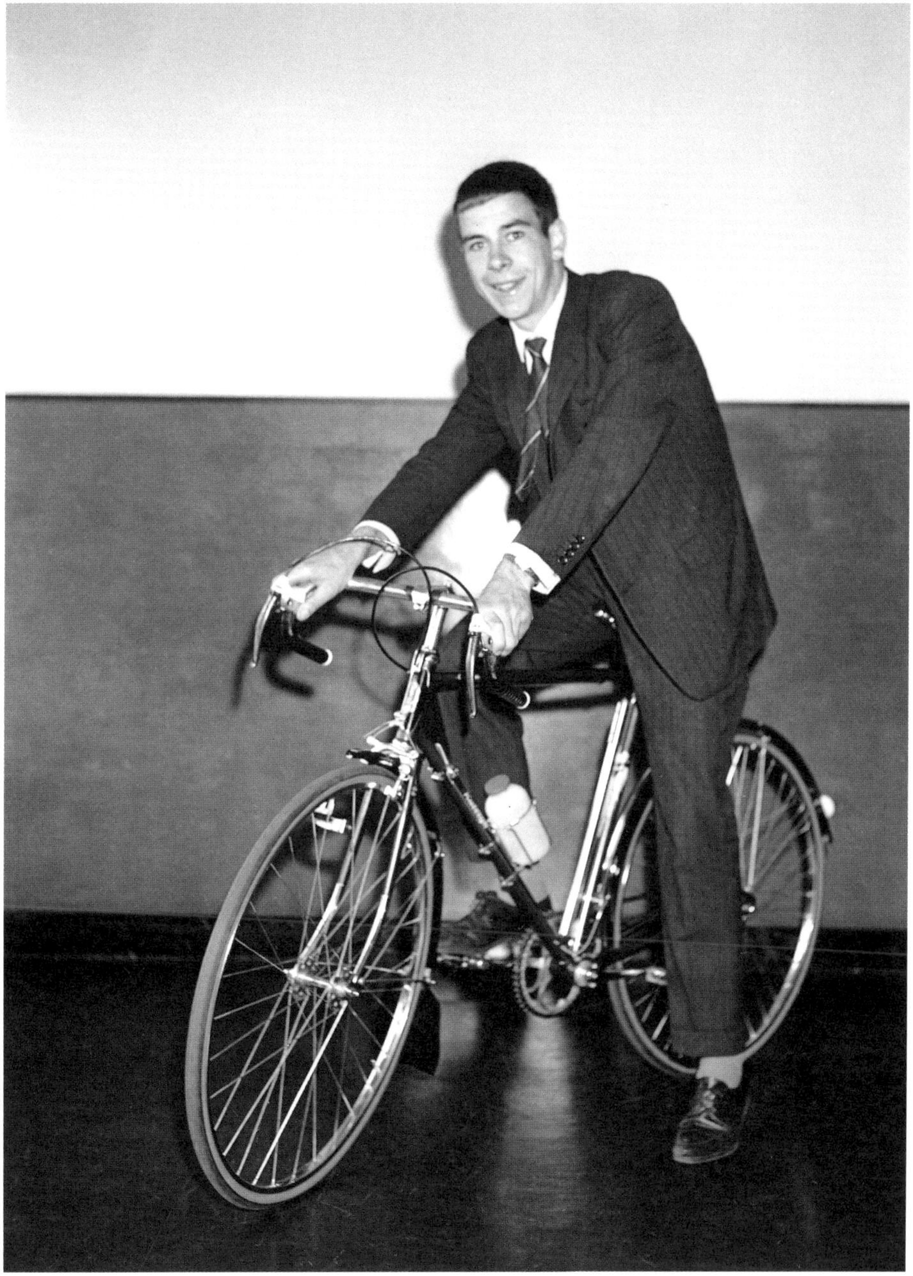

Seamus O'Hanlon, winner of Rás Tailteann 1962, on the Raleigh 'Gran Sport' bicycle with Campagnole 10-speed gears presented to him during his tour of Irish Raleigh Industries Ltd.

14 August 1962

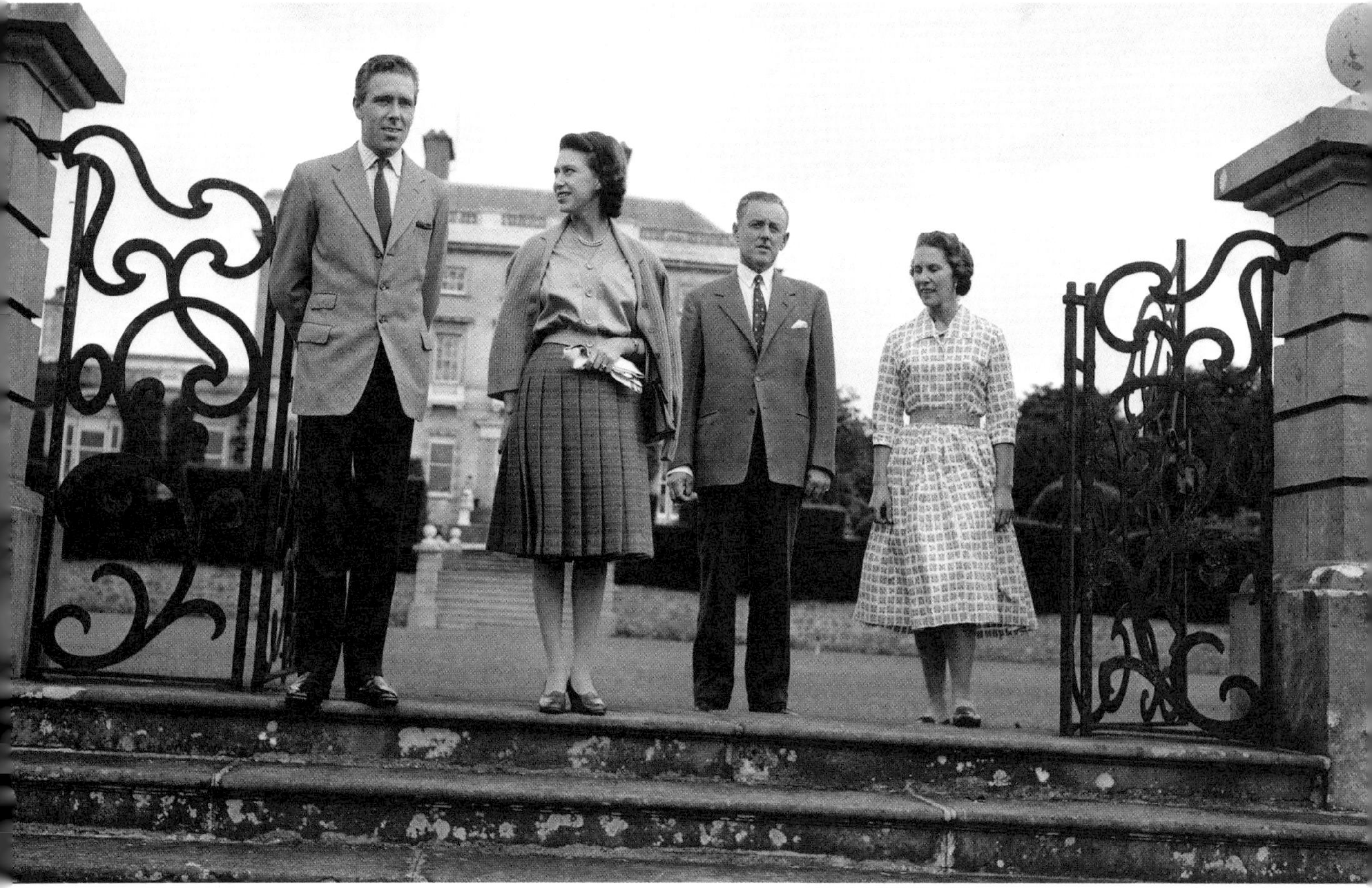

Princess Margaret on holidays in Ireland, pictured at Abbeyleix House with her husband, Lord Snowdon (left) and her hosts, Viscount and Viscountess de Vesci.

17 August 1962

Former US President Dwight Eisenhower golfing at Portmarnock. To his right is noted Irish golfer, Joe Carr.

23 August 1962

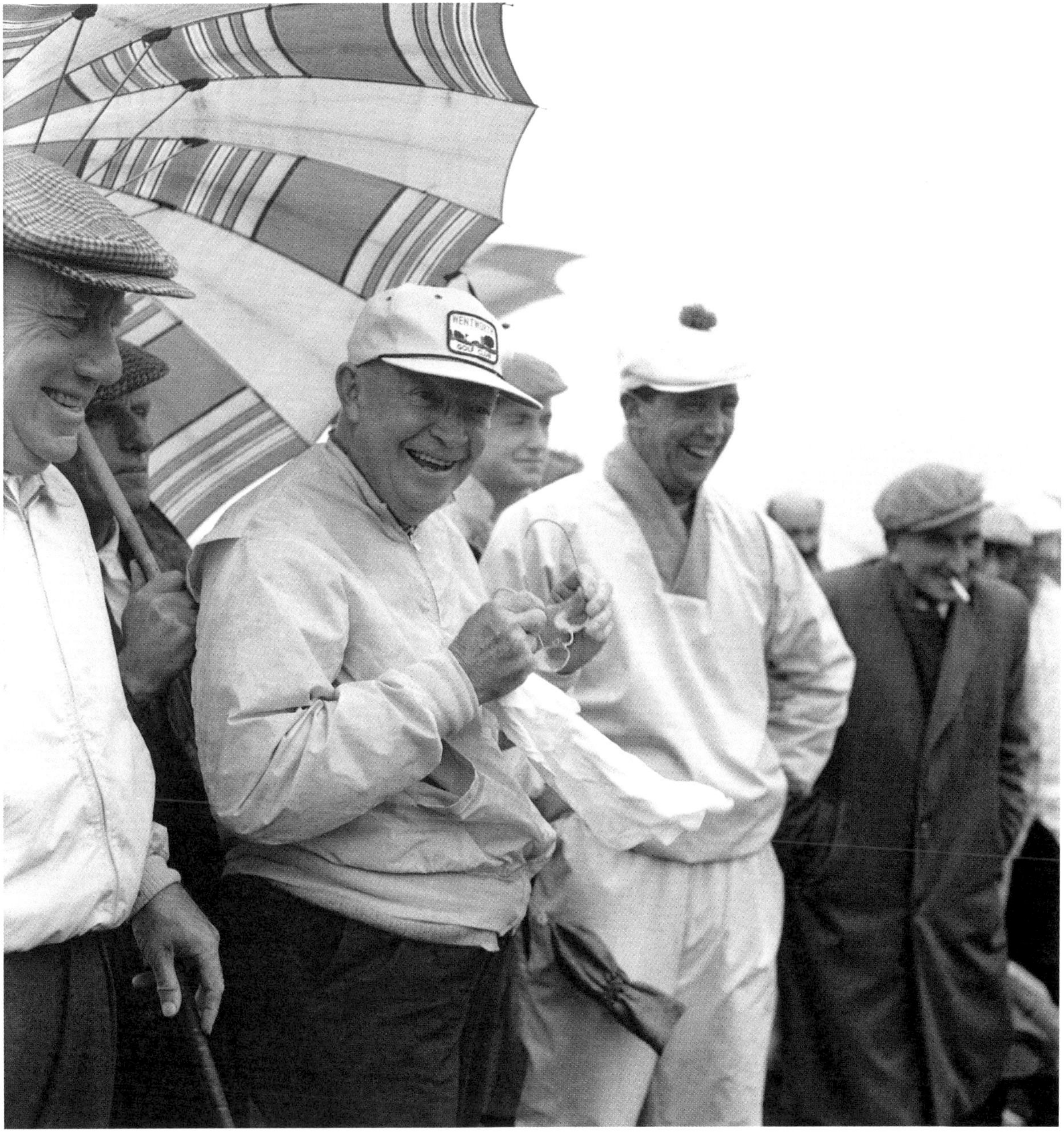
WENTWORTH

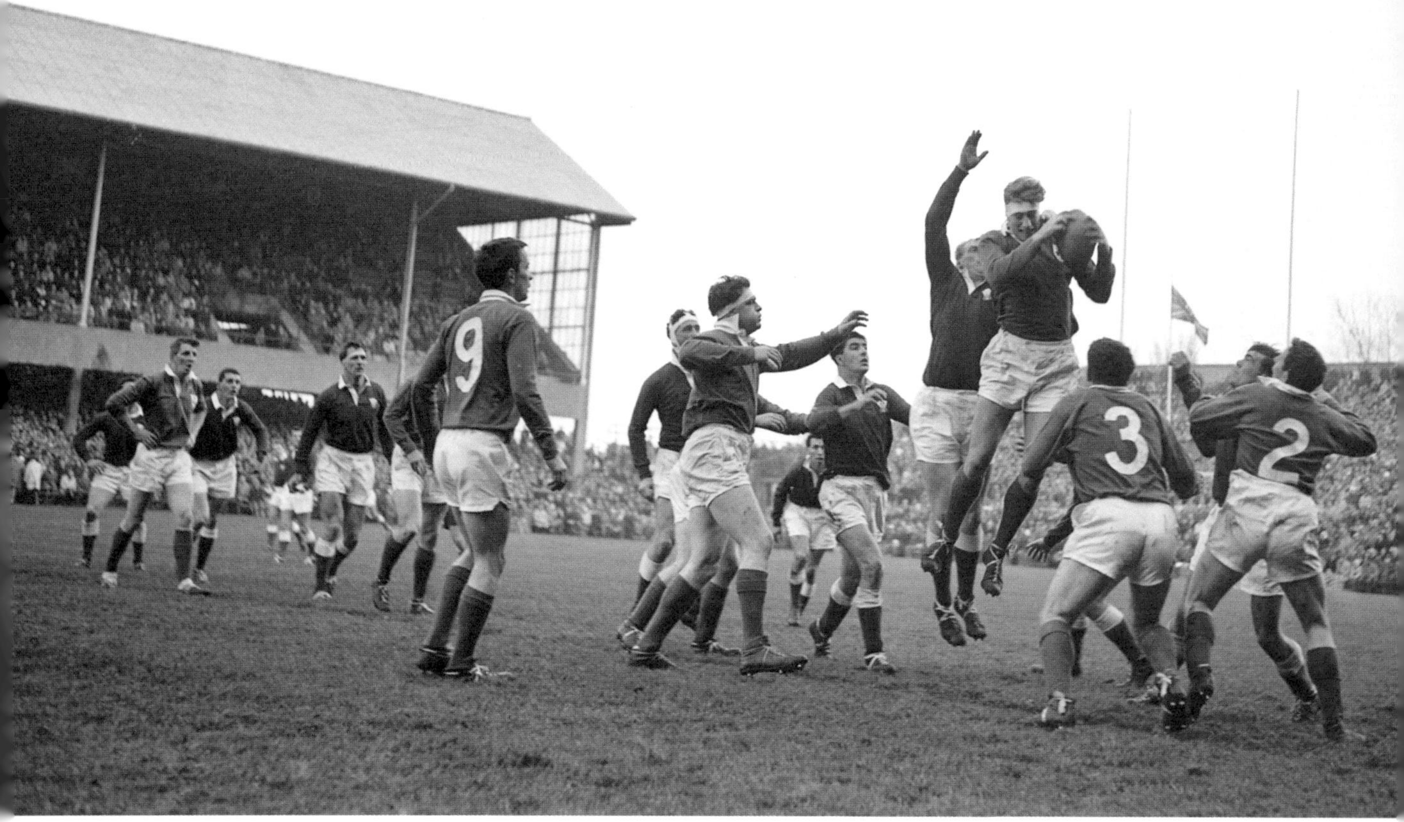
9
3
2

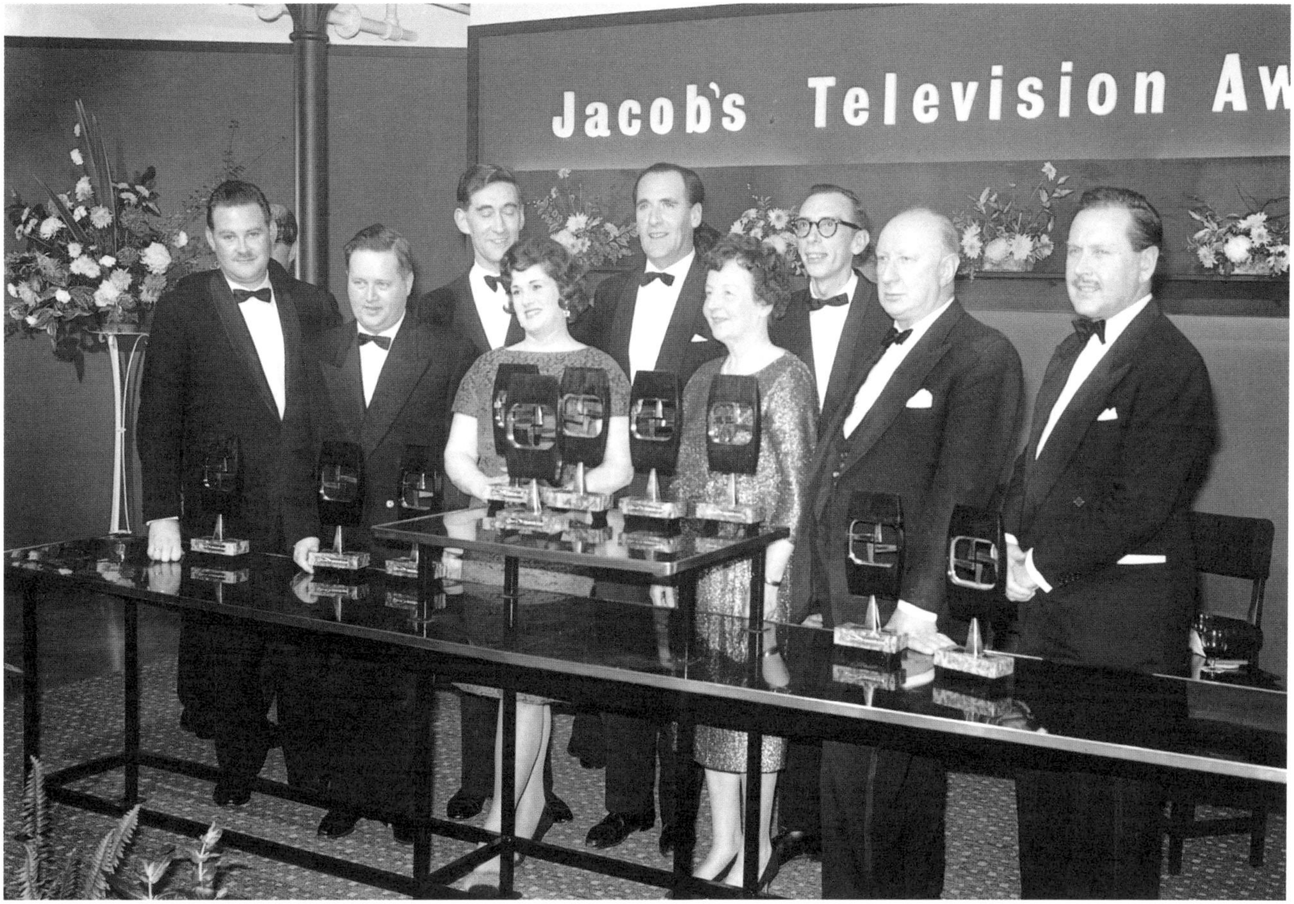

Recipients of Jacobs Television Awards in 1962 included Proinsias Mac Aonghusa and Micheál Ó hEithir (left and second from left), Charles Mitchell (centre), and Hilton Edwards (second from right).

4 December 1962

Willie John McBride captures the ball in the Ireland v Wales Five Nations Championship match at Lansdowne Road. The game ended in a 3-3 draw. McBride played 63 times for Ireland in a 13-year international career, 11 times as captain, and won 17 caps with the British and Irish Lions, captaining the unbeaten Lions team in the 1974 tour.

17 November 1962

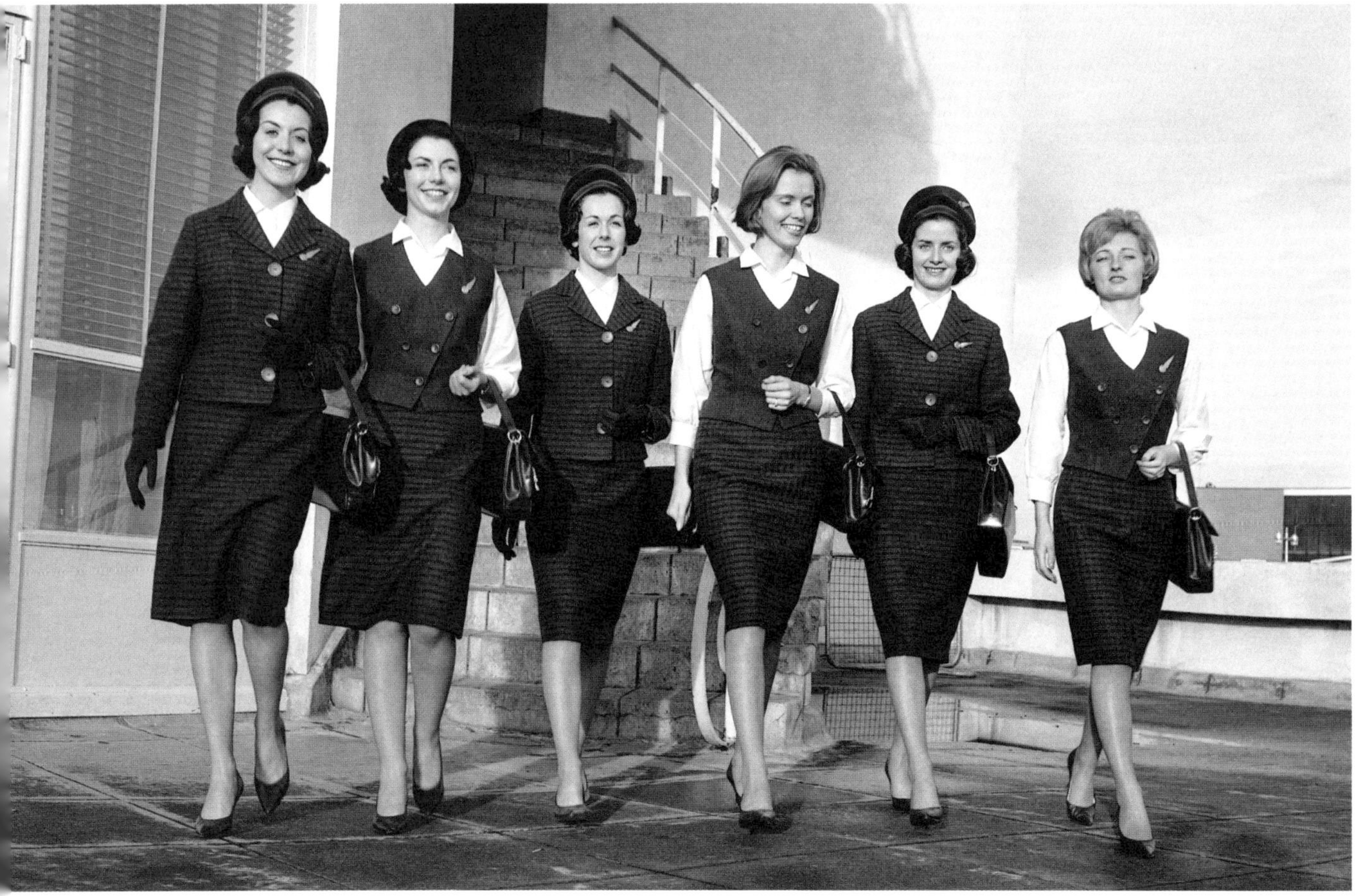

A group of Aer Lingus hostesses model their new uniform of Irish tweed. The three-piece ensemble in St Patrick's blue is worn with a sculpted beret and accessories in midnight blue. The material was designed and made by the McNutt Weaving Co., Downings, Co Donegal.

13 December 1962

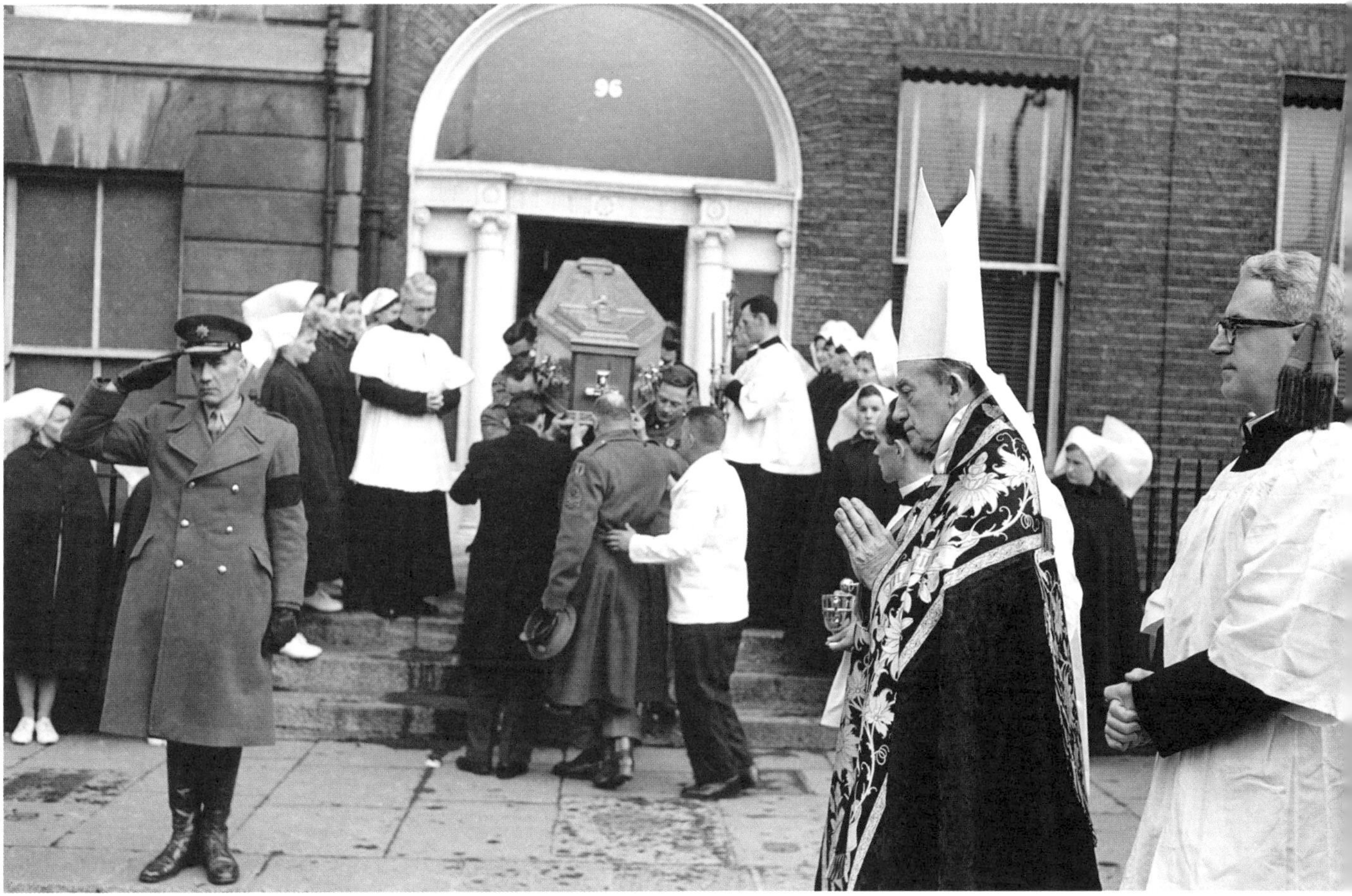

The remains of Cardinal D'Alton leave St Vincent's Nursing Home, Dublin, borne by members of the defence forces. Dr John Charles Mc Quaid, Archbishop of Dublin (in mitre), blessed the coffin as it was taken to the hearse. The cardinal was buried in St Patrick's Cathedral, Armagh.

2 February 1963

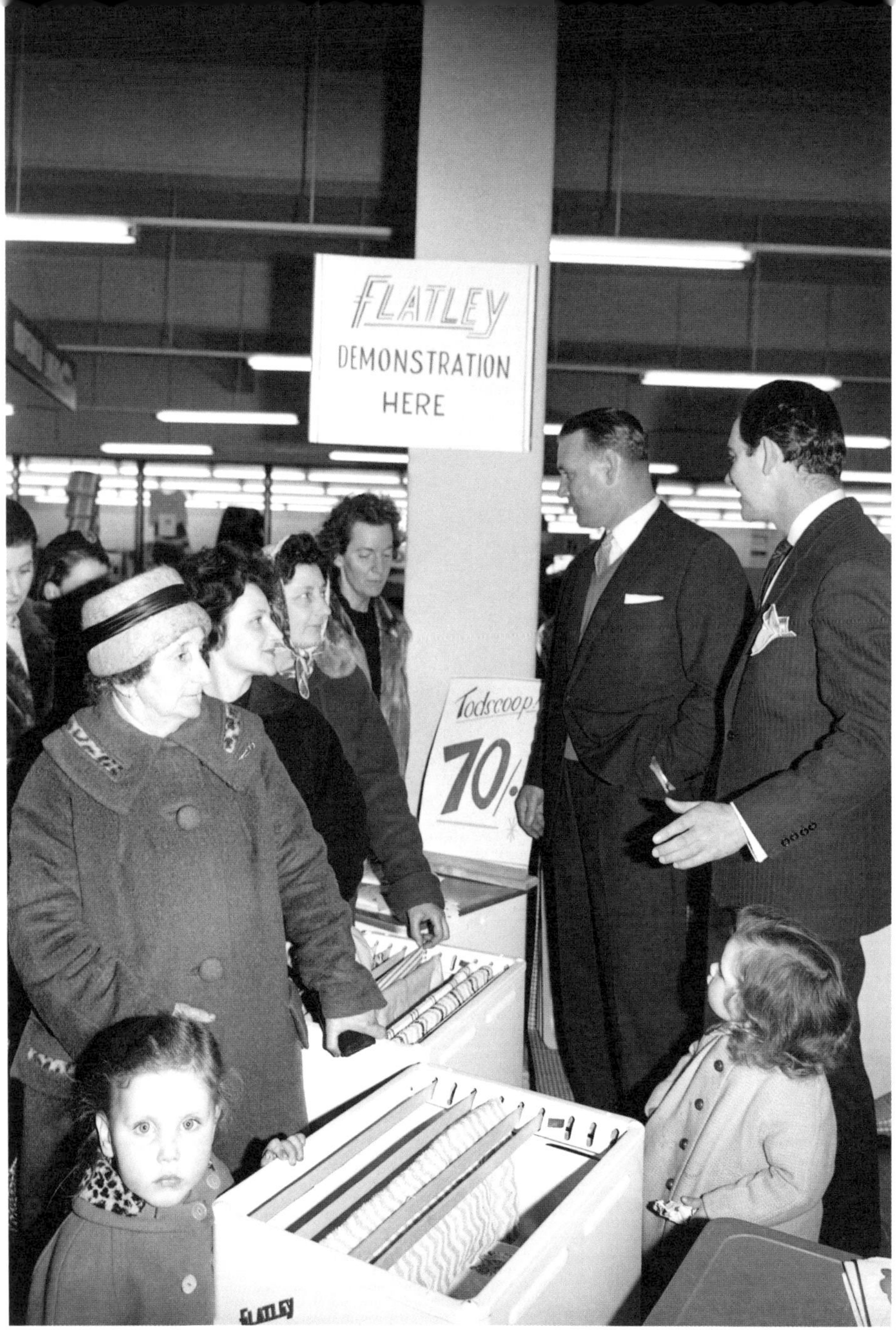

A demonstration of the Flatley Dryer at Todco Ltd. Basically a metal cabinet with a heater unit at the base and removable wooden slats for hanging clothes at the top, the clothes dryer was very popular for many years, and for a time was manufactured in Bantry, Co Cork. The inventor, A J Flatley, is standing immediately to the right of the pillar.

14 March 1963

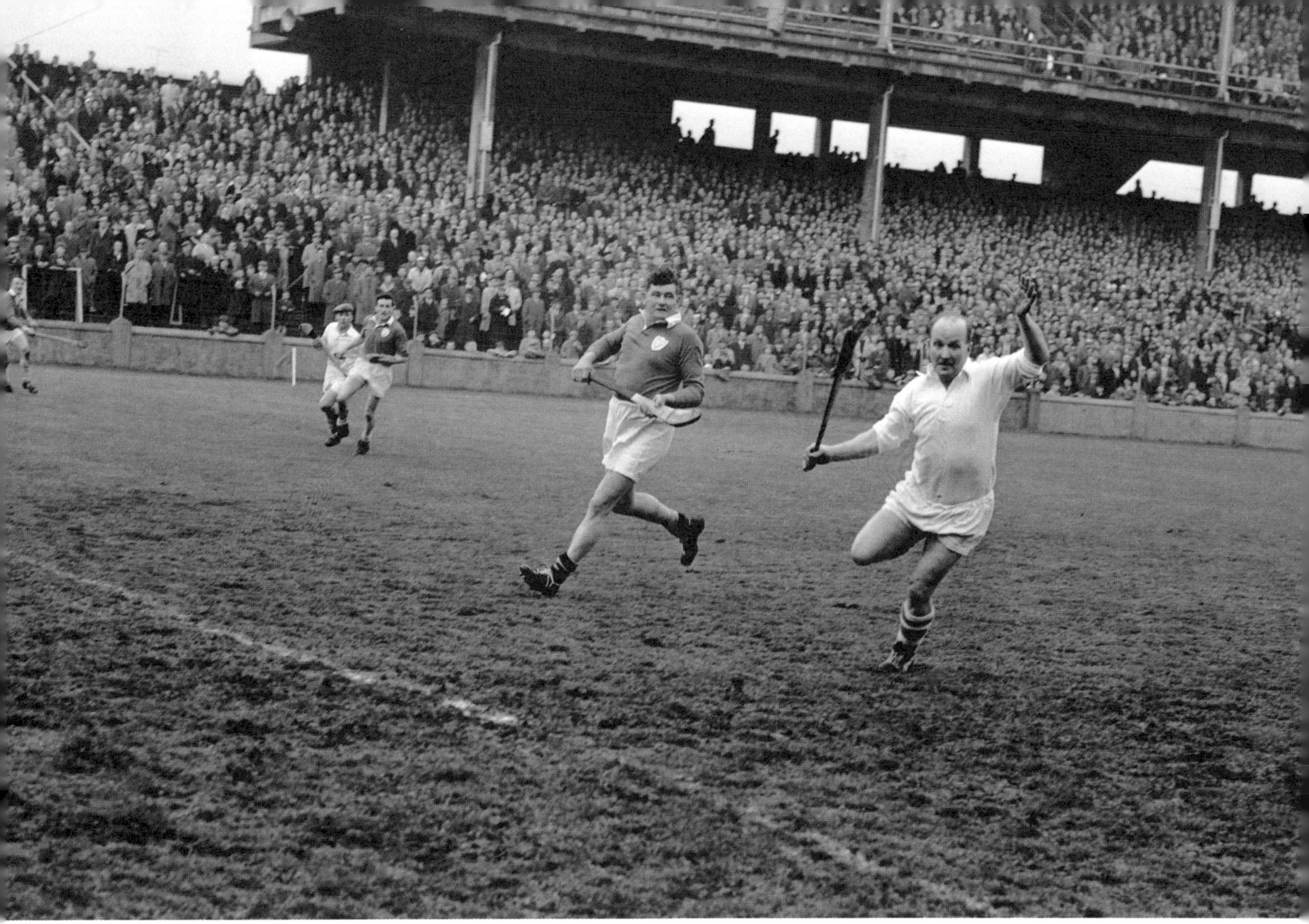

Famed Cork hurler, Christy Ring, in full flight in the 1963 Railway Cup Final, Leinster v Munster. (l to r): Lar Foley, Jimmy Doyle, John Nolan, Jim 'Link' Walsh, Christy Ring. Widely regarded as one of the greatest hurlers in the history of the game, he won eight senior All Ireland medals.

17 March 1963

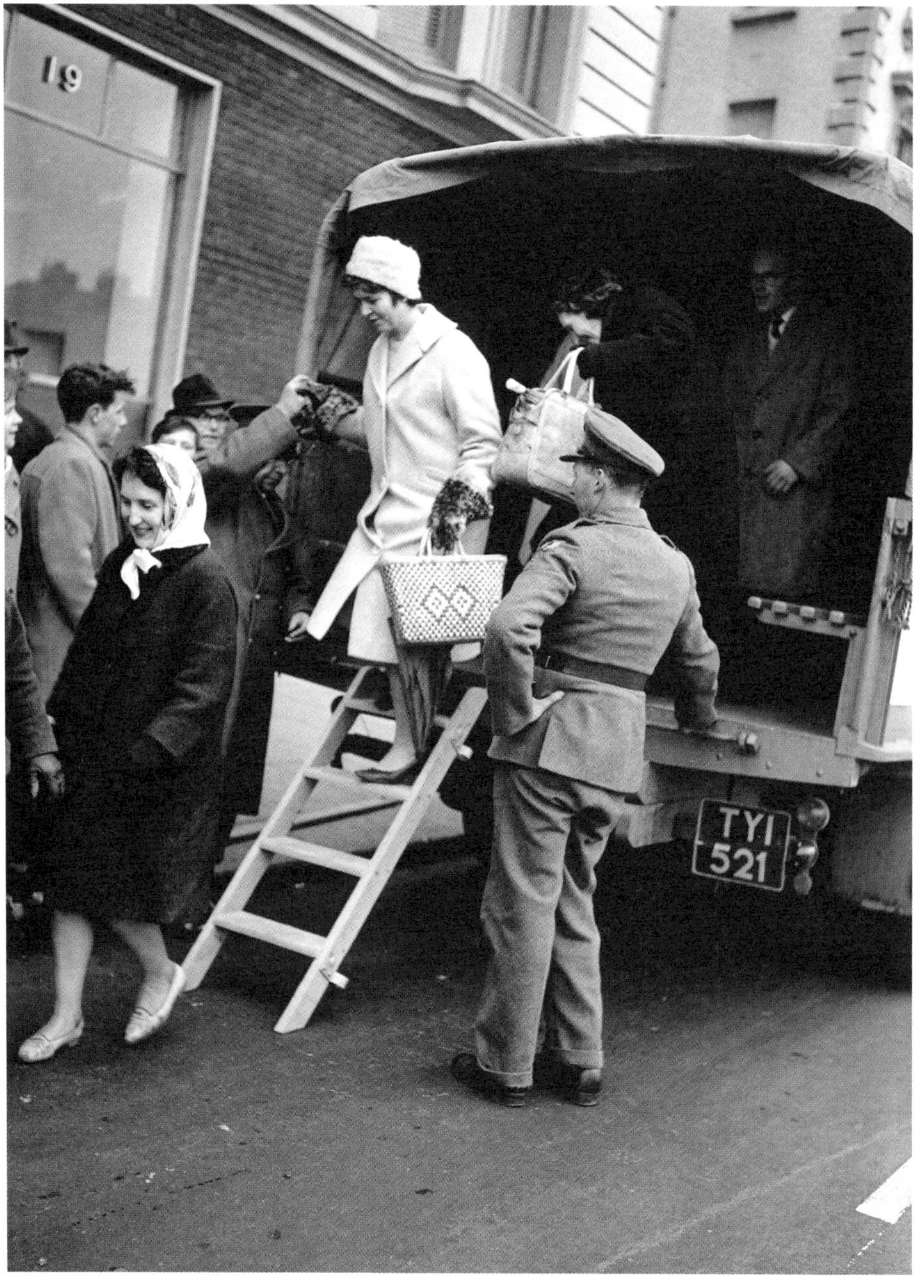

Bus strikes were a feature of the 1960s. Here, army lorries help get people to work.
9 April 1963

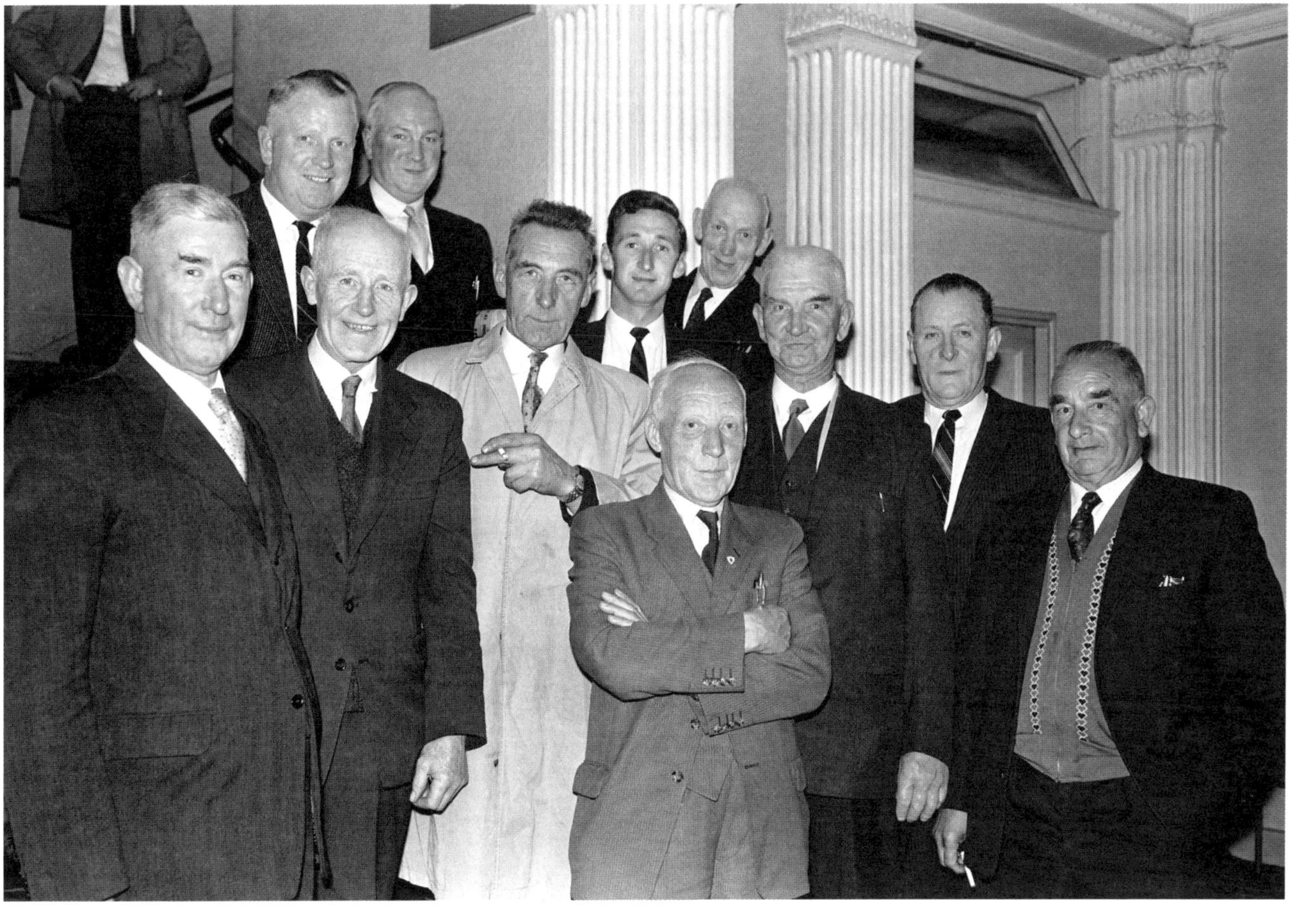

A group of former All-Ireland players, among whom were five who played in Croke Park on Bloody Sunday 1920, were guests at a showing of the Gael-Linn film 'Peil' at the Metropole cinema. Included are Paddy McDonnell, John Synott, Tommy Ryan, John McDonnell, Stephen Synott, Tony Herbert, Dan Dunne, Tommy Moore, Mattie Power, Tim O'Donnell and Pat Synott.

29 April 1963

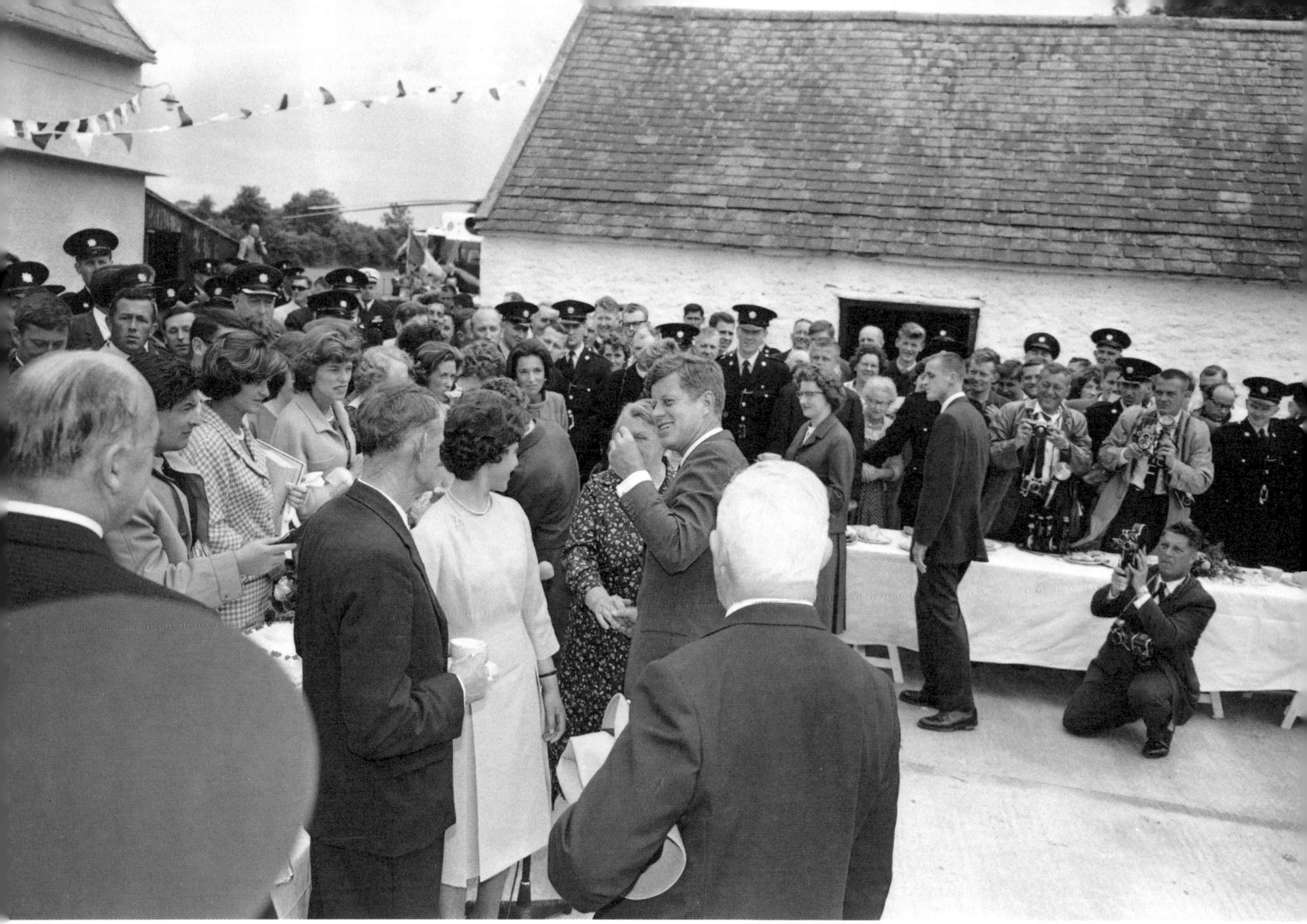

President Kennedy at Dunganstown, Co Wexford. In the background is the whitewashed building that was his ancestral family home. Postcards of the period carried his picture with the slogan 'From the White Cottage to the White House'.

26 June 1963

'There's no fireside like your own fireside'.
The President gets the obligatory cup of tea and
a proper 'welcome home' from his Wexford relatives.

26 June 1963

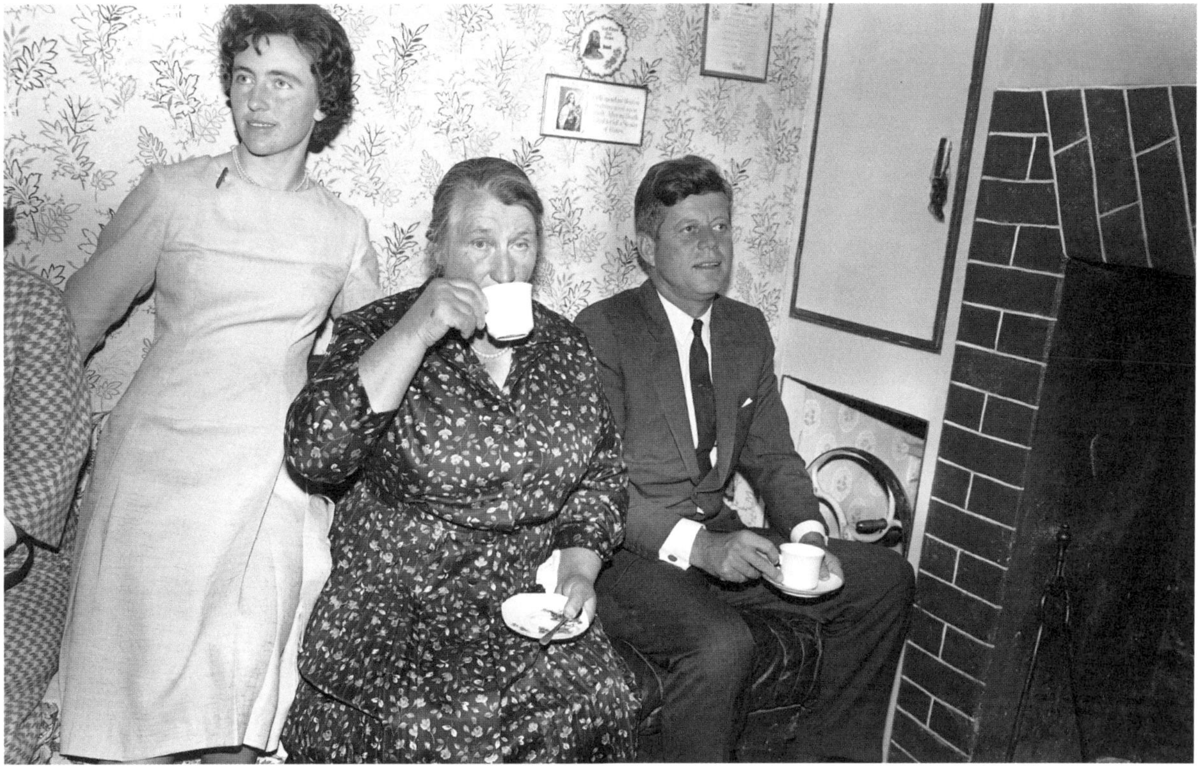

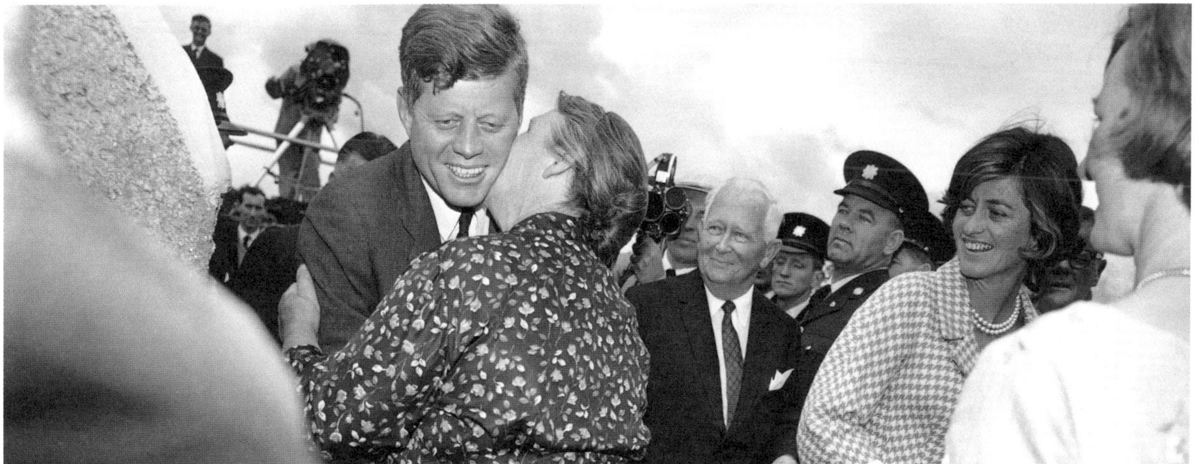

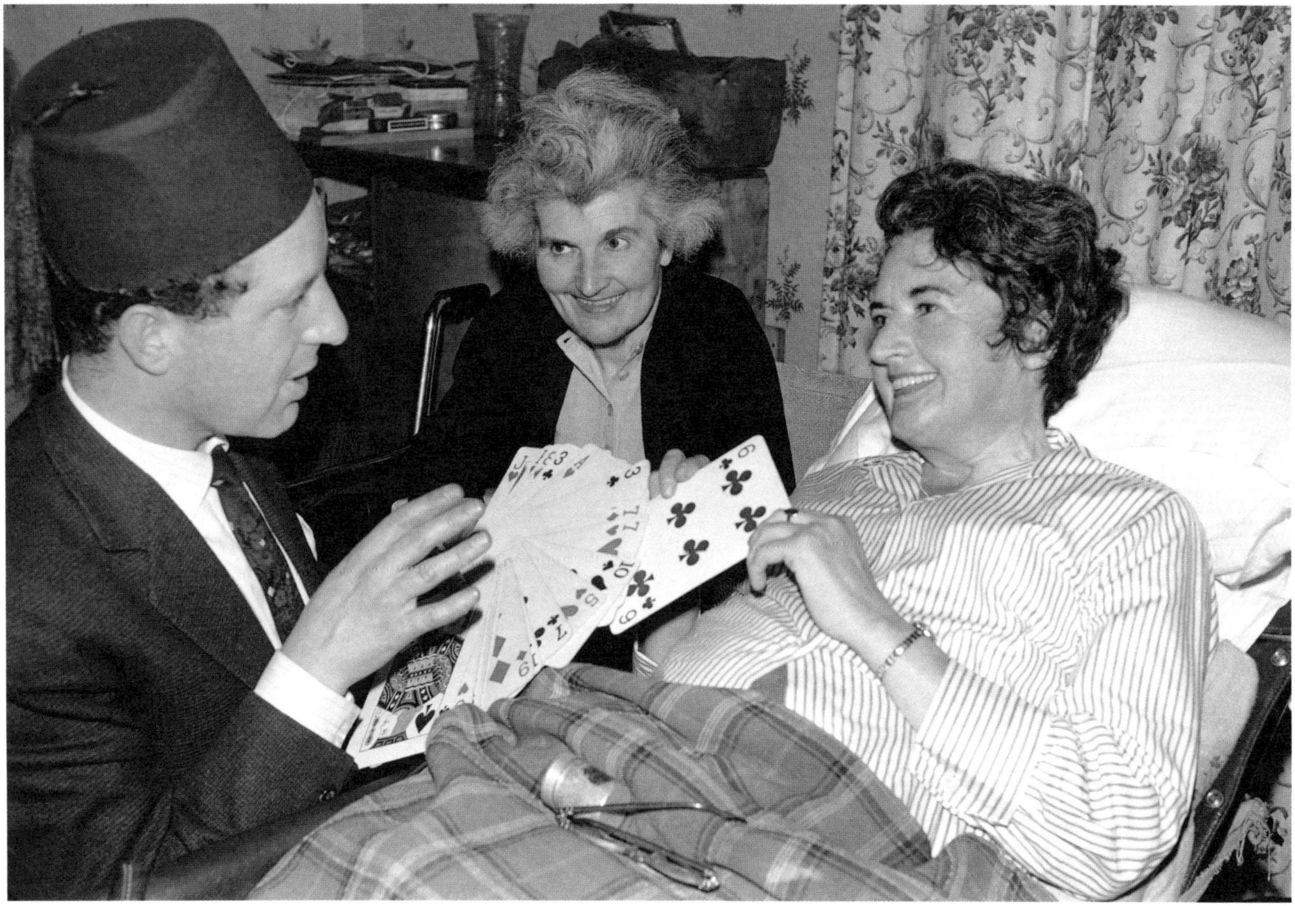

Pick a card – any card! Magician Albert le Bas entertains a hospital patient.

28 June 1963

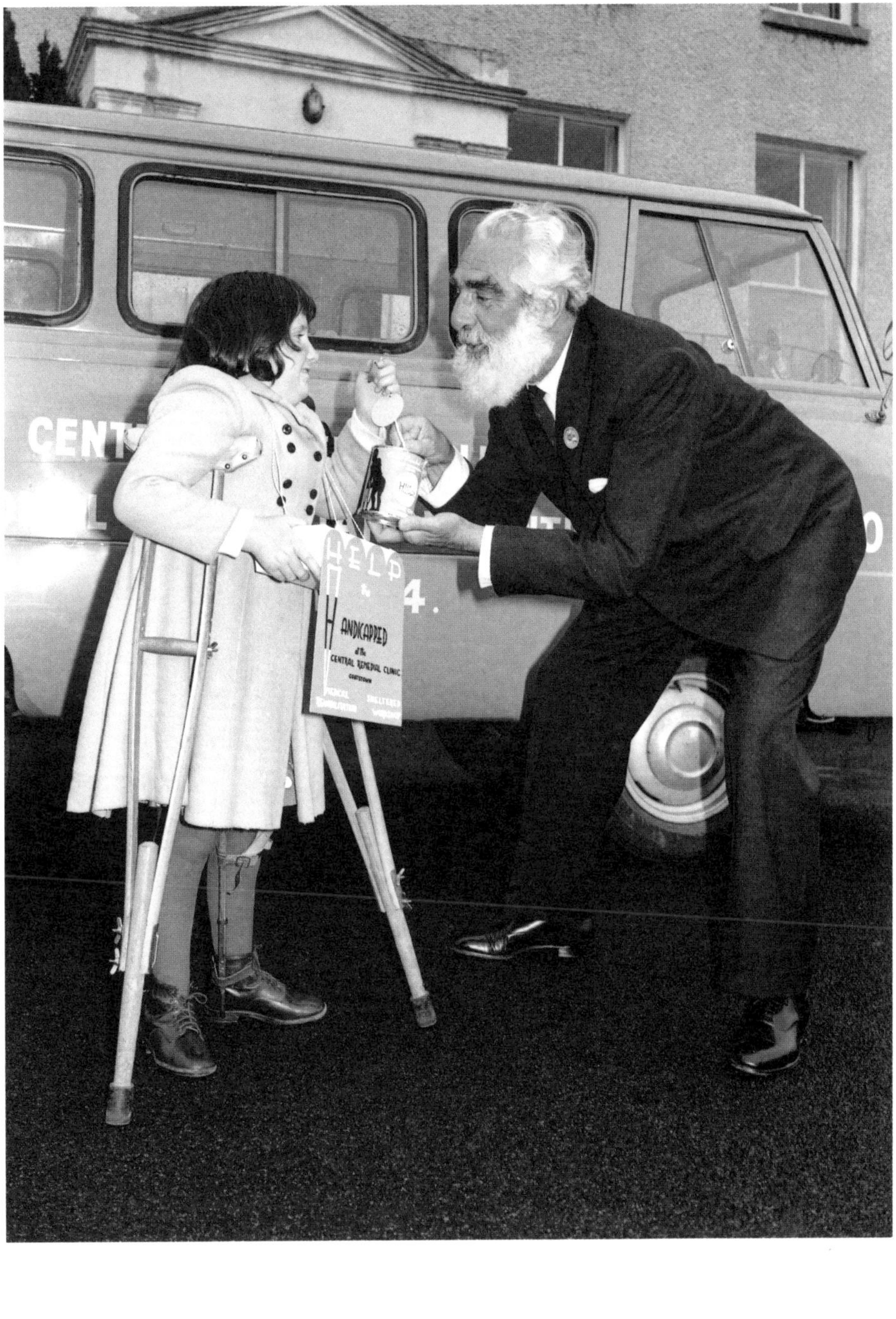

Entertainer Noel Purcell buys a flag from a young fund-raiser in a 'Help the Handicapped' campaign organized by the Central Remedial Clinic.

30 June 1963

The height of fashion! Aran knitwear, traditionally worn by fishermen in the West of Ireland, became a 'must-have' souvenir for visitors to Ireland. Its complicated patterns included single and double cable, 'tree of life', honeycomb and blackberry stitches, all said to have specific meanings.

13 July 1963

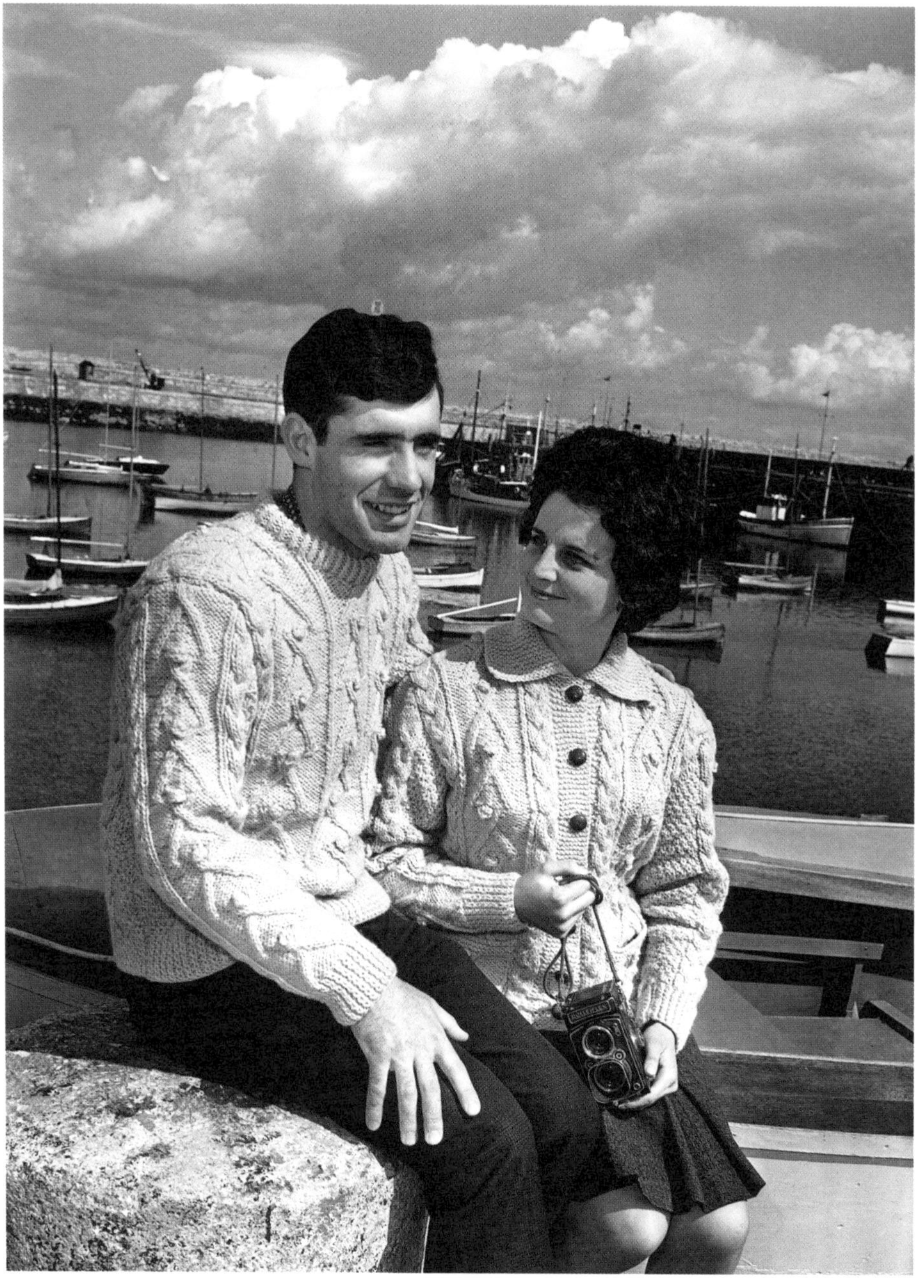

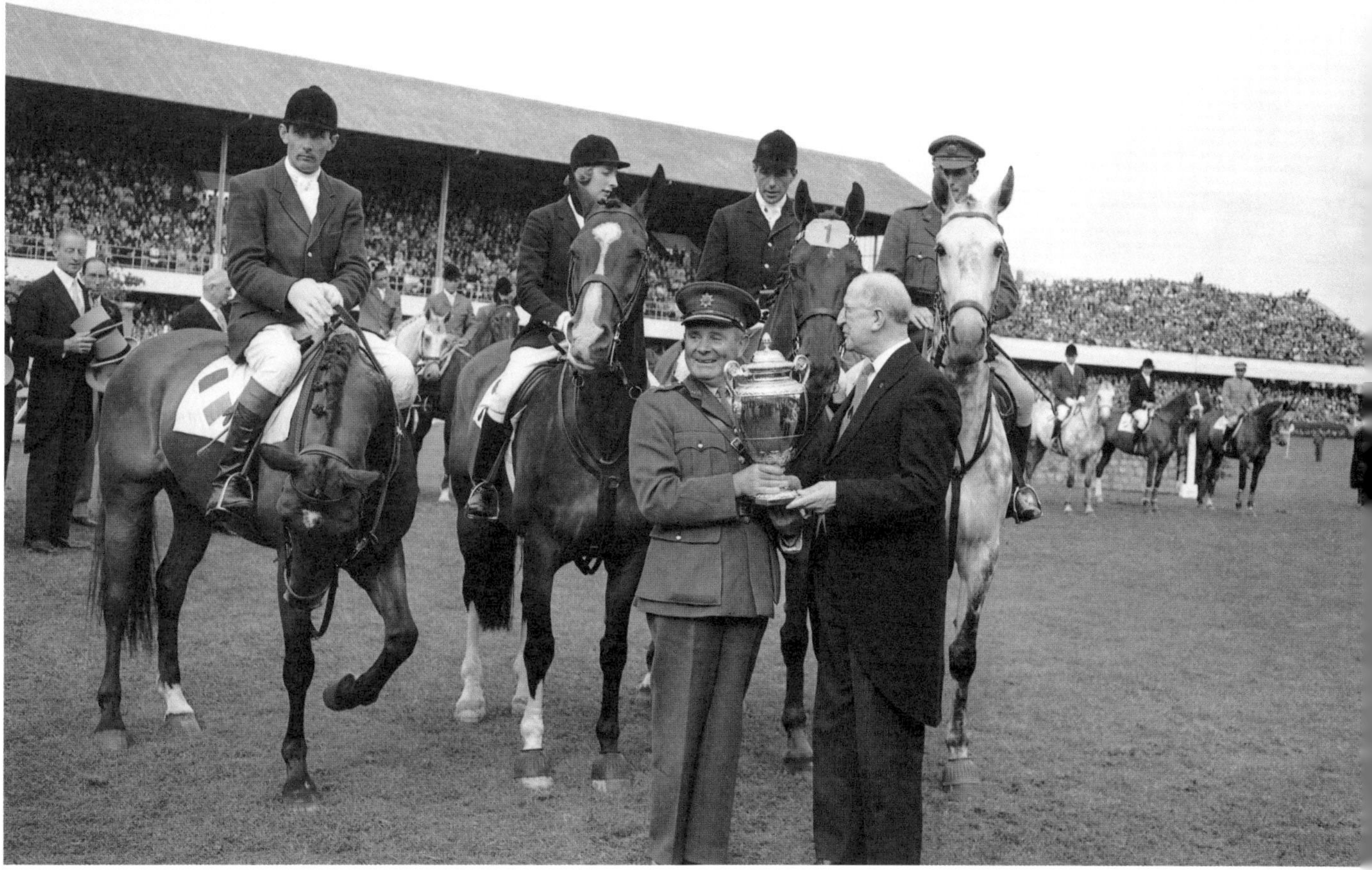

President de Valera presents the Aga Khan trophy to Col. J F Neylon, Chef d'Equipe of the winning Irish team. Mounted (l to r) are: Tommy Wade, The Hon. Diana Connolly-Carew, Seamus Hayes and Capt. Billy Ringrose.

8 August 1963

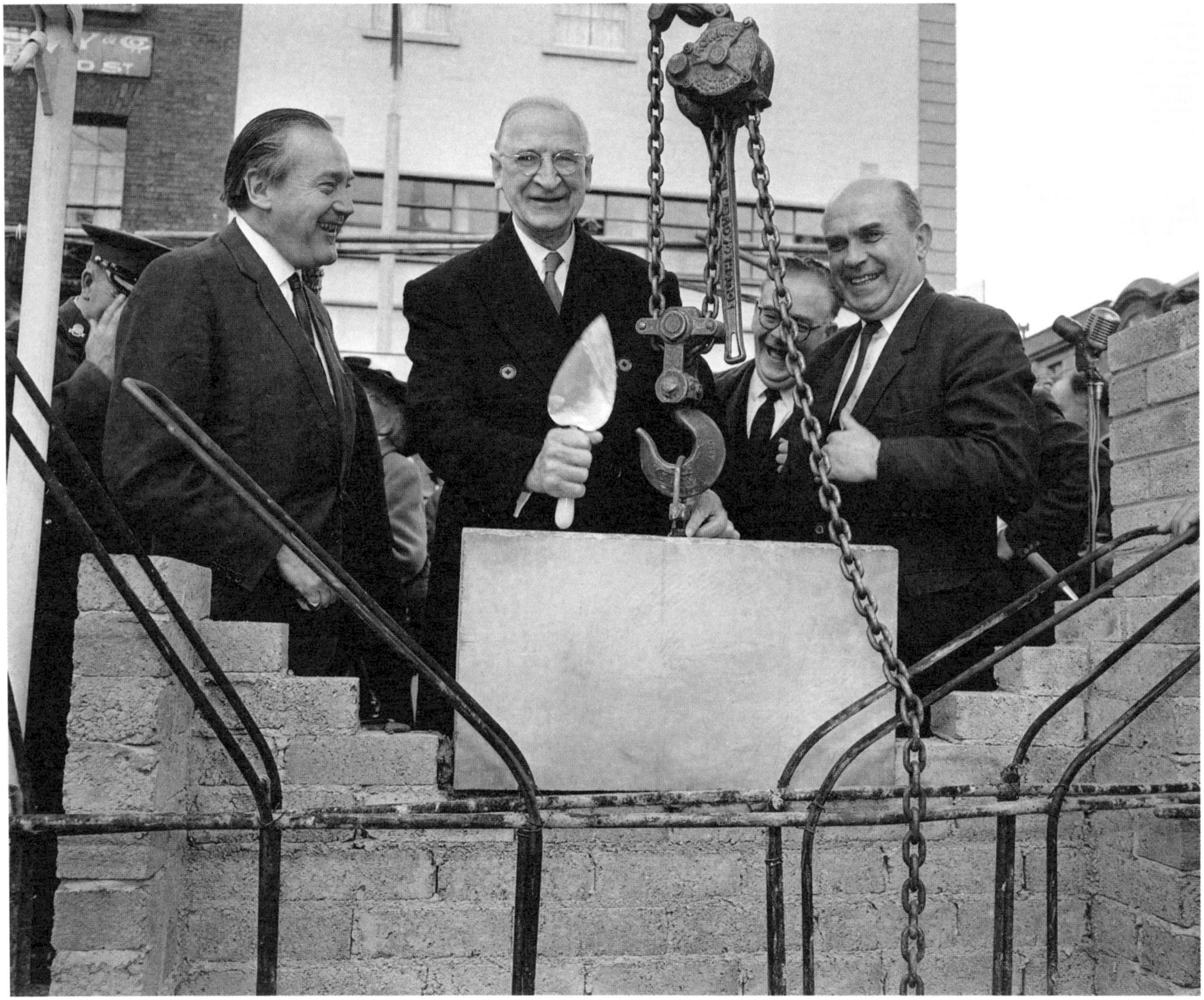

The President lays the foundation stone of the new Abbey Theatre. On the left is the architect Mr Michael Scott.

3 September 1963

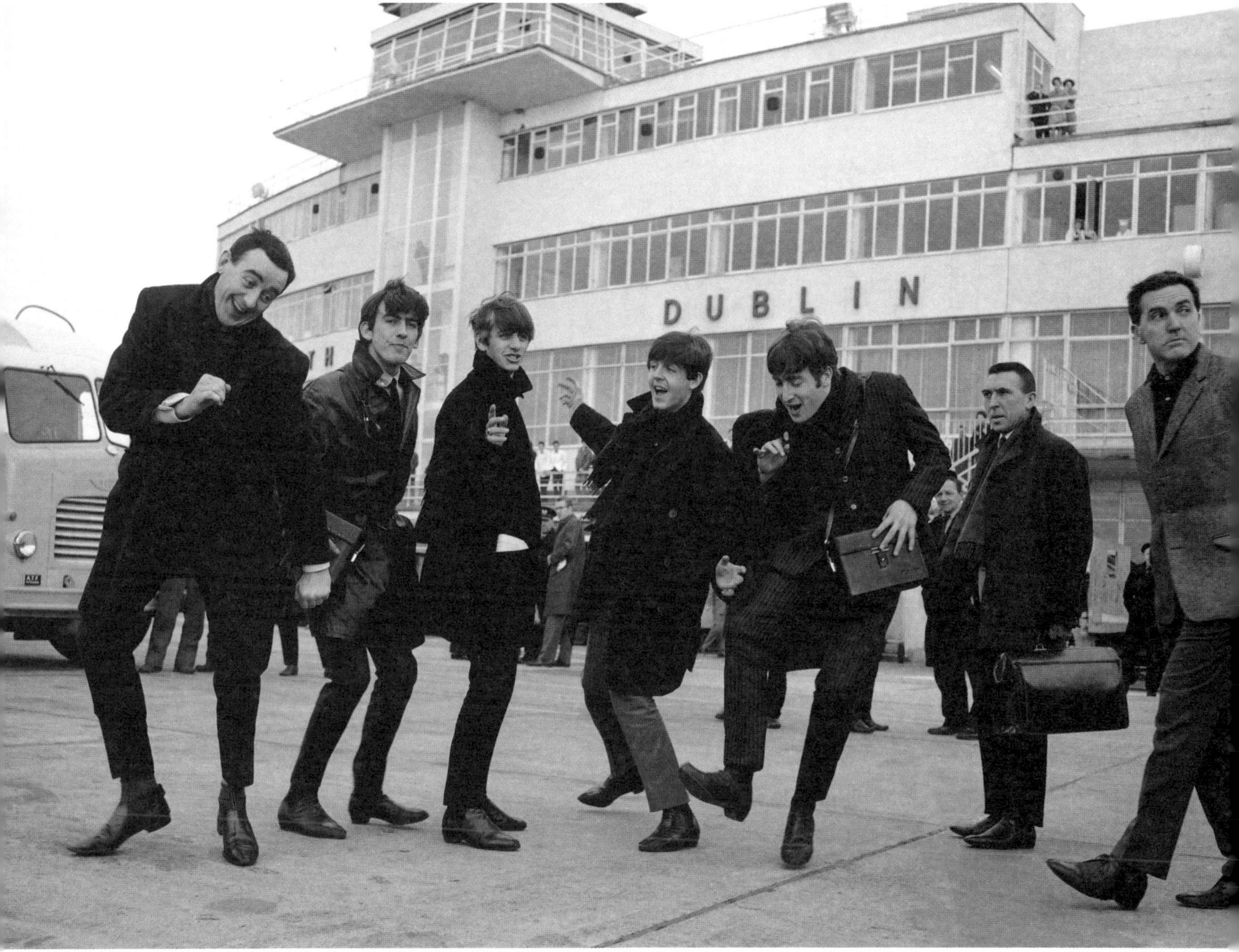

The Beatles arrive in Ireland to play their only gig in the country in the Adelphi Cinema on 7 November 1963. Alongside the Fab Four is radio & TV personality Paul Russell (left), with Frank Hall appearing on the right of the picture.

1 November 1963

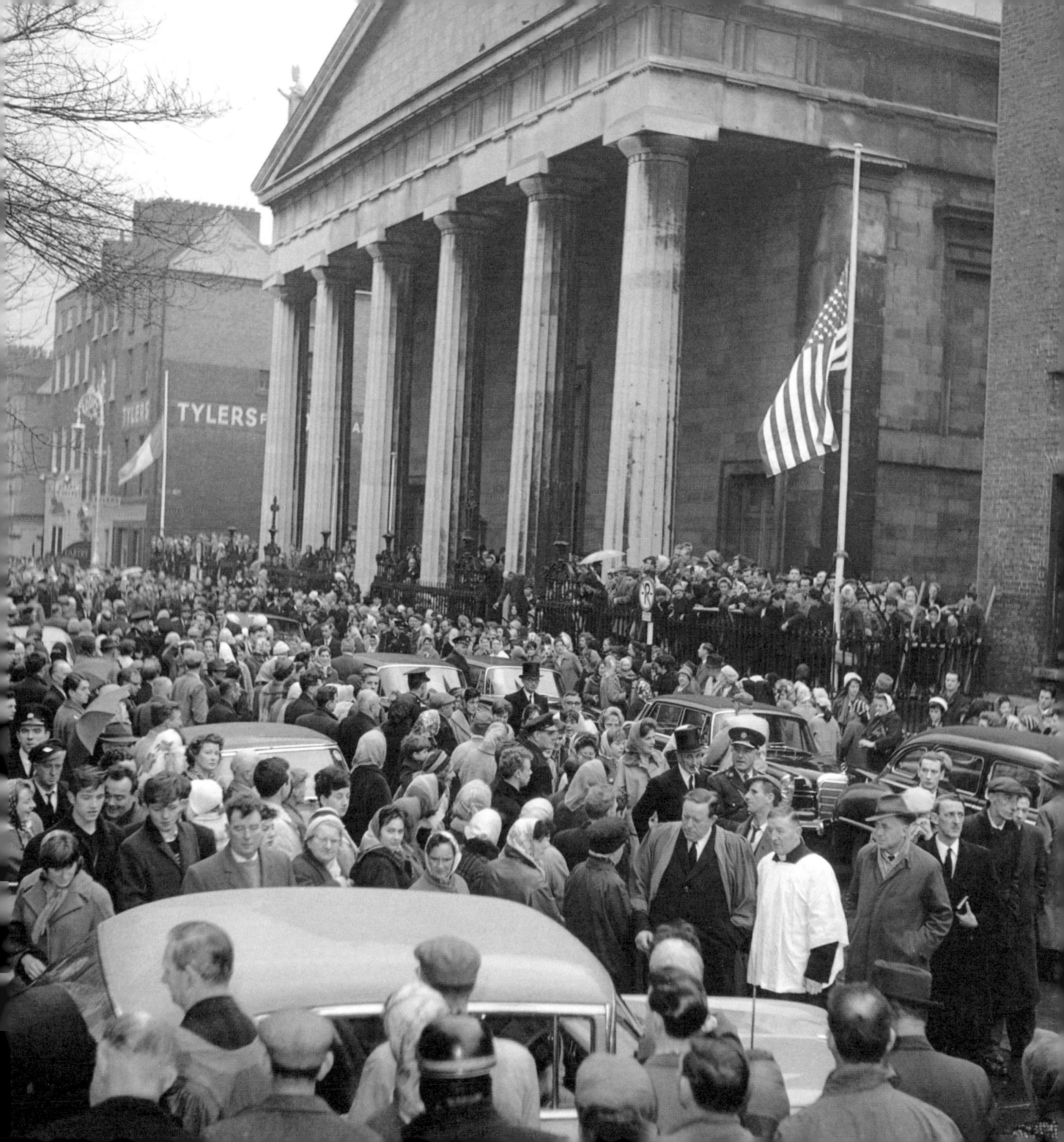
TYLERS
TYLERS

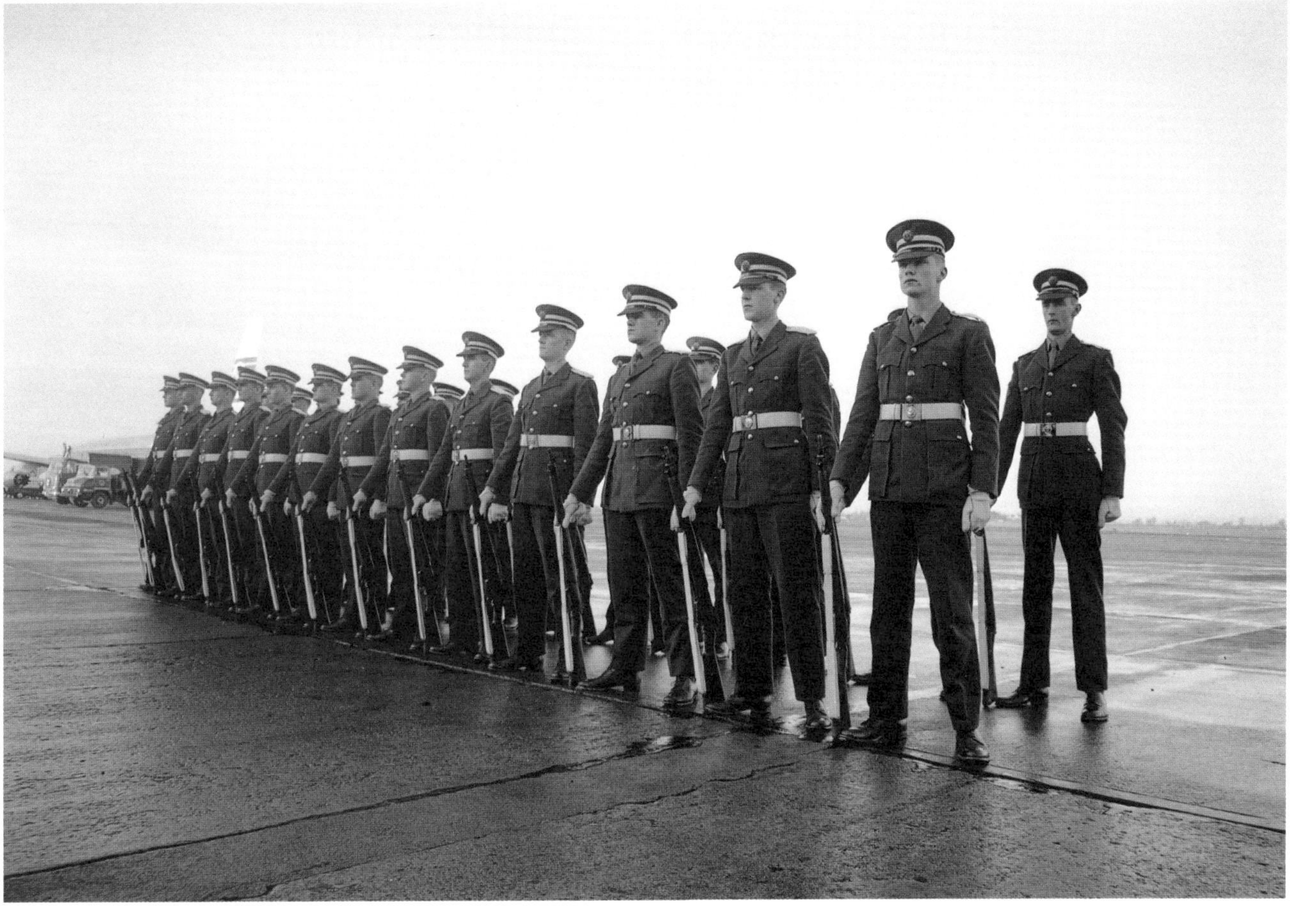

The twenty-six Irish Army Cadets who formed the guard of honour at President Kennedy's funeral return home. Kennedy had been so impressed by the cadets' precision drill at the wreath-laying ceremony in Arbour Hill on his visit to Ireland that he spoke of it often back in Washington, and his widow, Jackie Kennedy, made a special request to have the cadets involved in his funeral.

27 November 1963

Ireland mourns President Kennedy. Requiem Masses were held all over the country and businesses, schools and universities were closed. The picture shows crowds leaving the Pro-Cathedral after the Requiem Mass which was attended by Mrs de Valera, Taoiseach Sean Lemass, members of the government and of the diplomatic corps.

26 November 1963

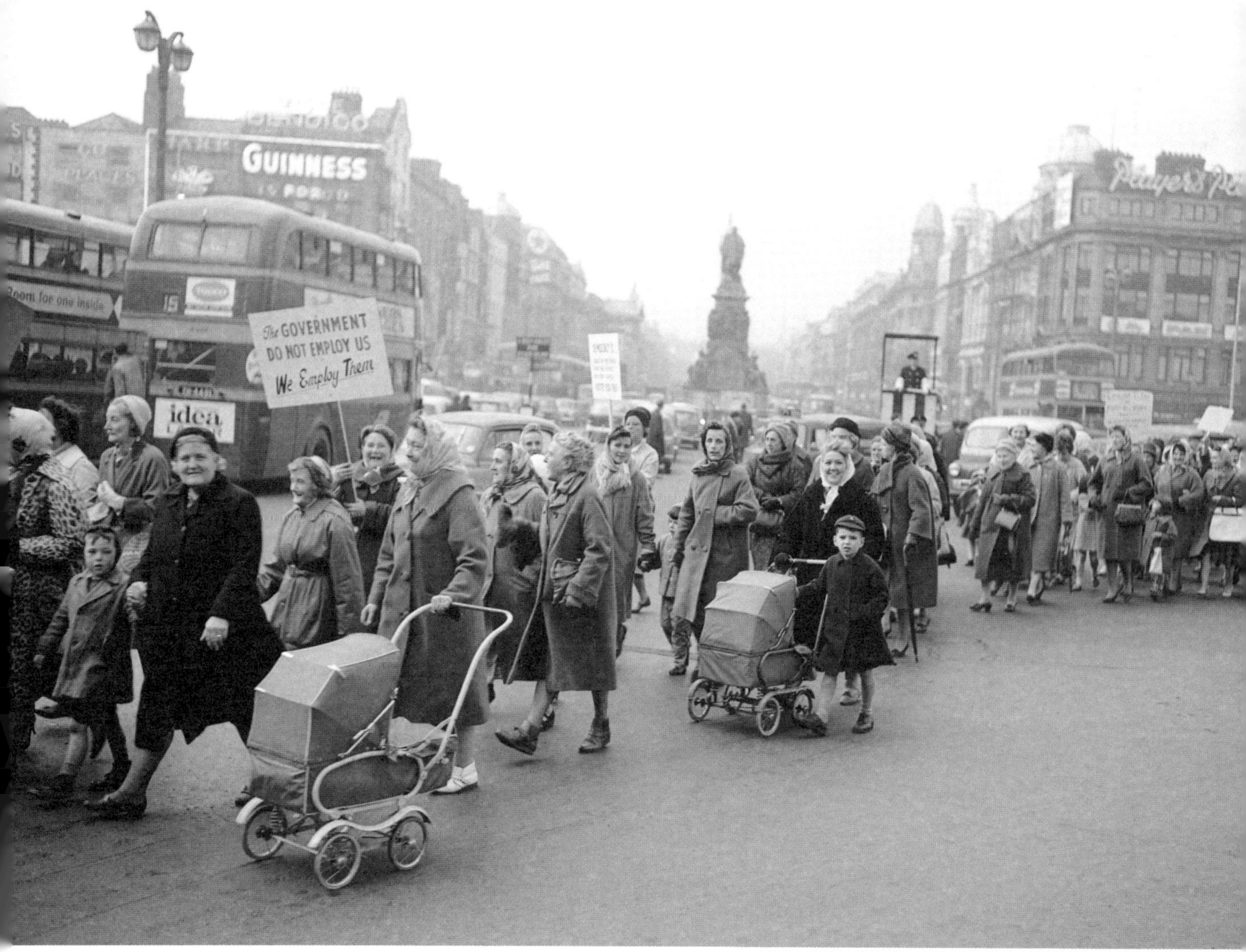

Housewives march in protest at the introduction of Turnover Tax, a new sales tax. The garda wearing white gloves in a raised booth to the centre right of the picture directed traffic on O'Connell Bridge.

14 November 1963

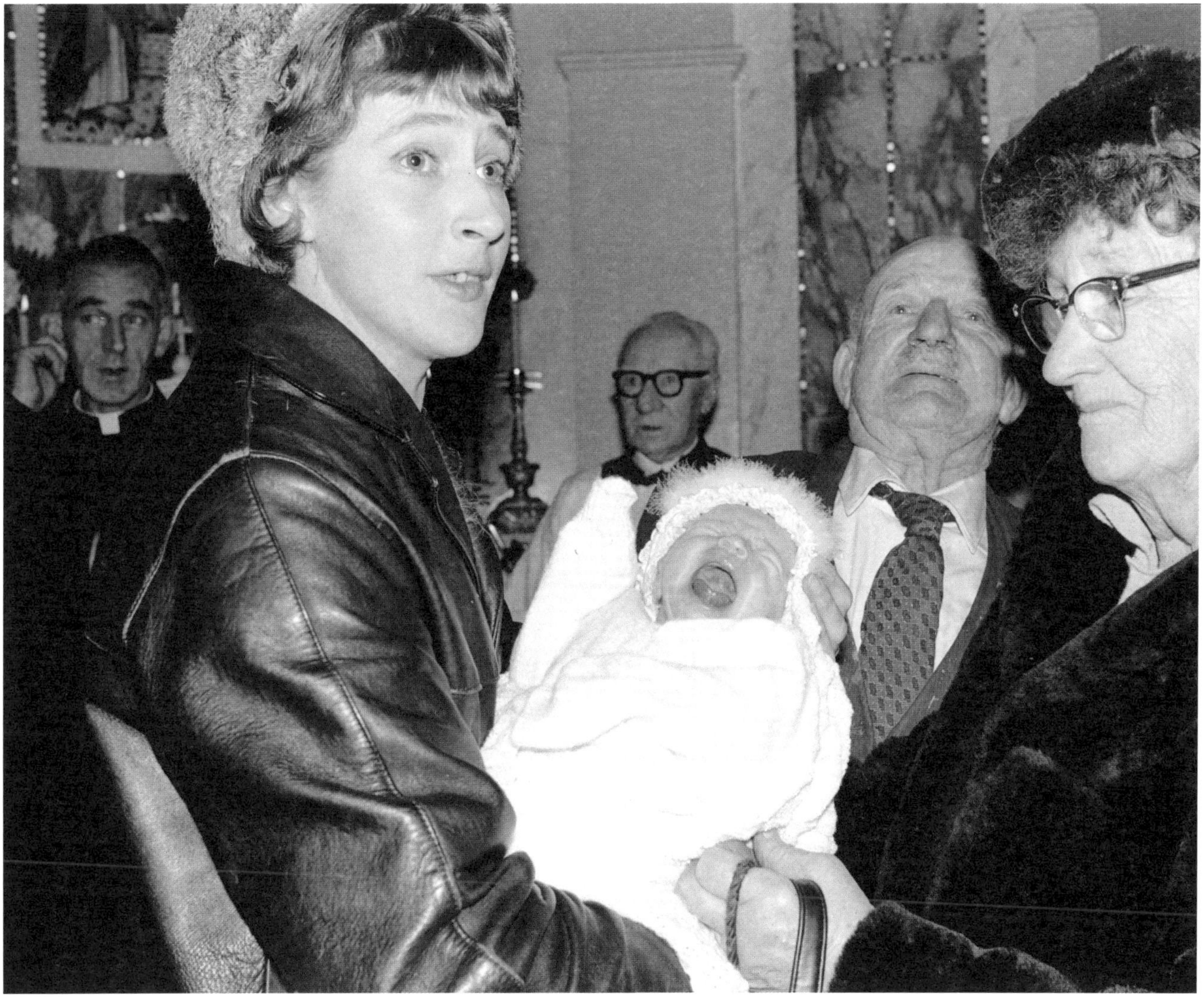

The baby daughter of Brendan and Beatrice Behan is christened Blanaid Orla Jacqueline Mairead at St Andrew's Church, Westland Row. Blanaid, in full voice, and wrapped in a 200-year-old Limerick lace shawl, is held by her godmother, Celia Salkeld (sister of Beatrice Behan) and watched over by her grandparents, Stephen and Kathleen Behan.

2 December 1963

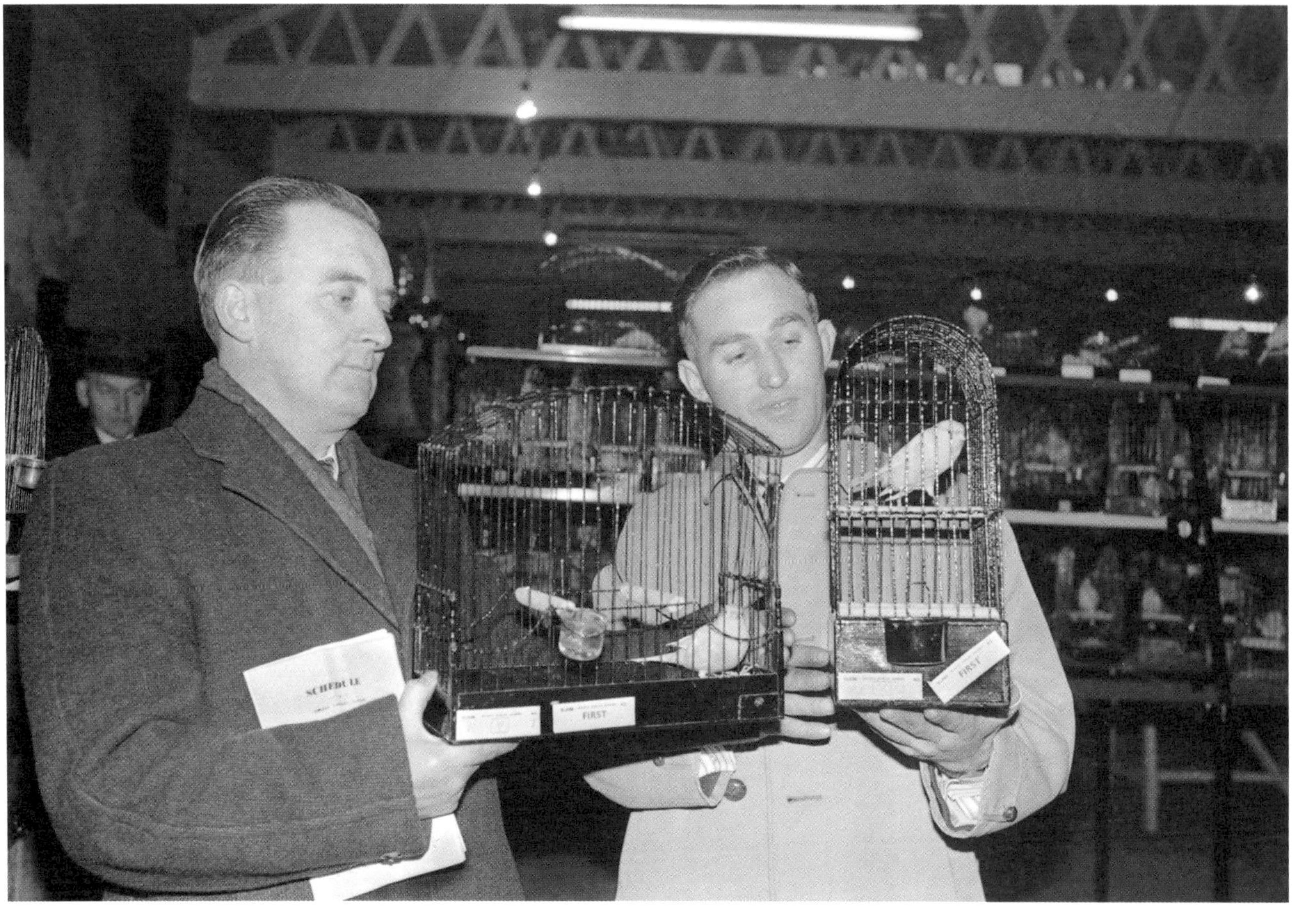

'I don't fancy your bird!' Prizewinners at the 16th annual Canary Show, Connolly Hall.

20 December 1963

The Clancy Bros and Tommy Makem, (on right), discard their trademark Aran jumpers and caps for a visit to Áras an Uachtaráin.

15 January 1964

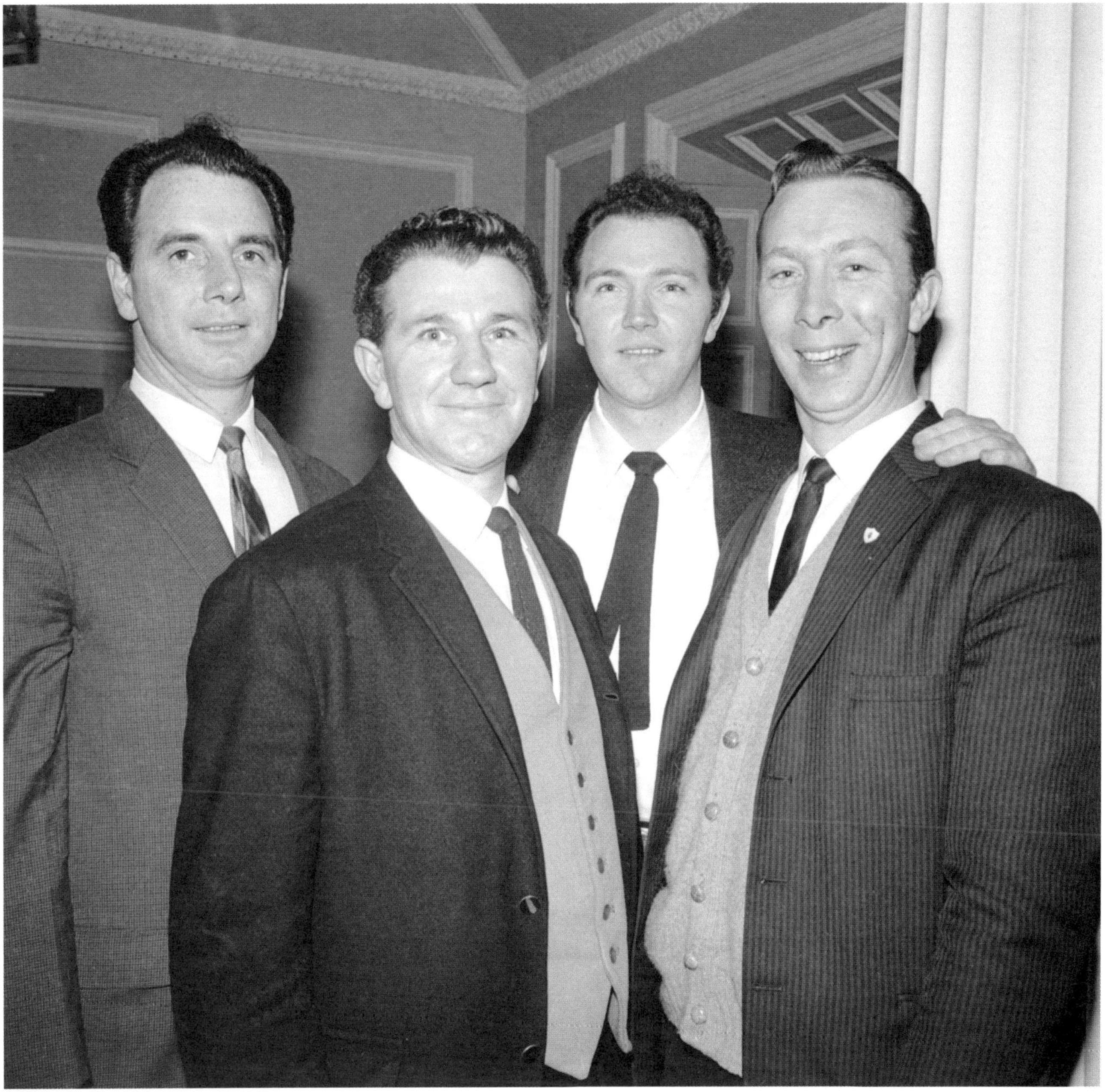

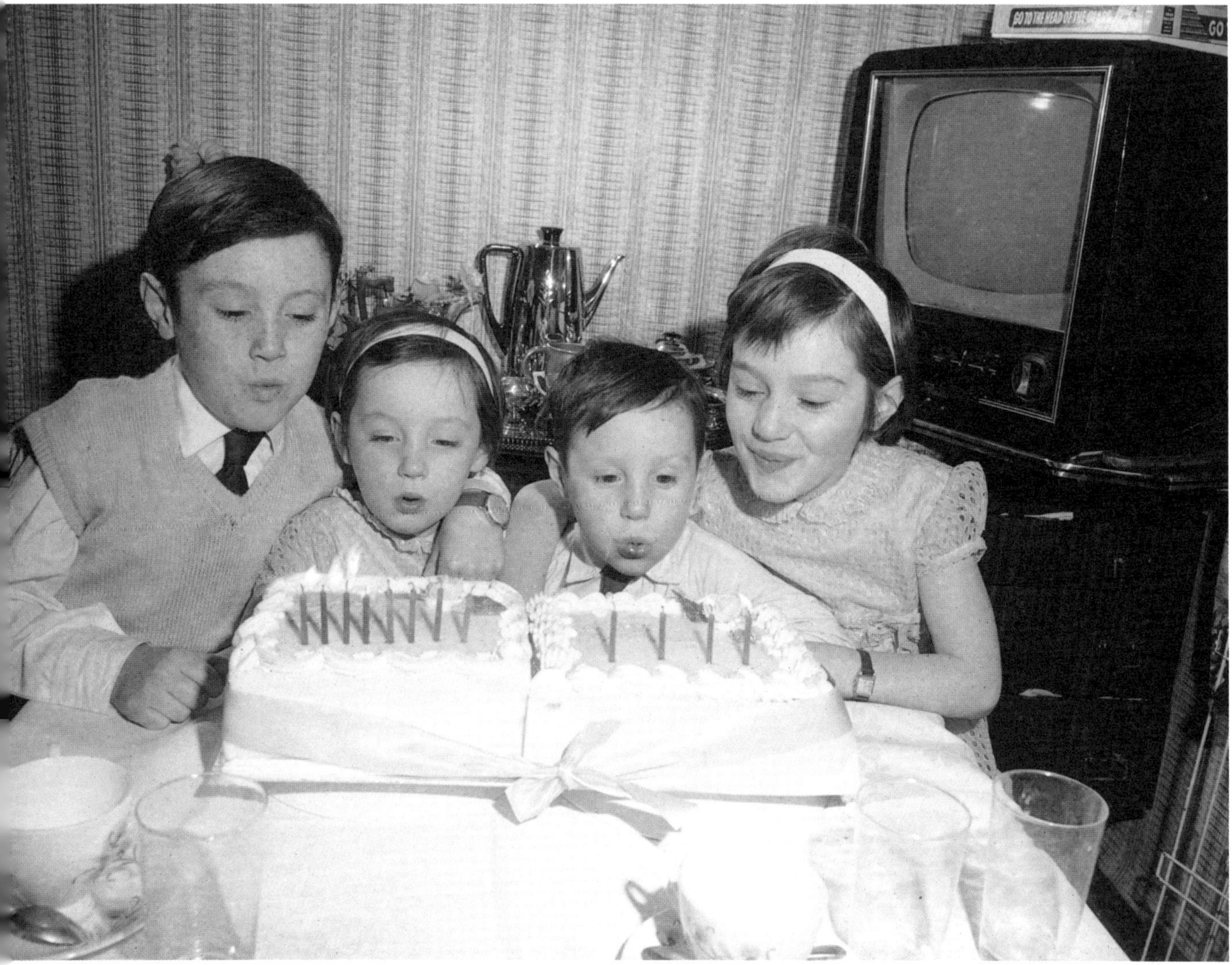

Imagine having an 'official' birthday only every four years! Here, two sets of Leap Year twins, Jimmy (8), Patricia and Robert (4), and Ann (8) MacDonnell, blow out the candles on their birthday cakes. All were born on 29th February.

28 February 1964

Prospective buyers discuss the catalogue at the RDS Boat Show.

10 March 1964

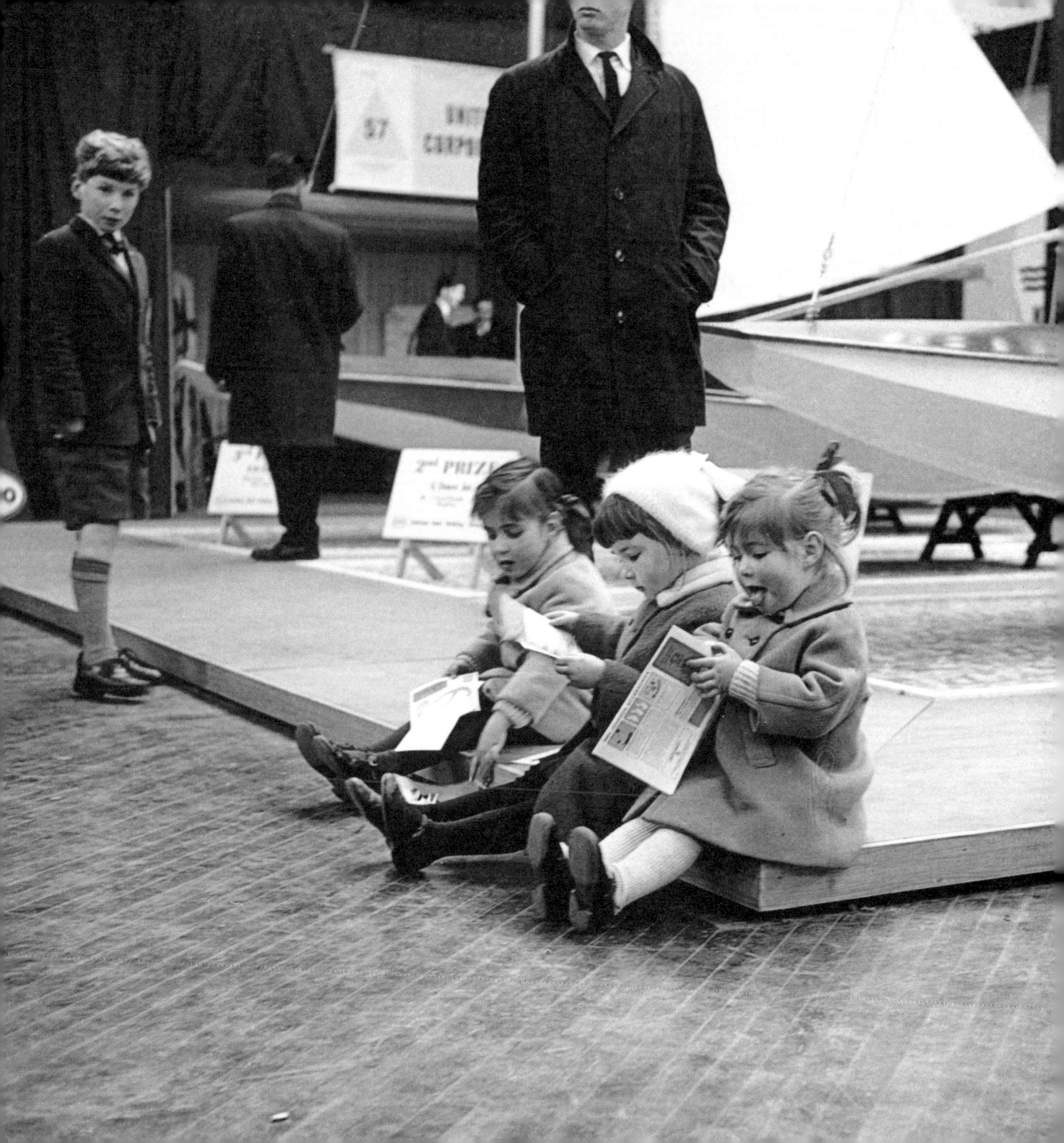
57

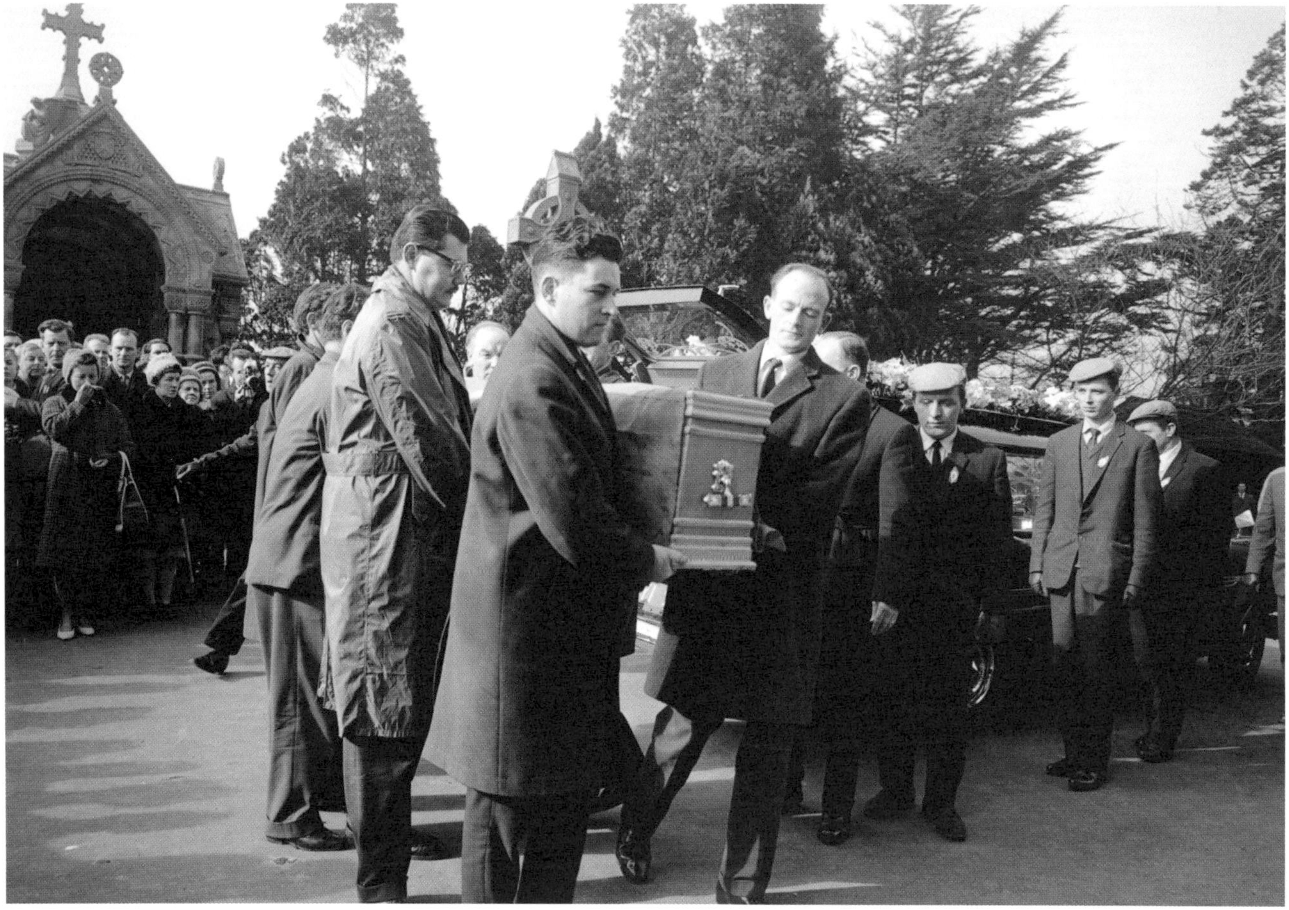

The funeral of Brendan Behan arrives at Glasnevin Cemetery. The hard-living playwright, novelist and poet was only forty-one when he died.

23 March 1964

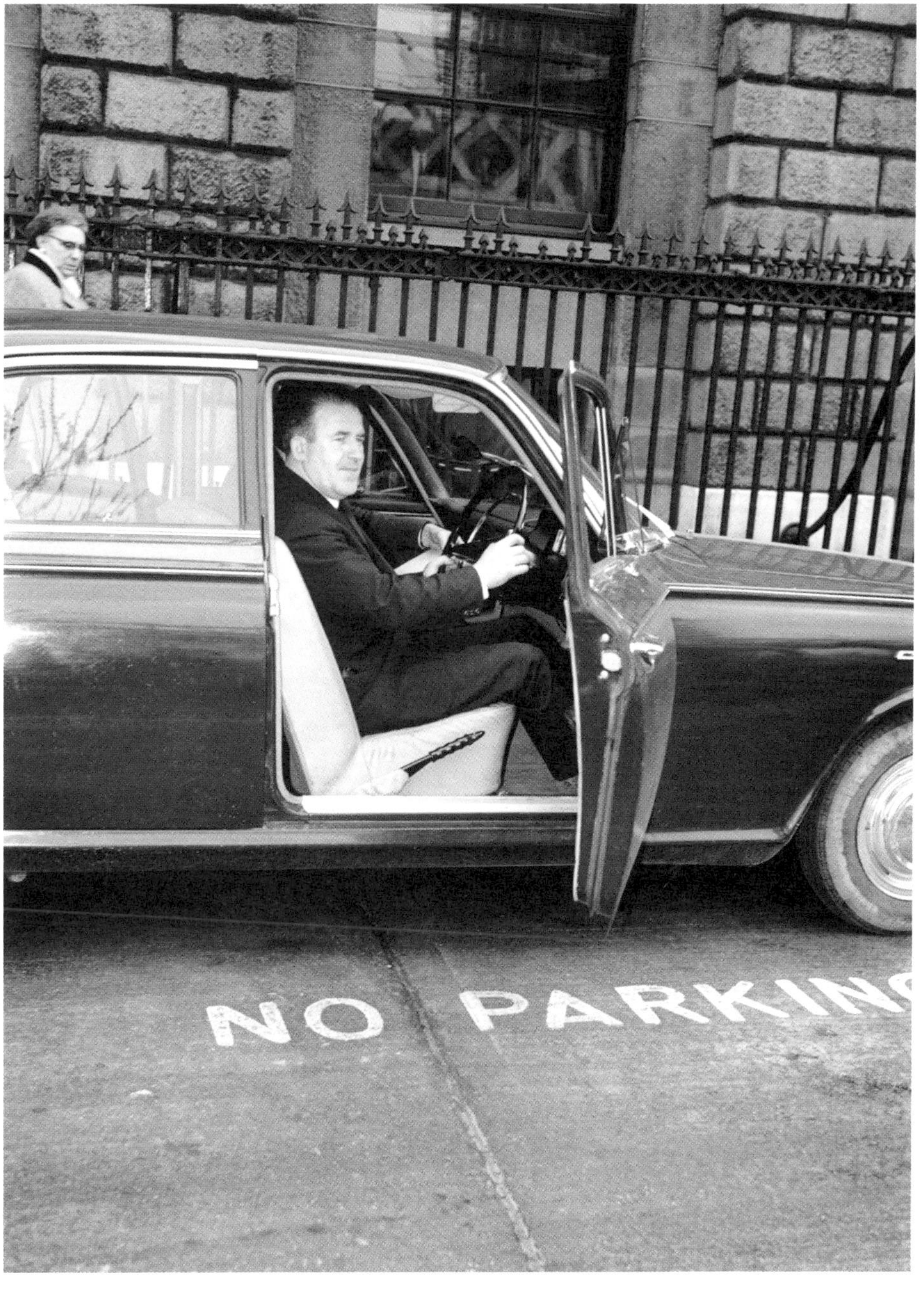

Neil Blaney, Minister for Local Government, takes the wheel to complete the new driving test. It was probably not a good idea to begin in a NO PARKING zone.

23 March 1964

Brendan Bowyer, lead singer with the Royal Showband, picks up their latest disc from HMV at the Gramophone Company. 1964 was a huge year for the band and included the hit for which Bowyer is most remembered 'The Hucklebuck', originally on the B-side of 'I Ran All the Way Home'.

26 May 1964

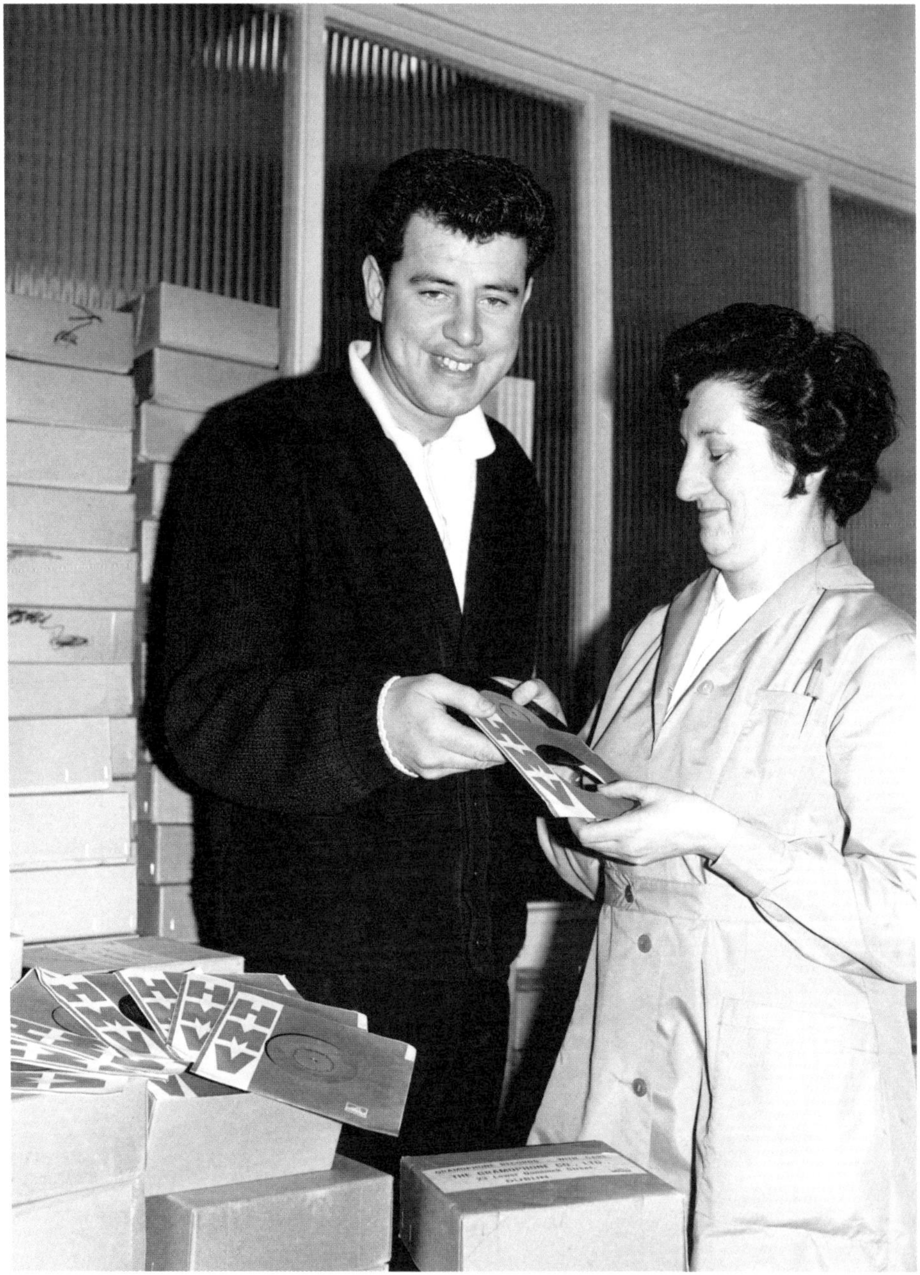

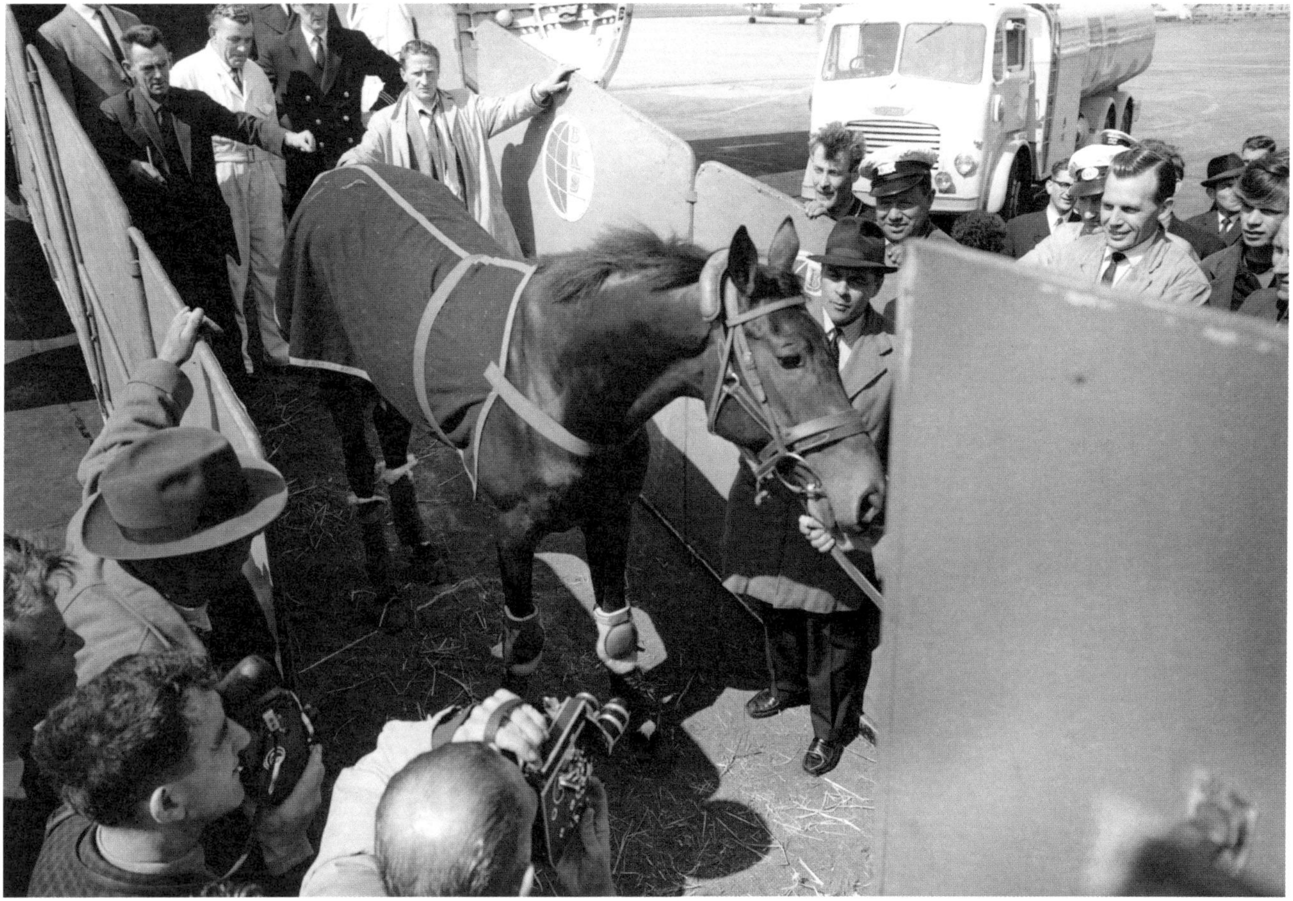

'Santa Claus', winner of the Epsom Derby, arrives home after his momentous victory. Mr Tim Rogers, (in hat), brother of trainer Mick Rogers, sees the horse unloaded from the BKS aircraft.

4 June 1964

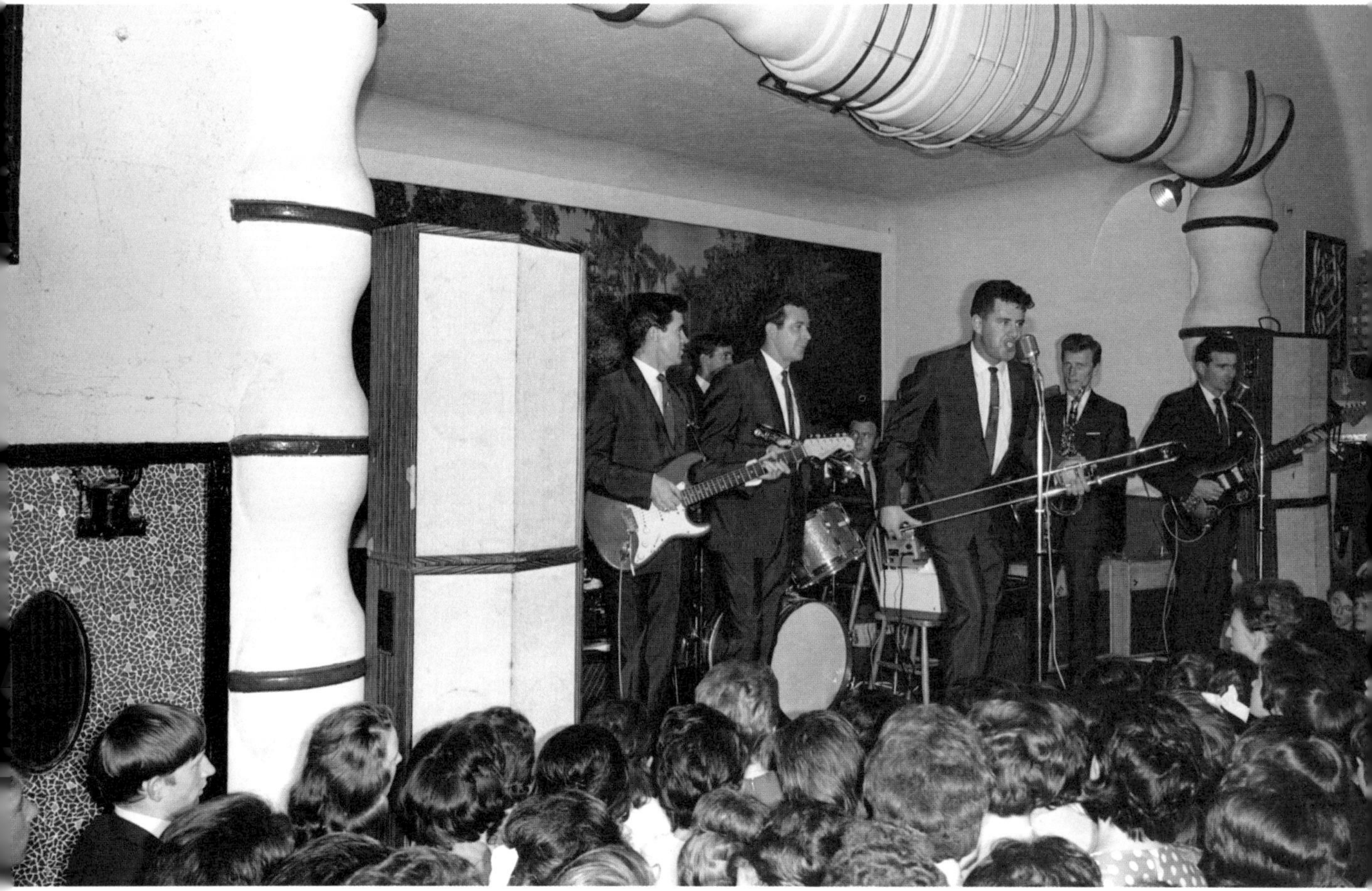

The Royal Showband perform to packed crowds at the Crystal Ballroom.

10 June 1964

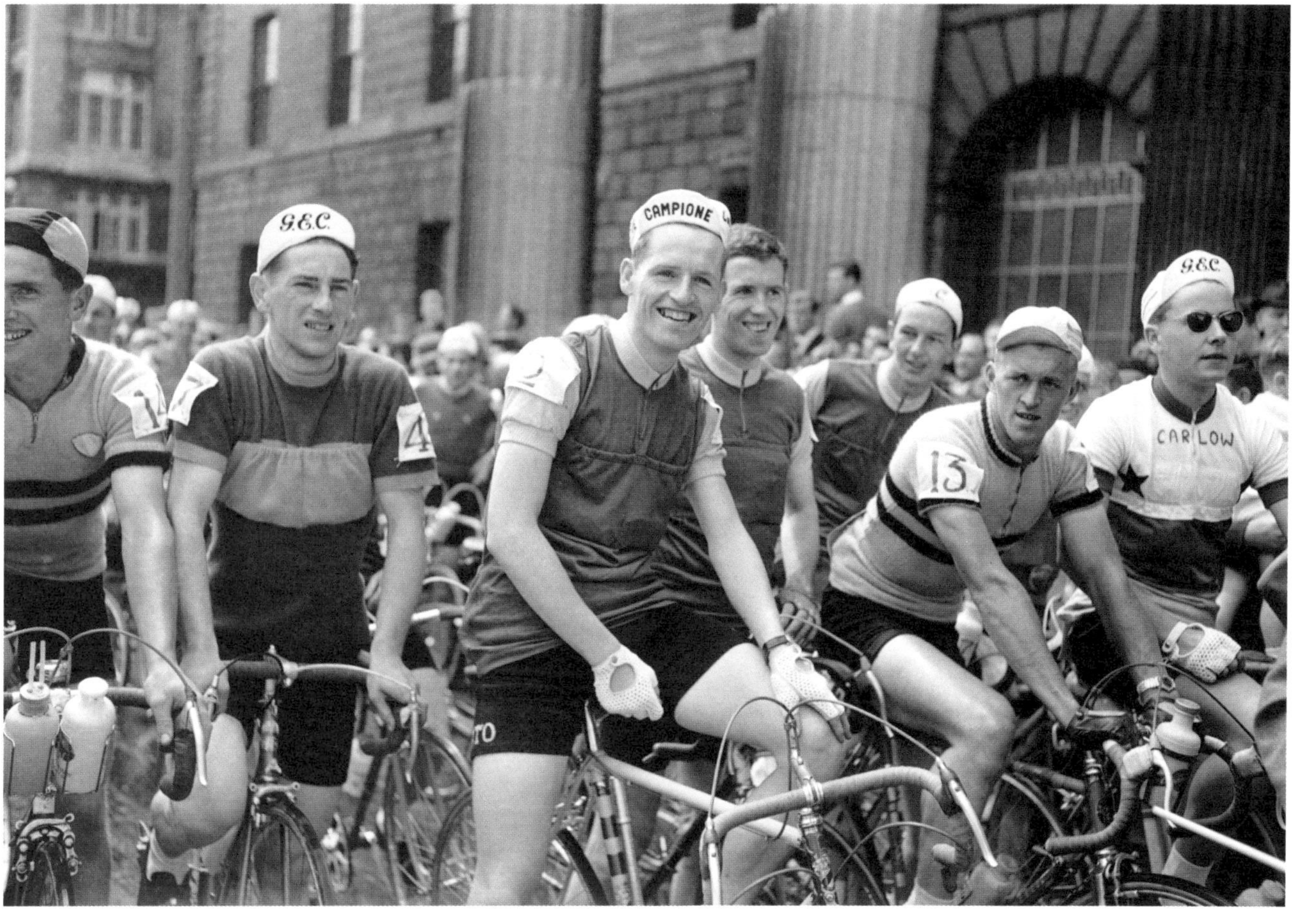

Competitors line up for the start of the Rás Tailteann.
5 July 1964

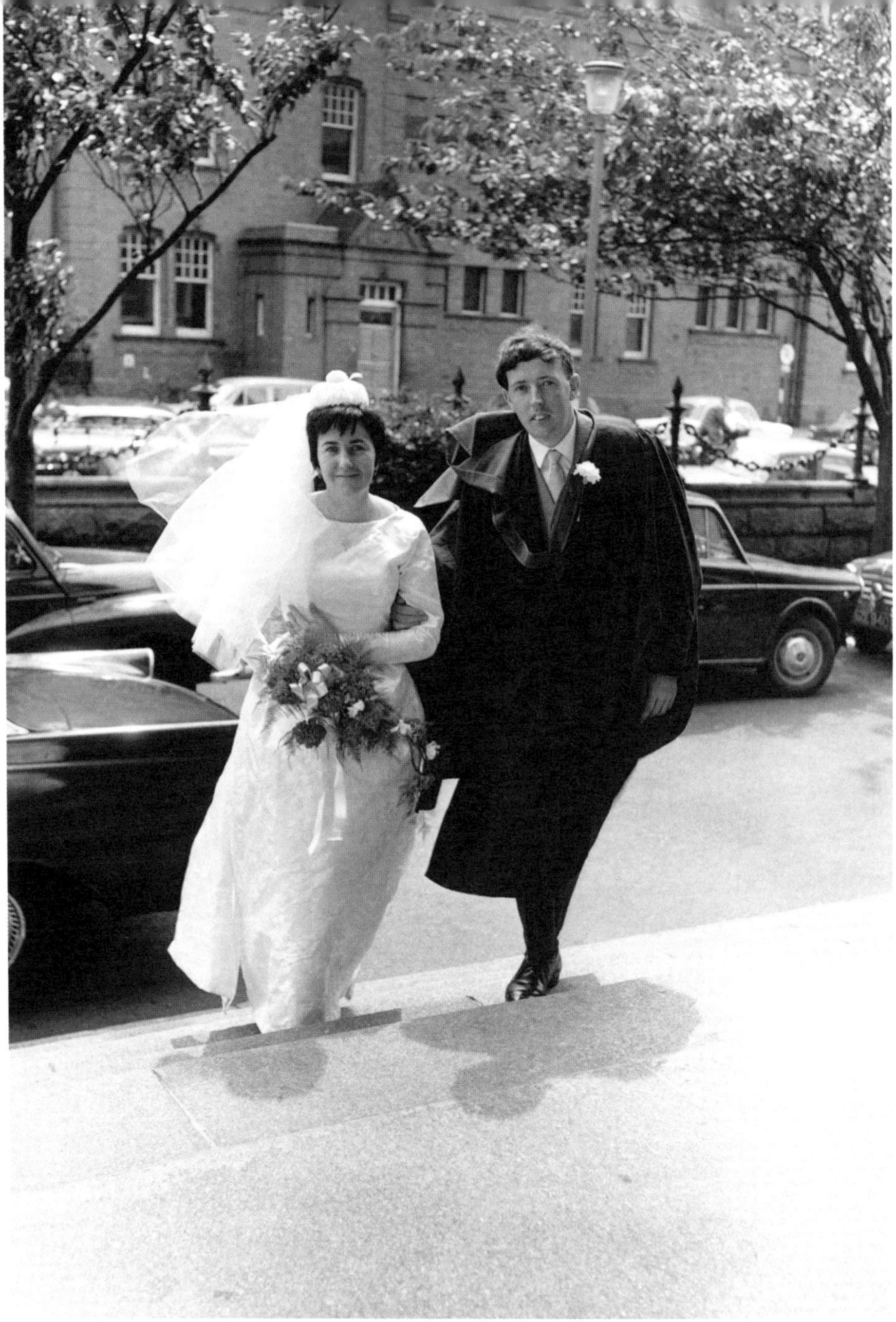

An unusual sight at UCD (Earlsfort Terrace) as groom John Quirke, Straffan, Co Kildare, arrives with his bride of 45 minutes, Mary Claire Harney, Stapleton Place, Dundalk, to receive his B.E. on Conferring Day.

14 July 1964

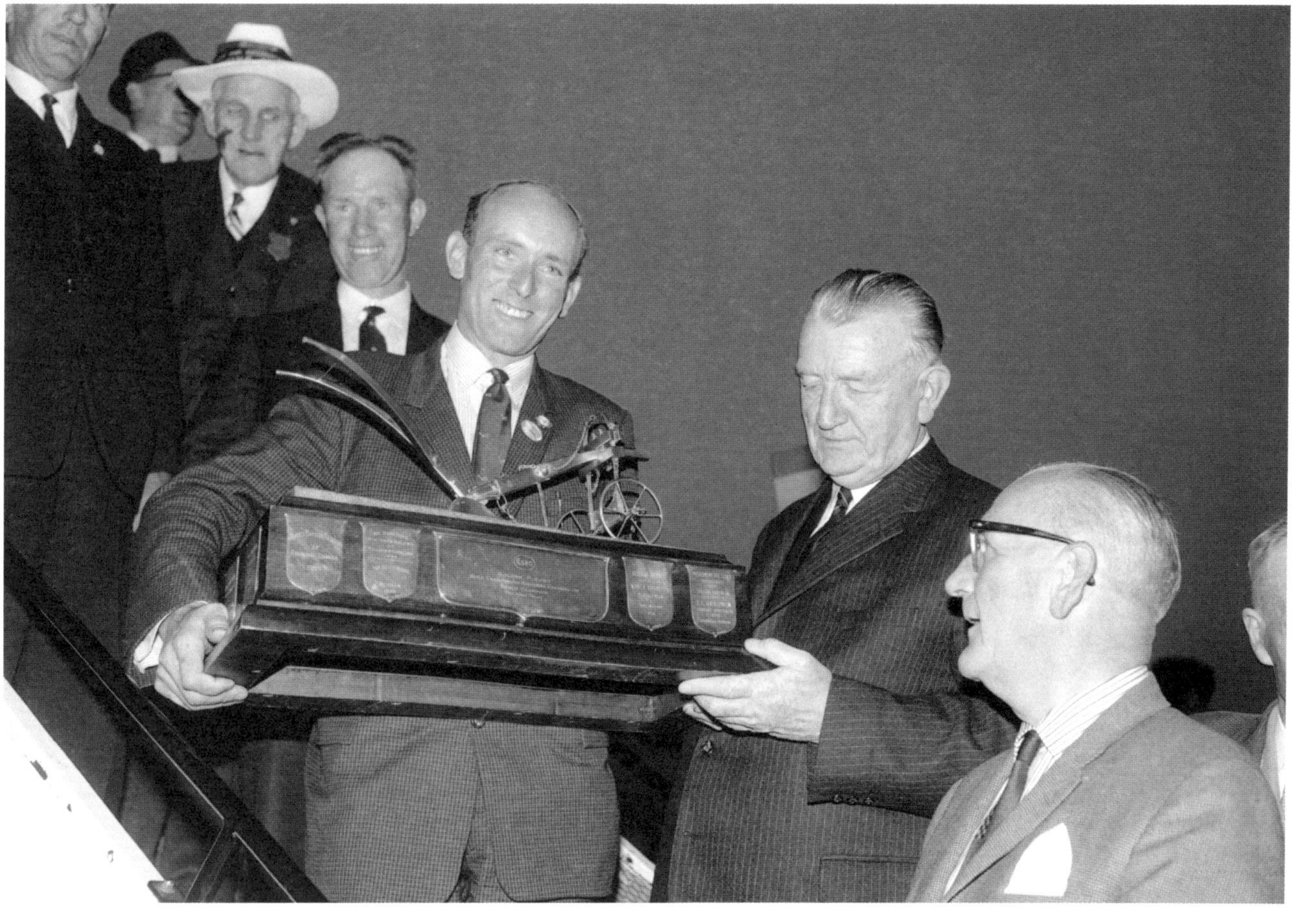

Charlie Keegan, from Wicklow, returns home from Austria with the Golden Plough trophy as World Champion Ploughman which he won against a field of 39 competitors.

4 October 1964

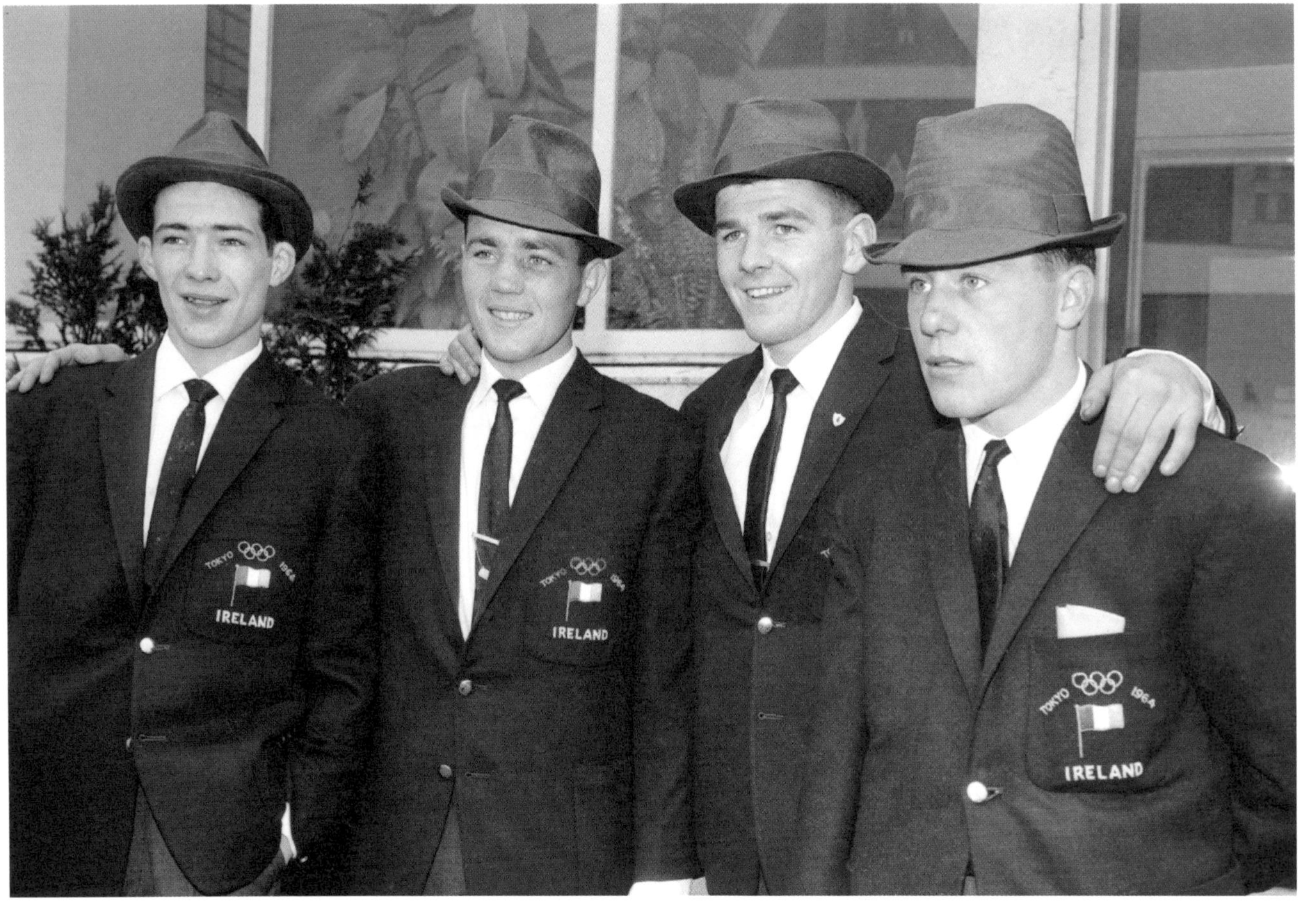

The four Irish boxers who represented Ireland at the Olympic Games in Tokyo. L to R: Sean McCafferty, Belfast, Brian Anderson, Donegal, Jim McCourt, Belfast and Paddy Fitzsimons, Belfast. McCourt won a bronze medal.

8 October 1964

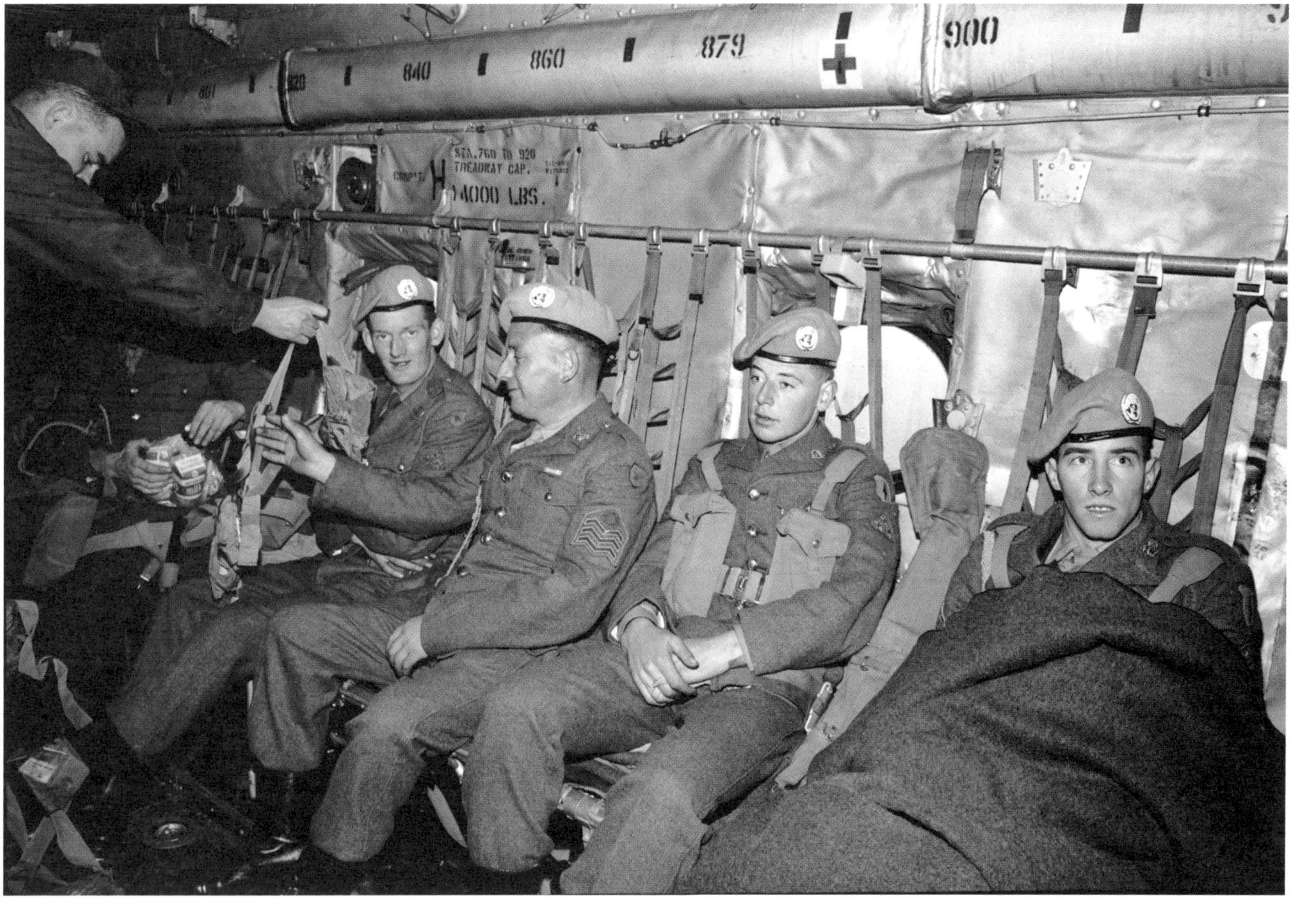

Irish Army troops on their way to Cyprus to serve with the UN peacekeeping force.

13 October 1964

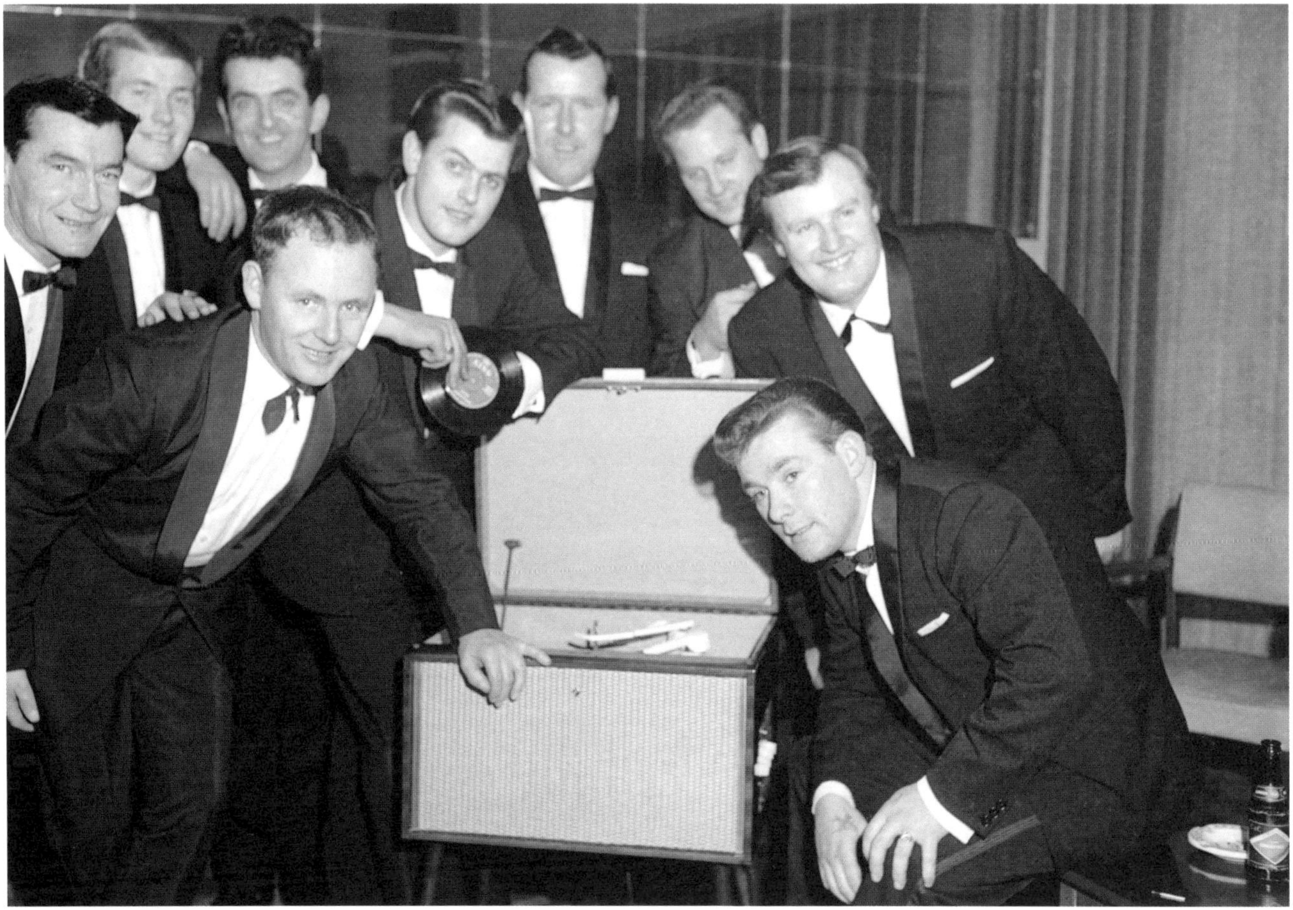

The Regal Showband, Cork, listen to their first recording 'Love Me', released under the King label. L to R, back row: Kevin Lynch, Mike Ahern, Gordon Hanley, vocalist Declan Ryan, Paddy Kennedy (Manager), Benno Haussmann. Front left is band leader John Minehane, and seated, right, is Jimmy Cotter.

9 November 1964

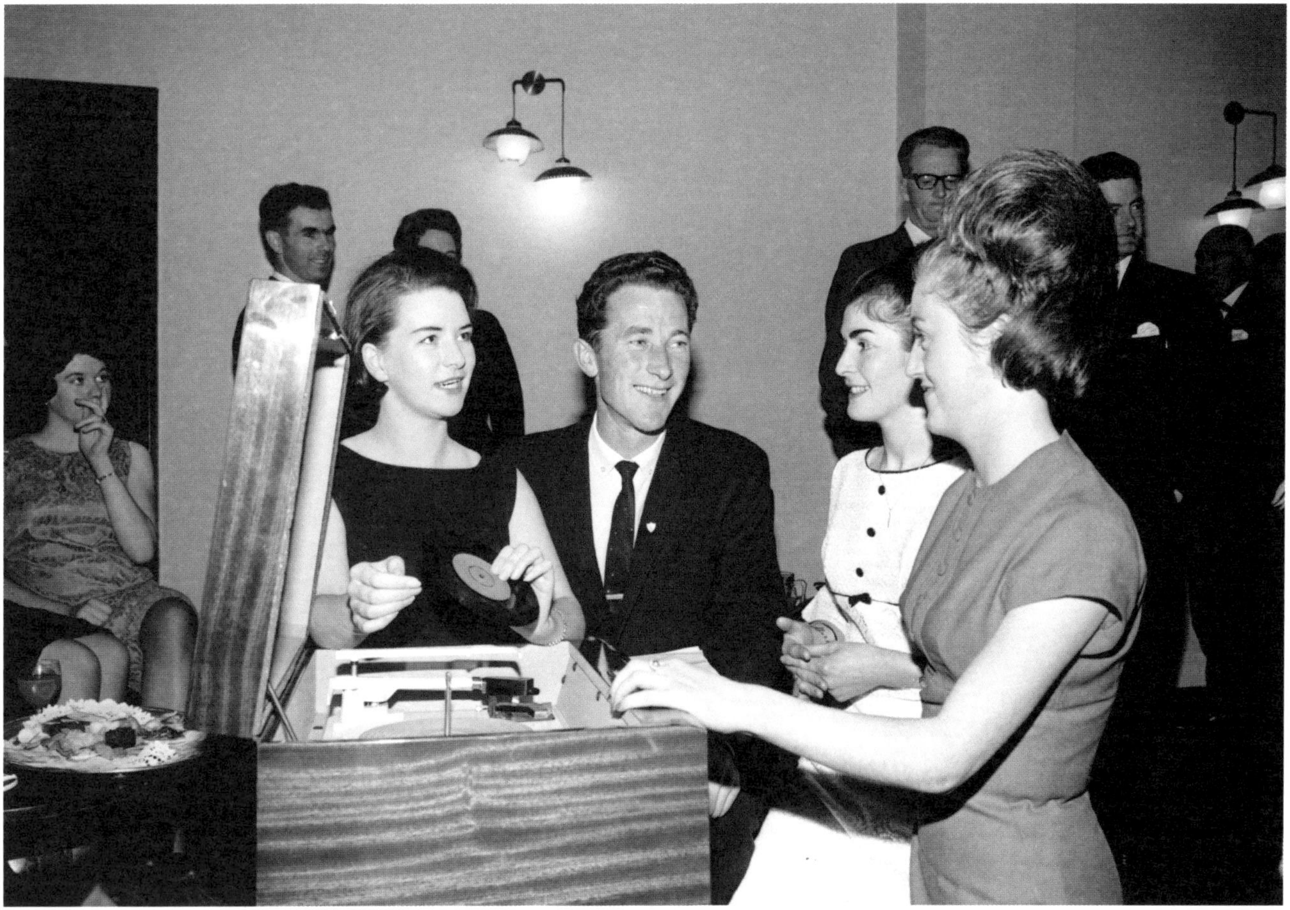

At the release of a Jim Reeves tribute disc by
the Mighty Avons showband, lead singer Larry
Cunningham, from Granard, Co Longford
is pictured with (l to r) Miss Pauline Walker,
Monaghan, Miss Phyllis Mortimer, Enniskillen, and
Miss Mary Mullen, Kiltegan, Co Wicklow.

16 November 1964

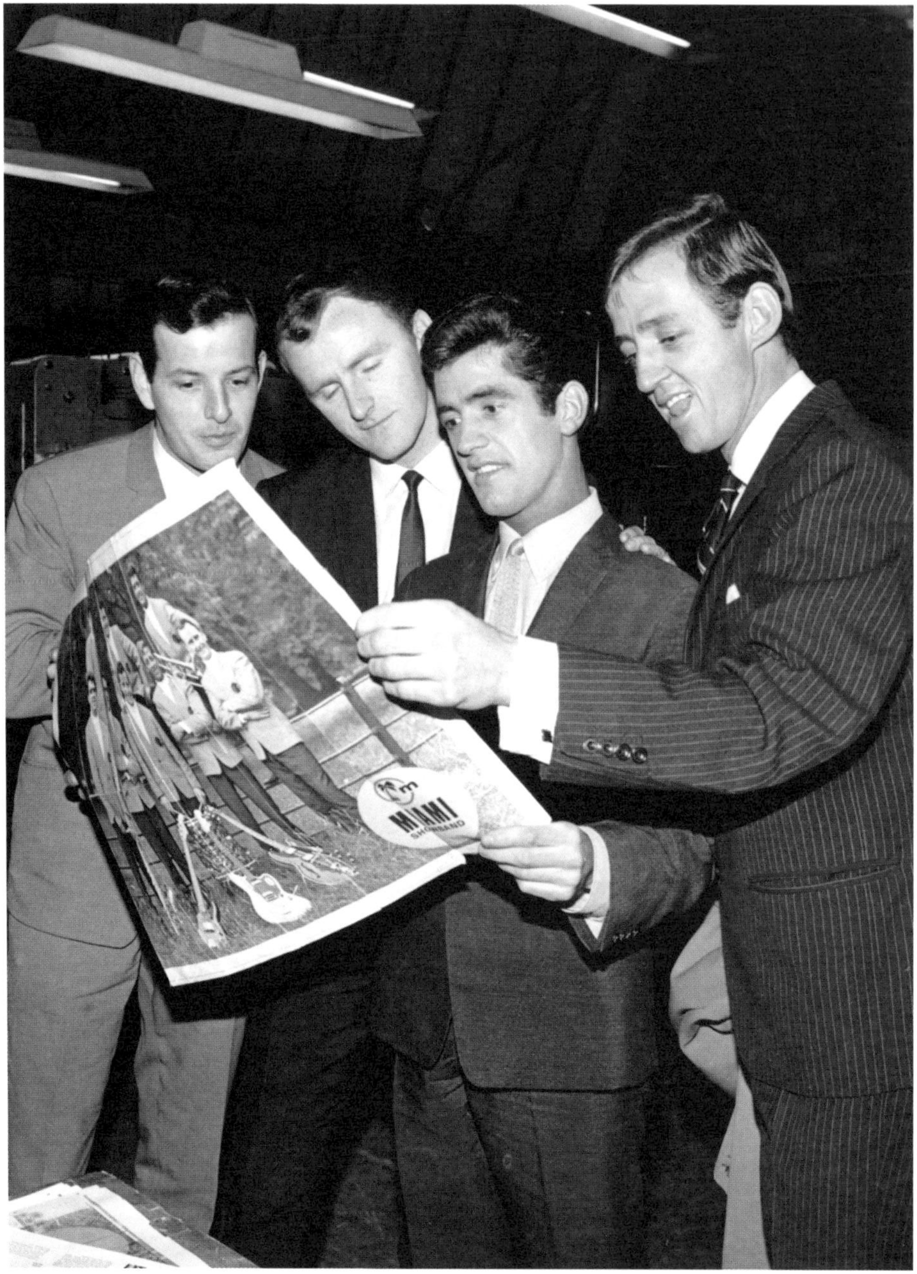

Dickie Rock (right) and other members of the Miami Showband check their pictures at Baily Gibson Printers.

12 December 1964

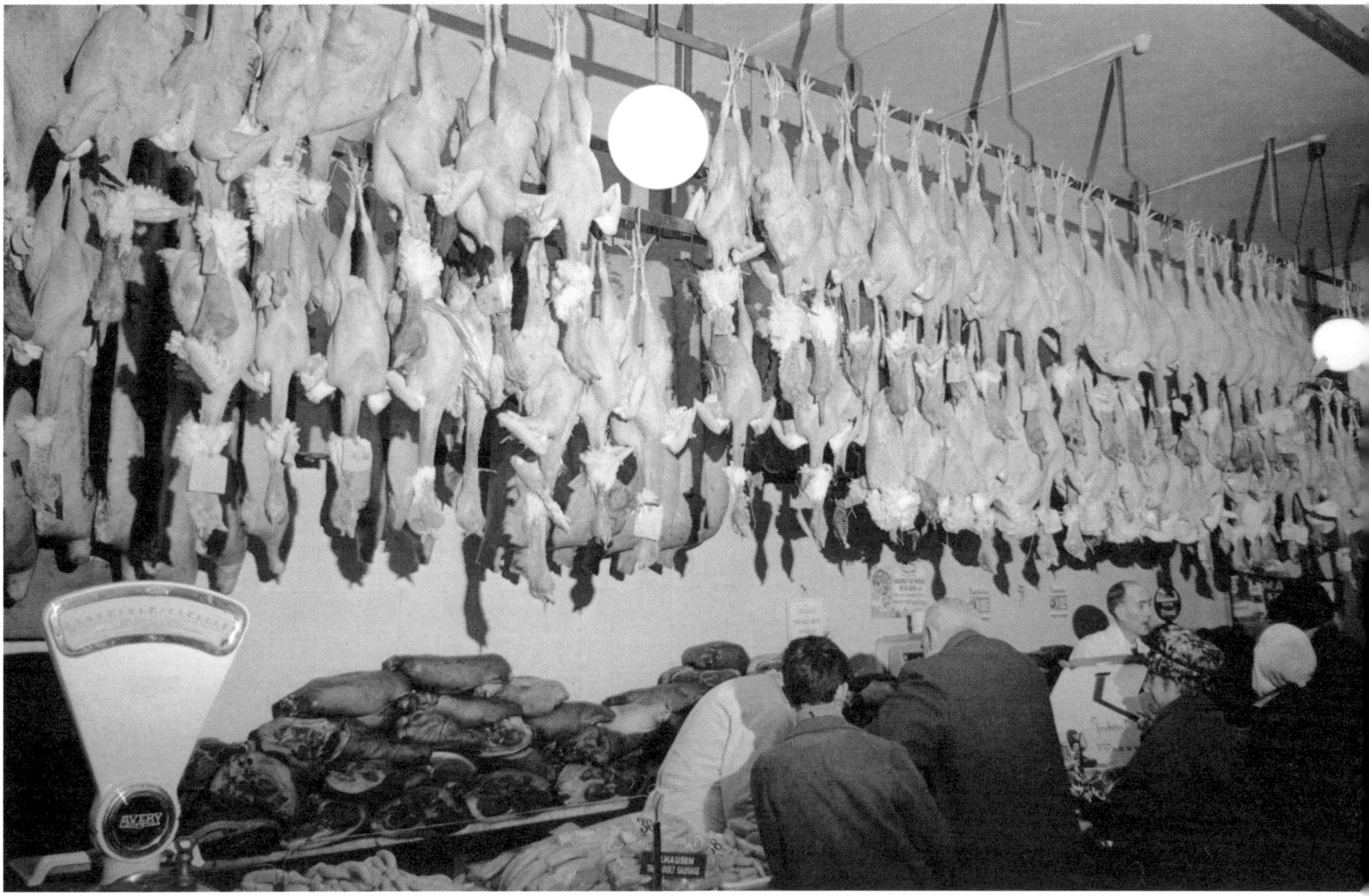

Trussed, plucked and hung, these turkeys in Findlaters shop, O'Connell Street, await the Christmas table.

18 December 1964

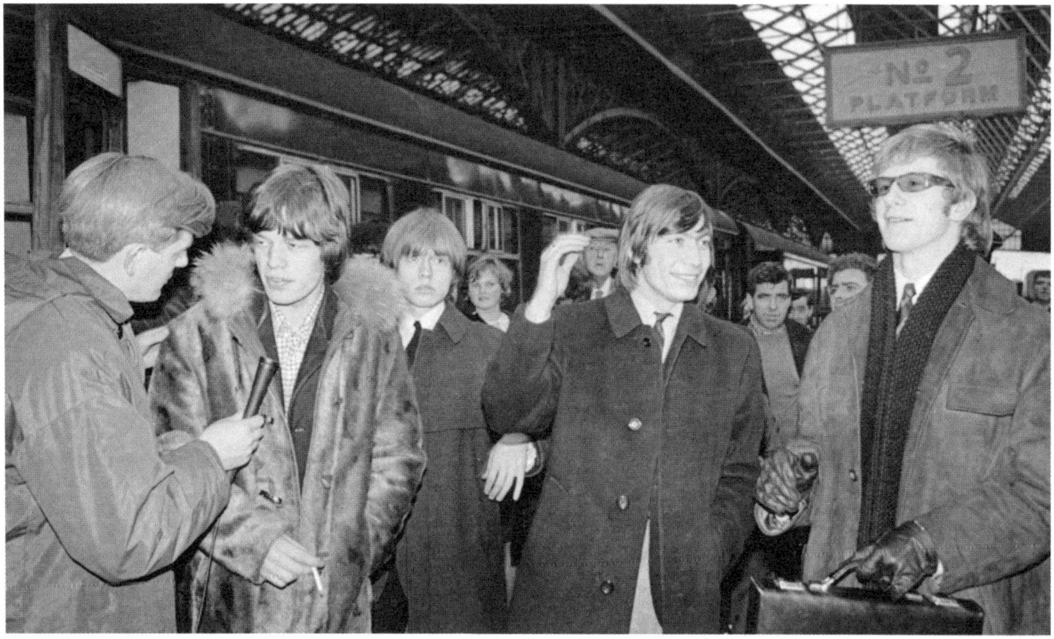

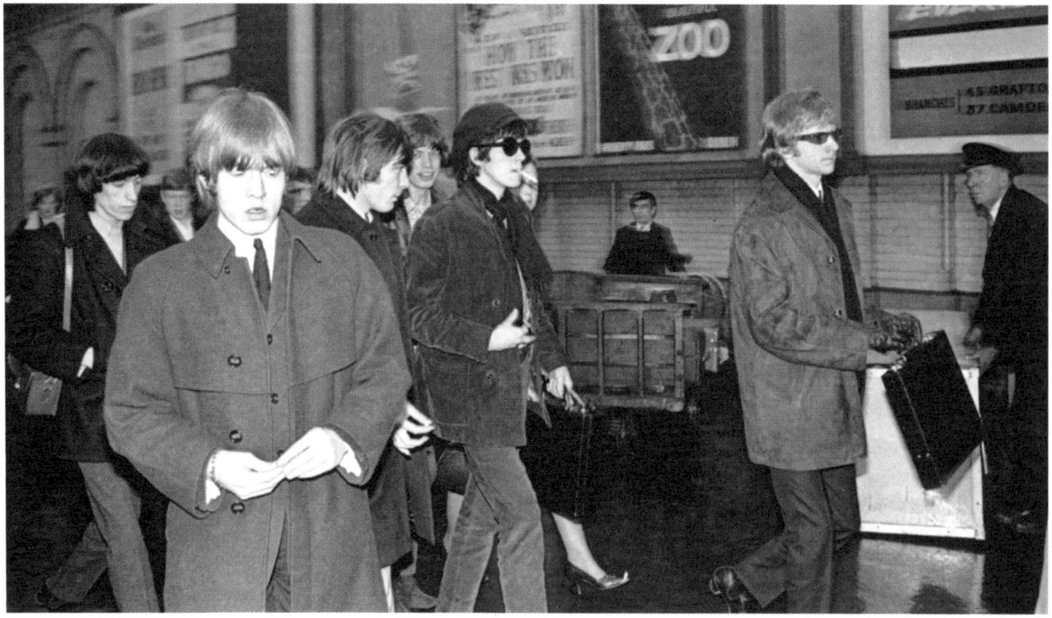

The Rolling Stones arriving at Amiens St station from Belfast to perform in the Adelphi. Bottom, from left: Bill Wyman, Brian Jones, Charlie Watts, Mick Jagger, Keith Richards.

9 January 1965

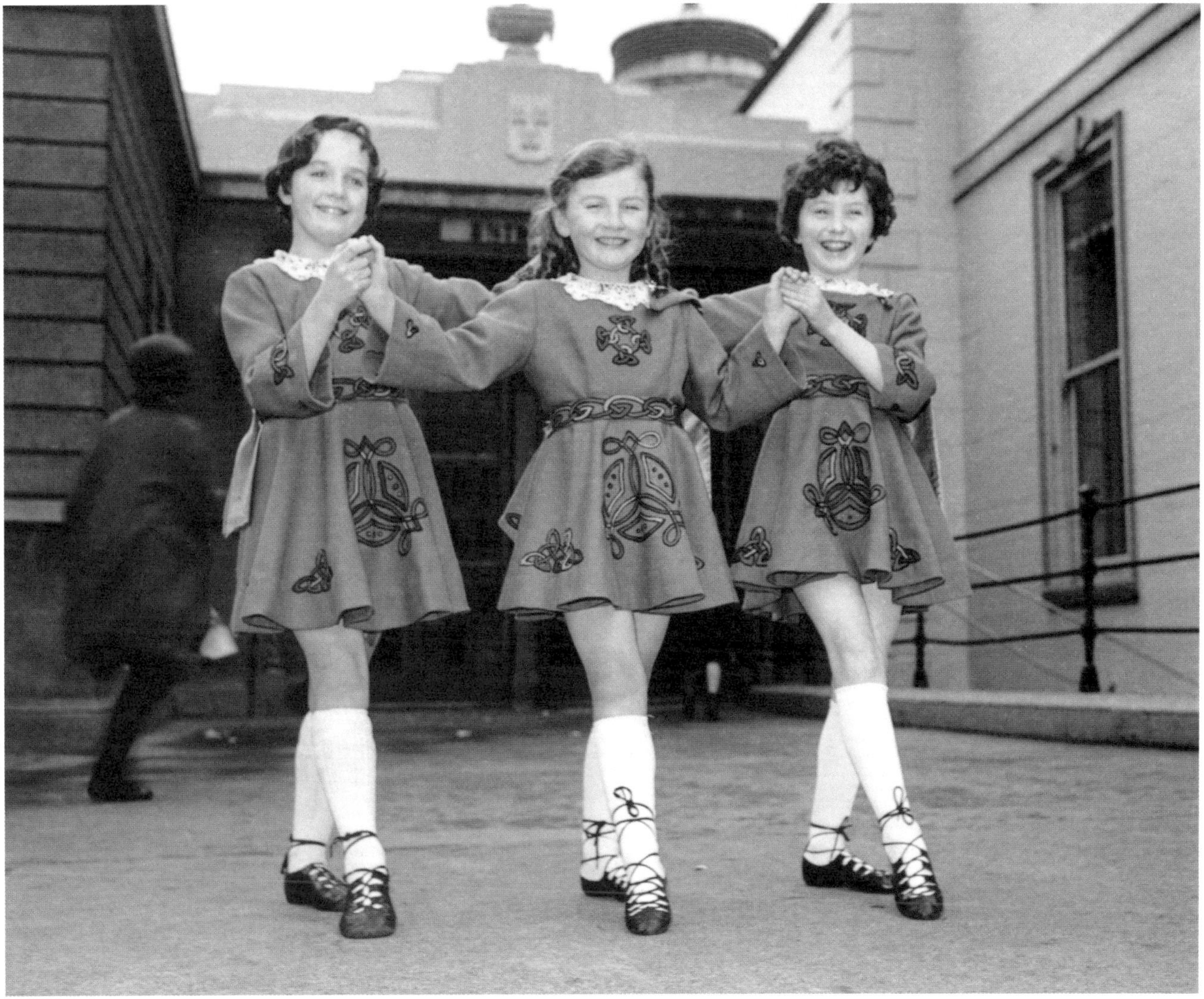

Three young Limerick lasses line up prior to competing in the Irish Dancing Championships.
L to R: Máire Ní Charthaigh, Deirdre Ní Chearbhaill and Magella Nic Mathúna, all from Scoil Rince Ui Ruairc.

21 February 1965

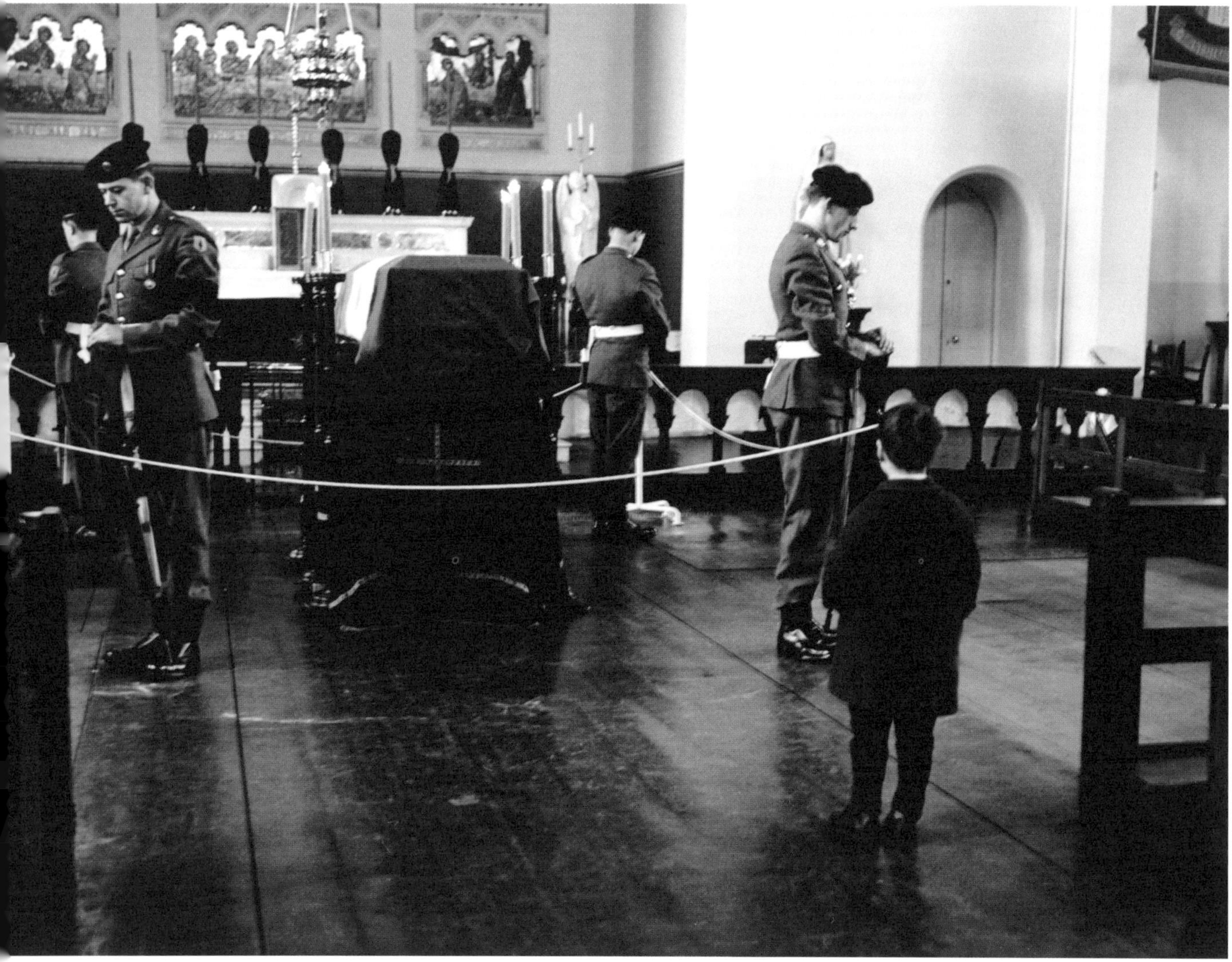

A young boy pays his respects as the body of Roger Casement lies in state at Arbour Hill. Casement had been hanged at Pentonville Prison in 1916. In 1965 his remains were repatriated to Ireland and he was given a state funeral, after which he was buried with full military honours in the Republican plot in Glasnevin Cemetery.

14 February 1965

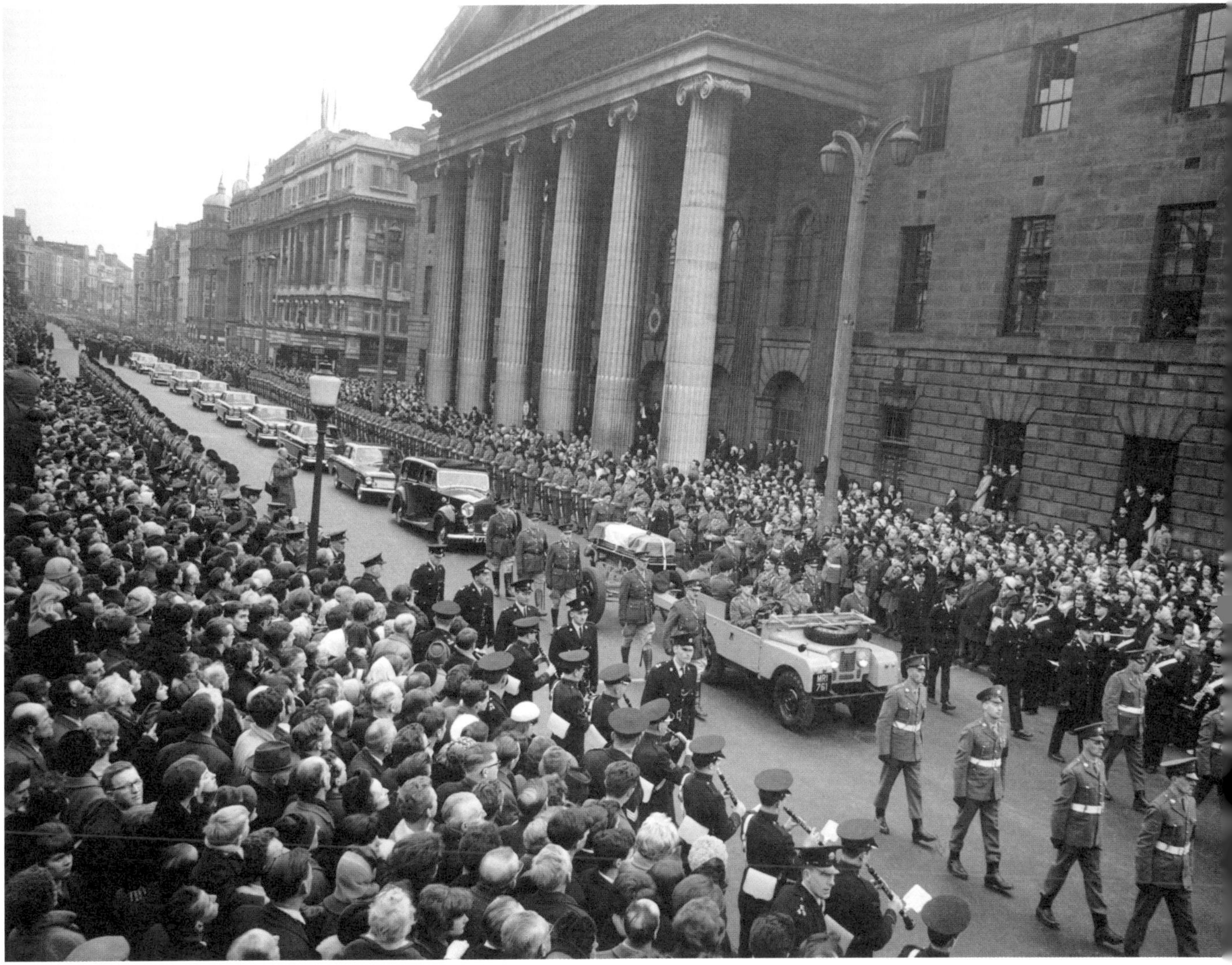

Thousands line the streets as Casement's funeral passes by the GPO.

18 February 1965

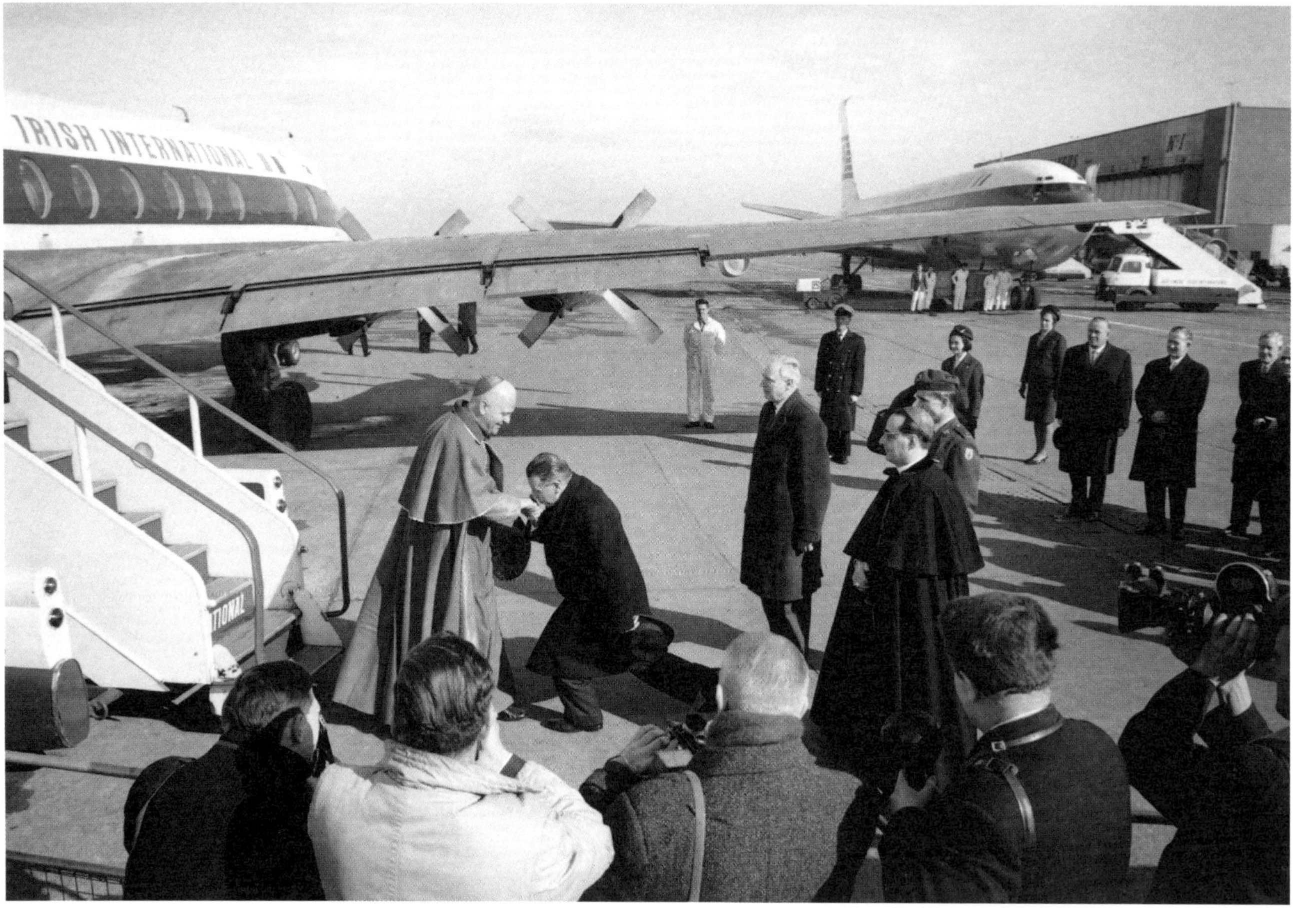

William Cardinal Conway is greeted in the customary manner by Taoiseach Sean Lemass on his return from Rome where he had been elevated to the cardinalate.

2 March 1965

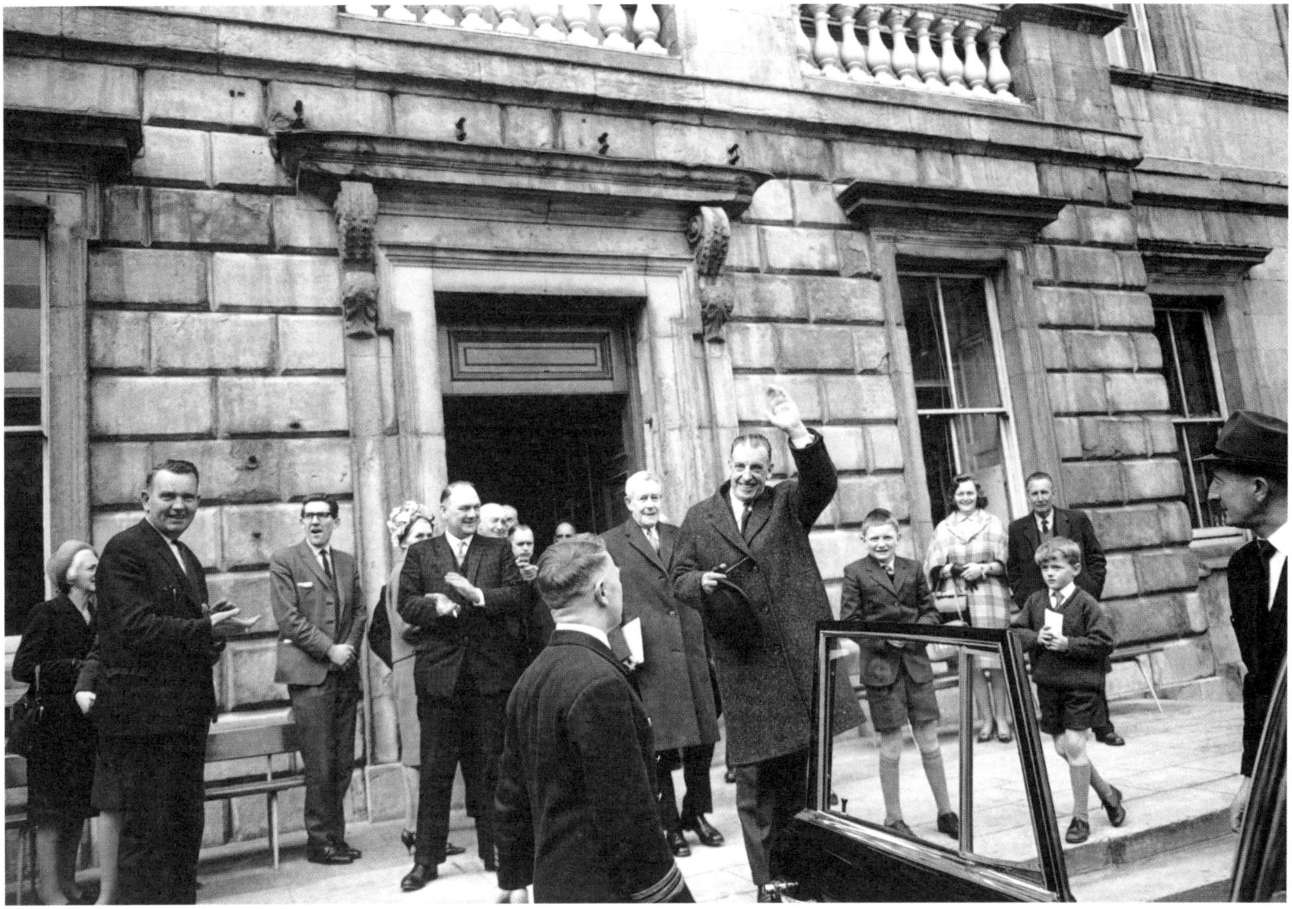

Sean Lemass waves to supporters as he leaves Leinster House following his re-election as Taoiseach.

11 April 1965

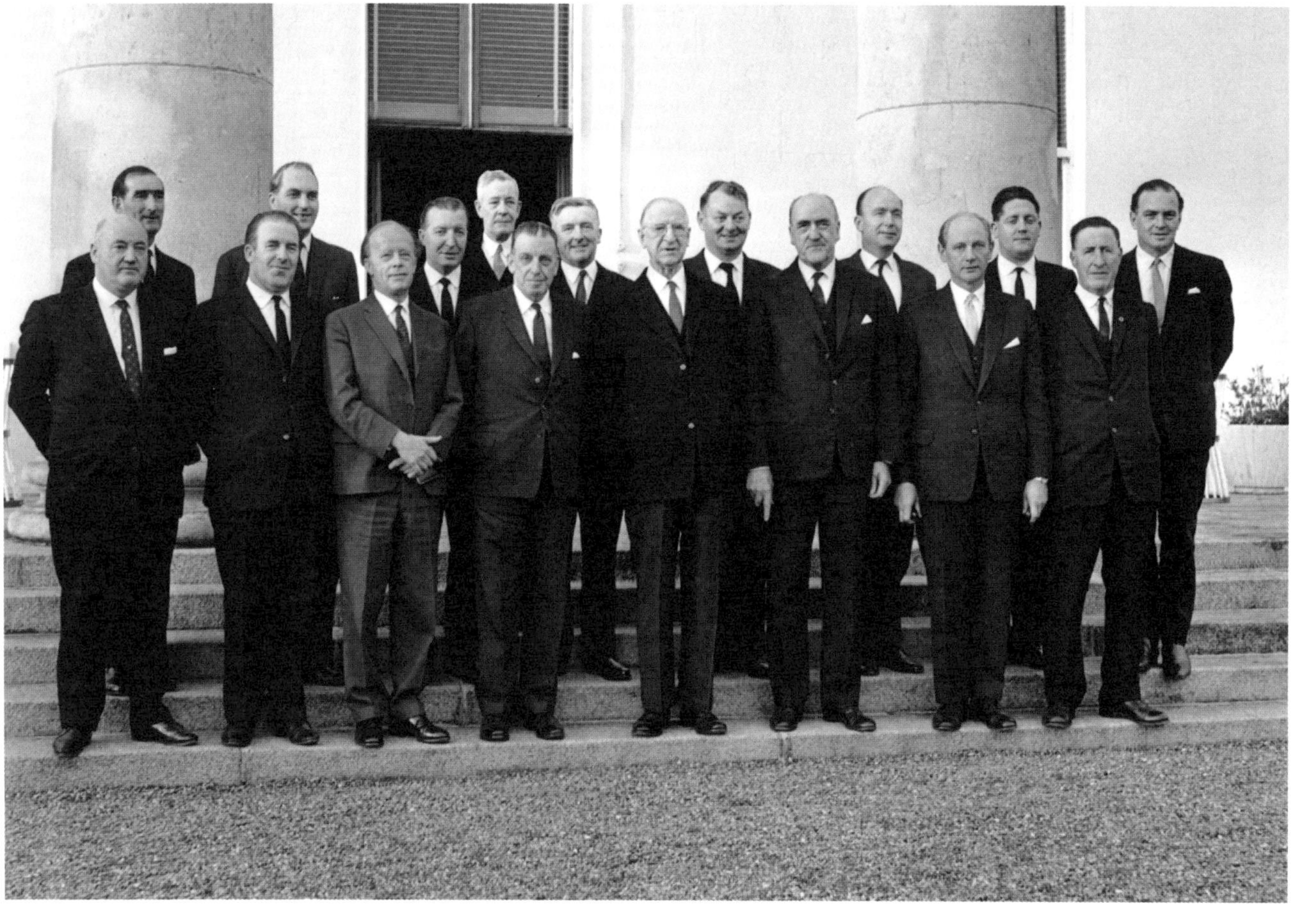

De Valera receives the new Cabinet at Áras an Uachtaráin. L to R, front row: Joseph Brennan, Neil Blaney, Erskine Childers, Taoiseach Sean Lemass, the President, Frank Aiken, Jack Lynch, Kevin Boland. Back row: Sean Flanagan, George Colley, Charles Haughey, Michael Hilliard, Micheál O Moráin, Patrick Hillery, Brian Lenihan, Donogh O'Malley.

21 April 1965

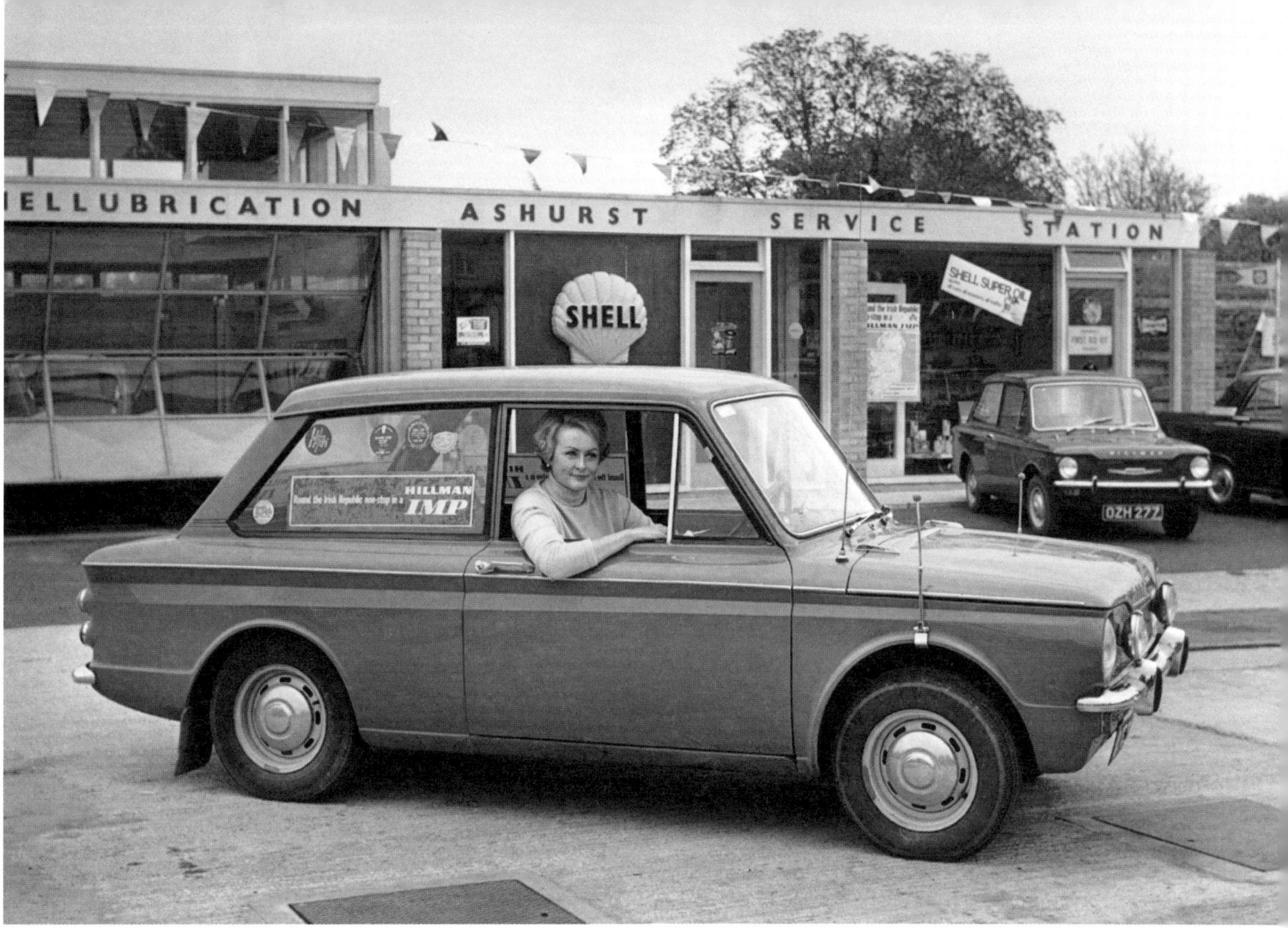

Rally driver Rosemary Smith after completing
a non-stop Round Ireland Endurance Run
in her Hillman Imp.

11 May 1965

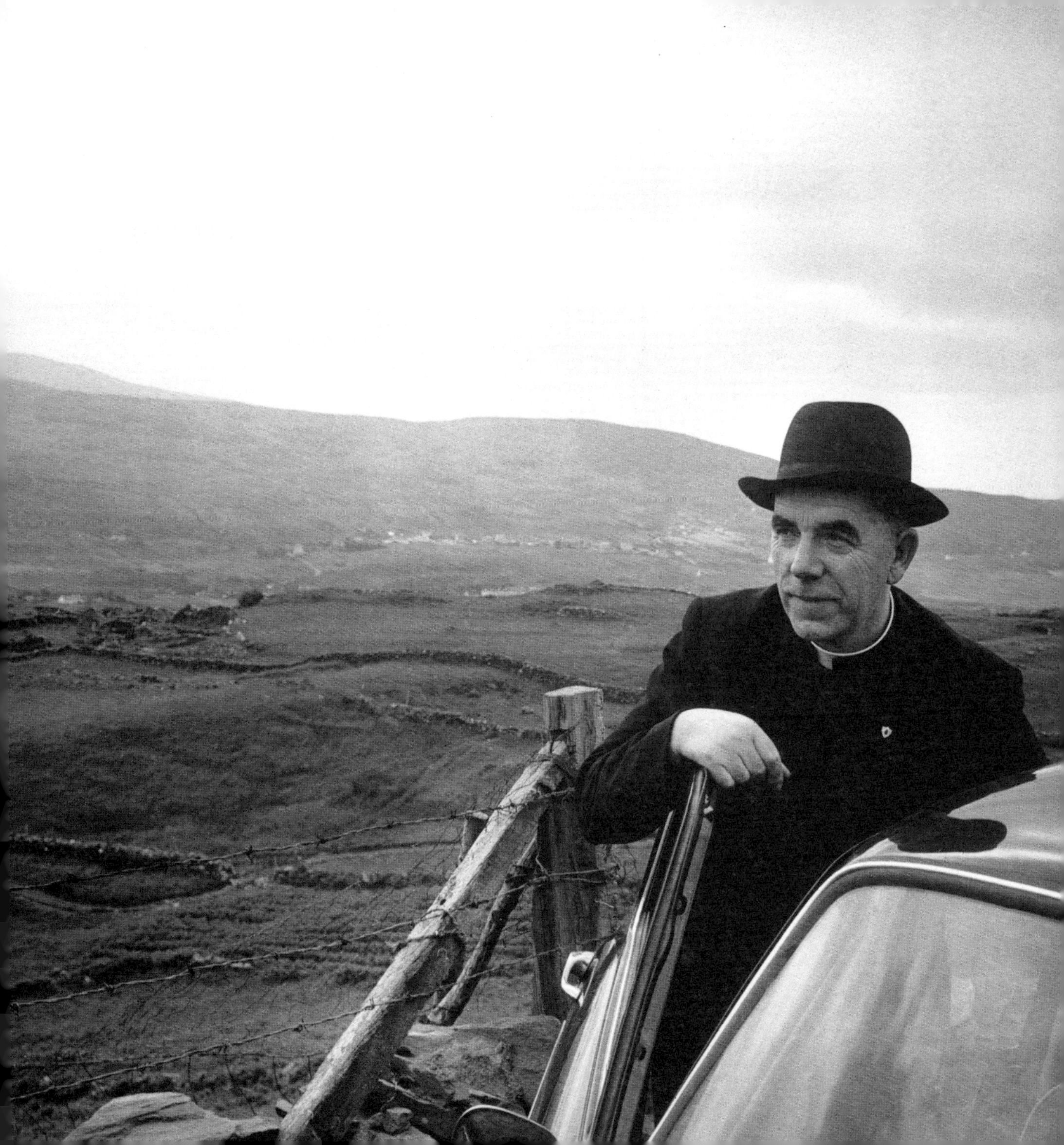

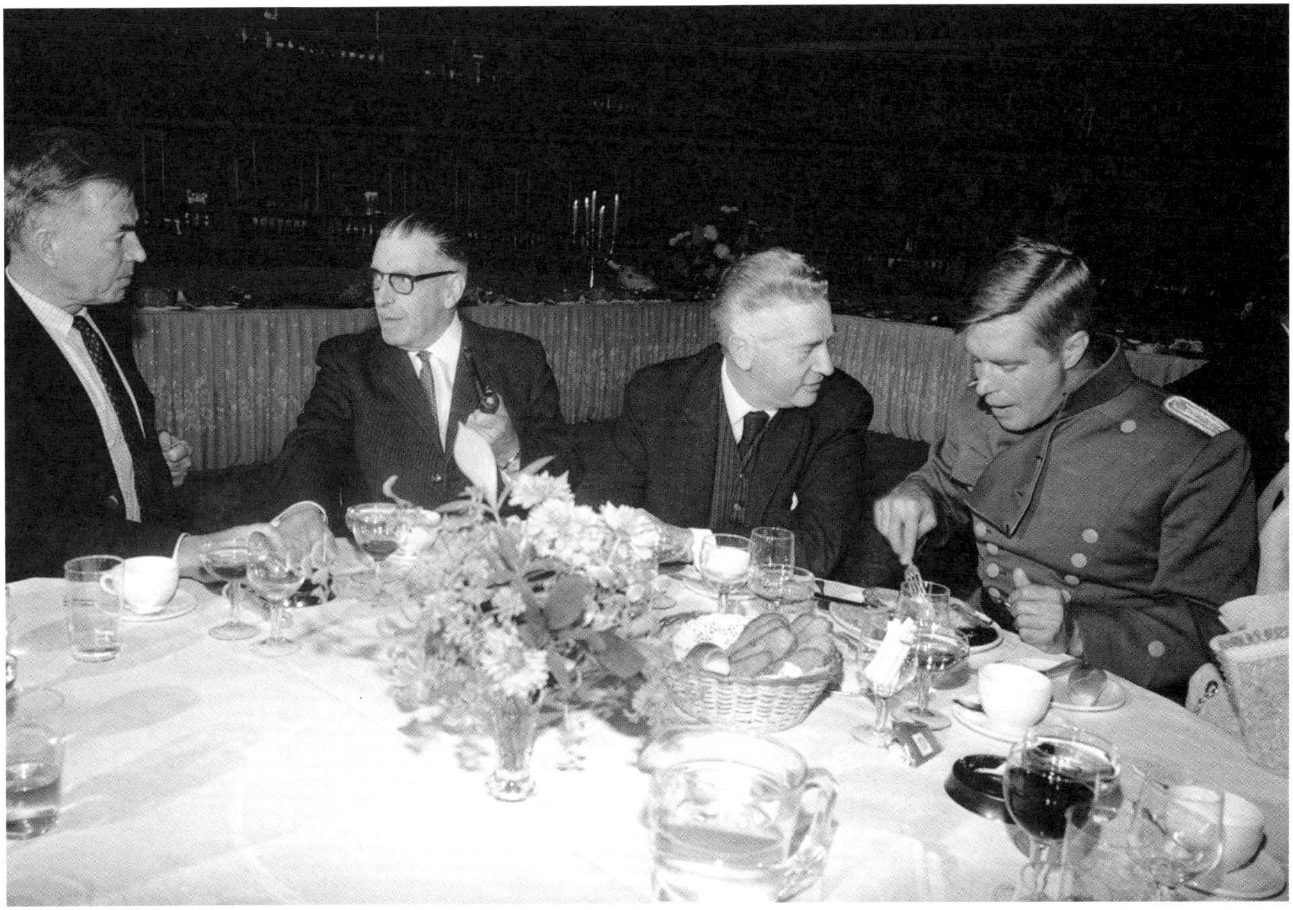

Actors James Mason (left) and George Peppard (right) at lunch with Taoiseach Sean Lemass during the filming of 'The Blue Max' in Ardmore Studios.

16 September 1965

Fr James McDyer, curate of Glencolumcille, Co Donegal became a byword for rural regeneration through his activities in the small parish to which he was appointed in 1951. He succeeded in building a community centre, bringing electricity to the area, and establishing a Folk Village and Museum, which still thrive.

6 July 1965

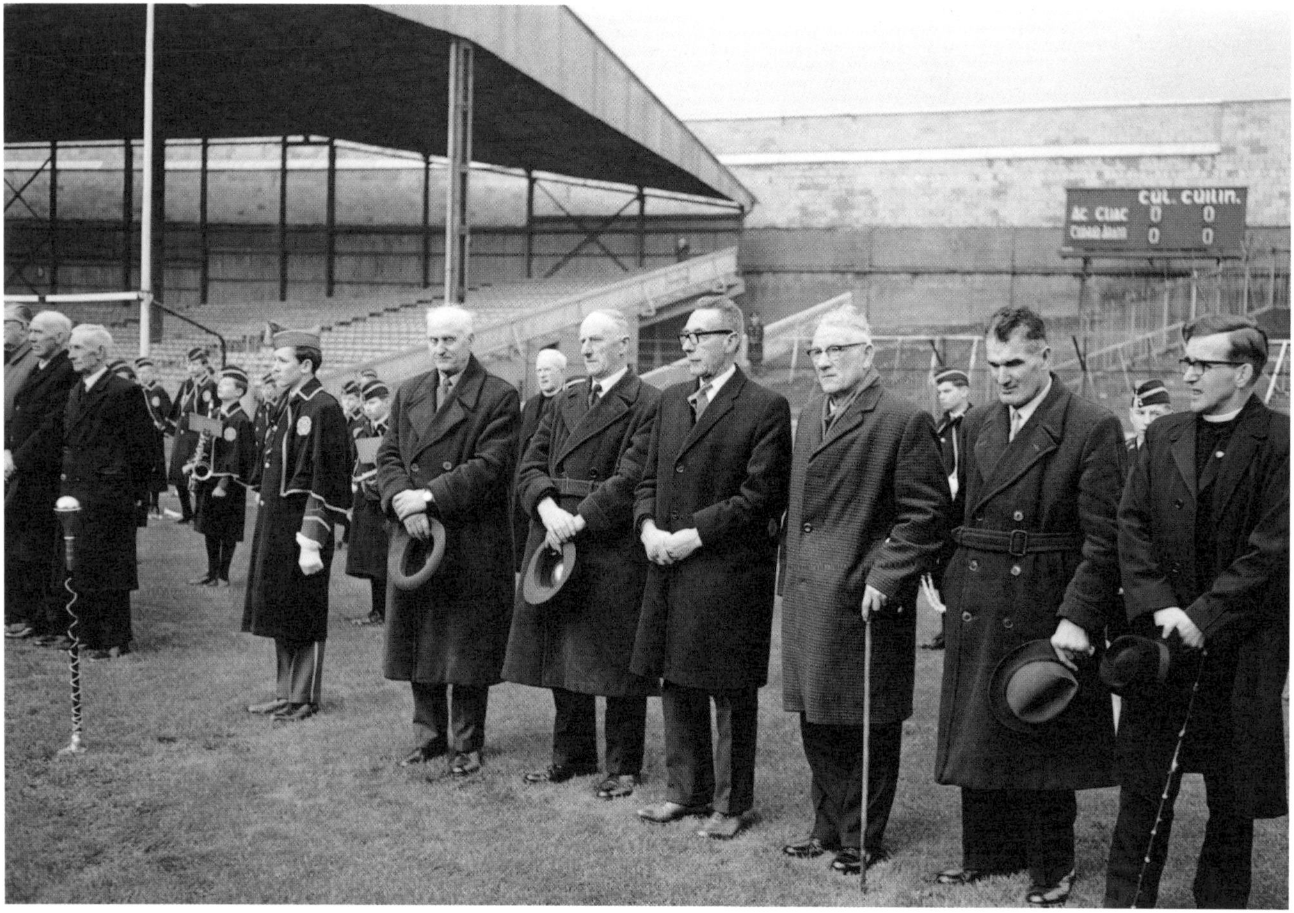

Former players remember the 14 who were shot dead in Croke Park on Bloody Sunday 1965 as they attended a Dublin v Tipp match. Among the dead were Tipperary fullback Michael Hogan, after whom the Hogan Stand is named.

21 November 1965

The Kish lighthouse keeper heads for his station carrying the Christmas pudding and other goodies presented to him to make up for not being home for Christmas. The lighthouse, erected in 1965 was automated in 1992.

10 December 1965

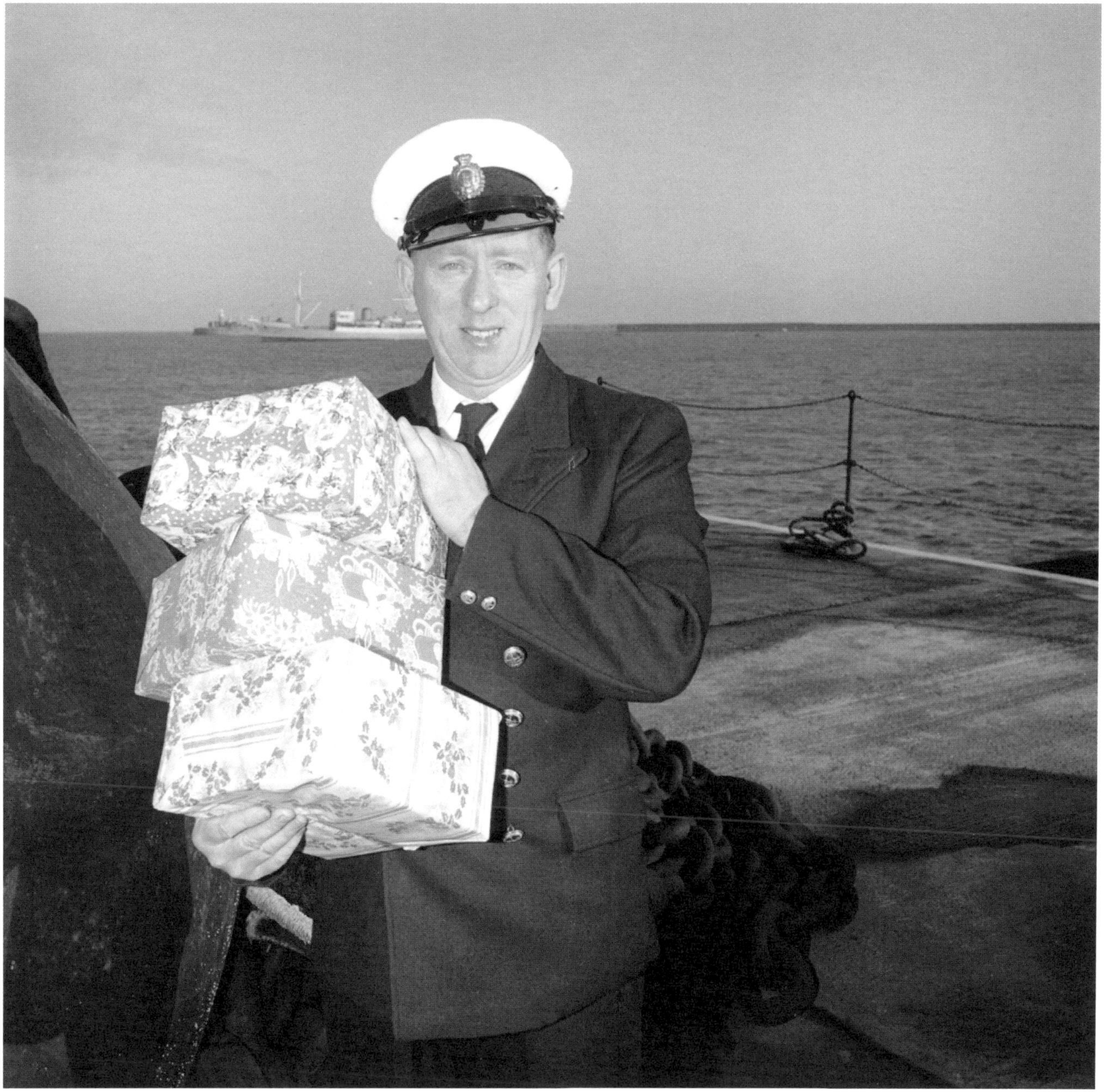

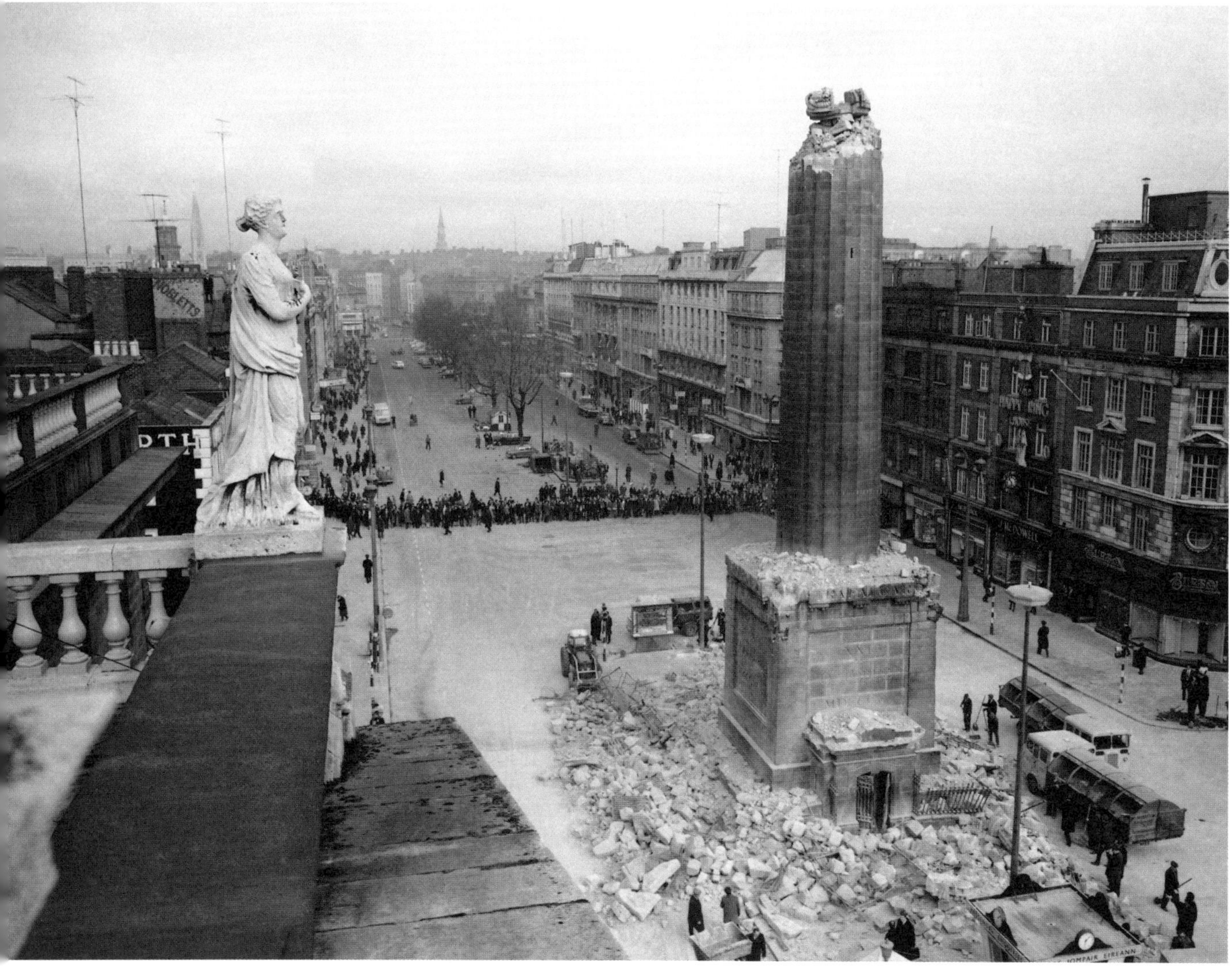

A statue on top of the GPO gets a good look at the decapitated Nelson's Pillar, blown up by a republican bomb in the early hours of the morning. A well-known landmark and meeting place, the Pillar also offered a great view over the city, and its 168 steps could be climbed for a fee of sixpence.

8 March 1966

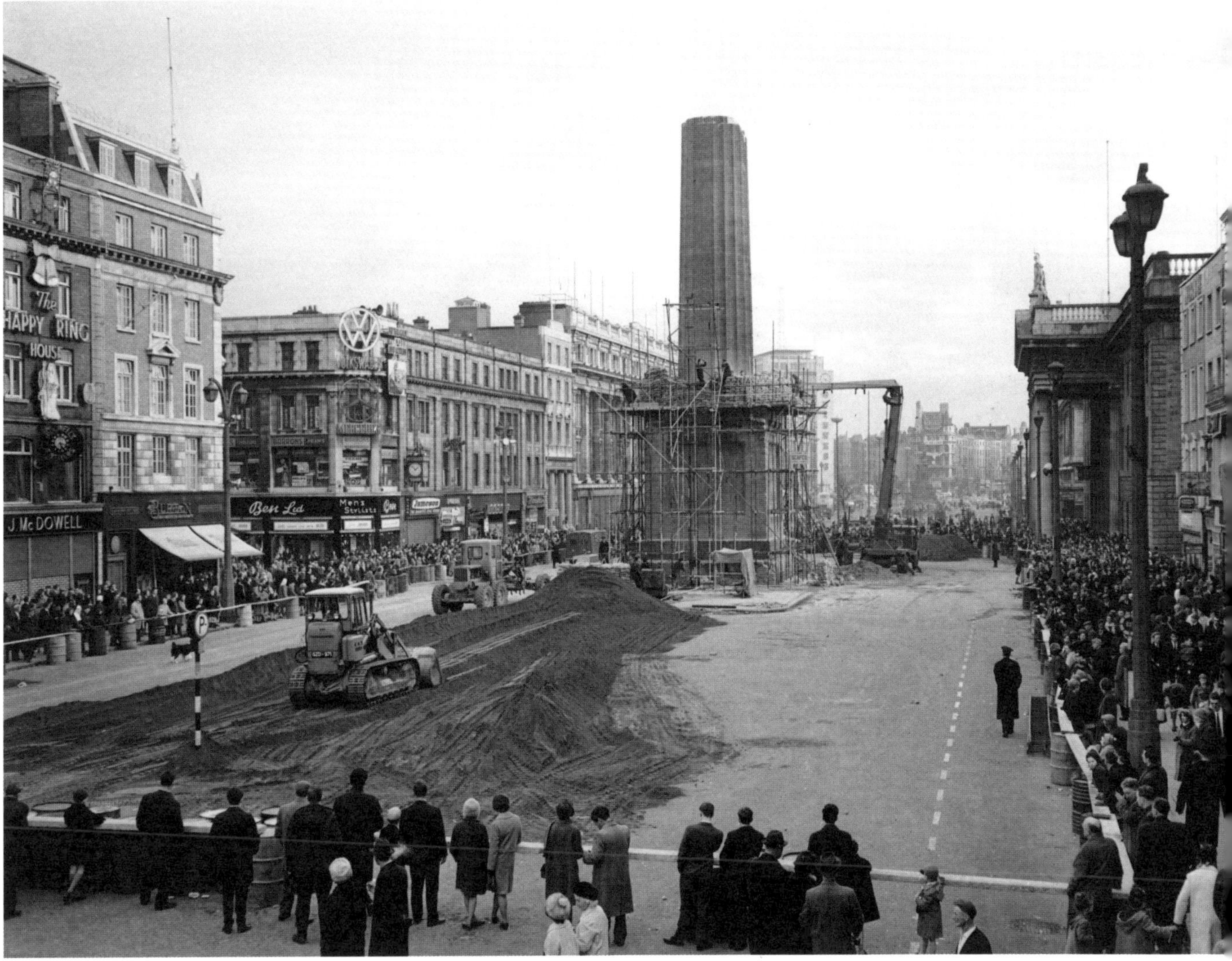

An area around the site is cordoned off in preparation
for the army demolition of what is left of the Pillar.

13 March 1966

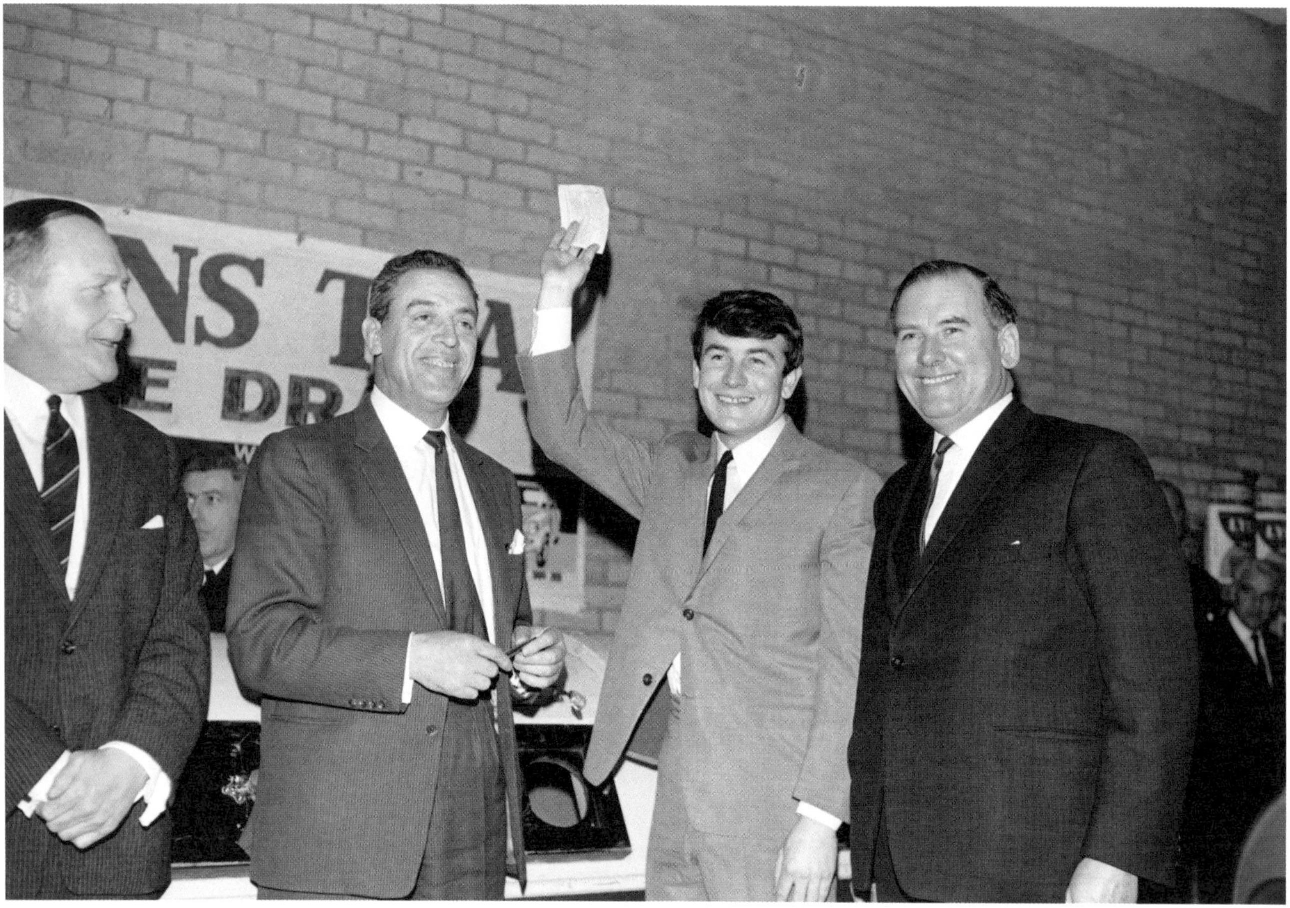

Butch Moore, lead singer with the Capitol Showband, pulls the winning name in the 14th Lyons Tea Free Draw, with (2nd left) stage, film and TV actor Eddie Byrne. Also in the picture are Joint Managing Directors of Lyons, Mr Jim O'Meara (right) and Mr George Patterson (left).

28 February 1966

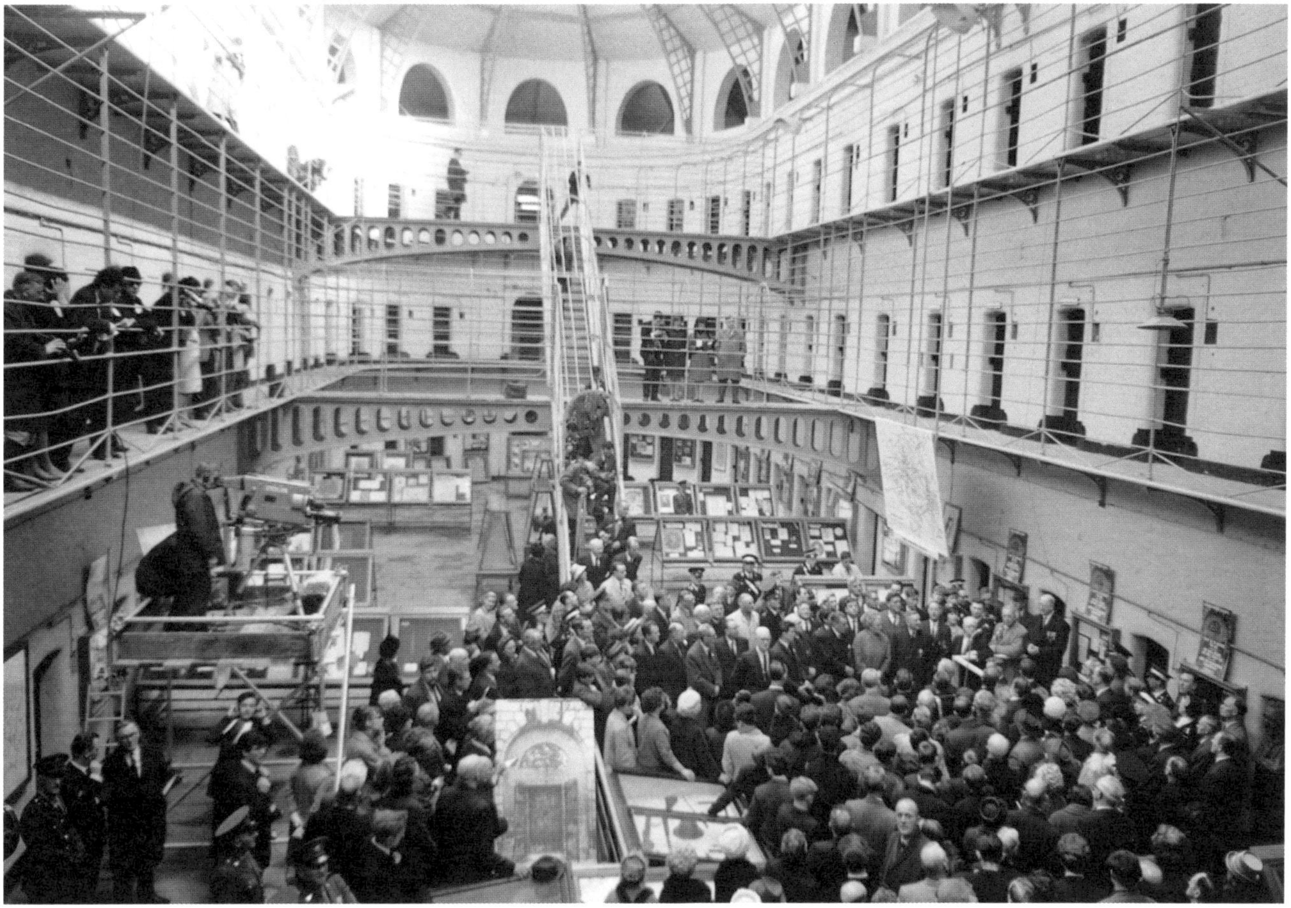

As part of the 1916 Jubilee Commemorations
Kilmainham Gaol Historical Museum is opened.

10 April 1966

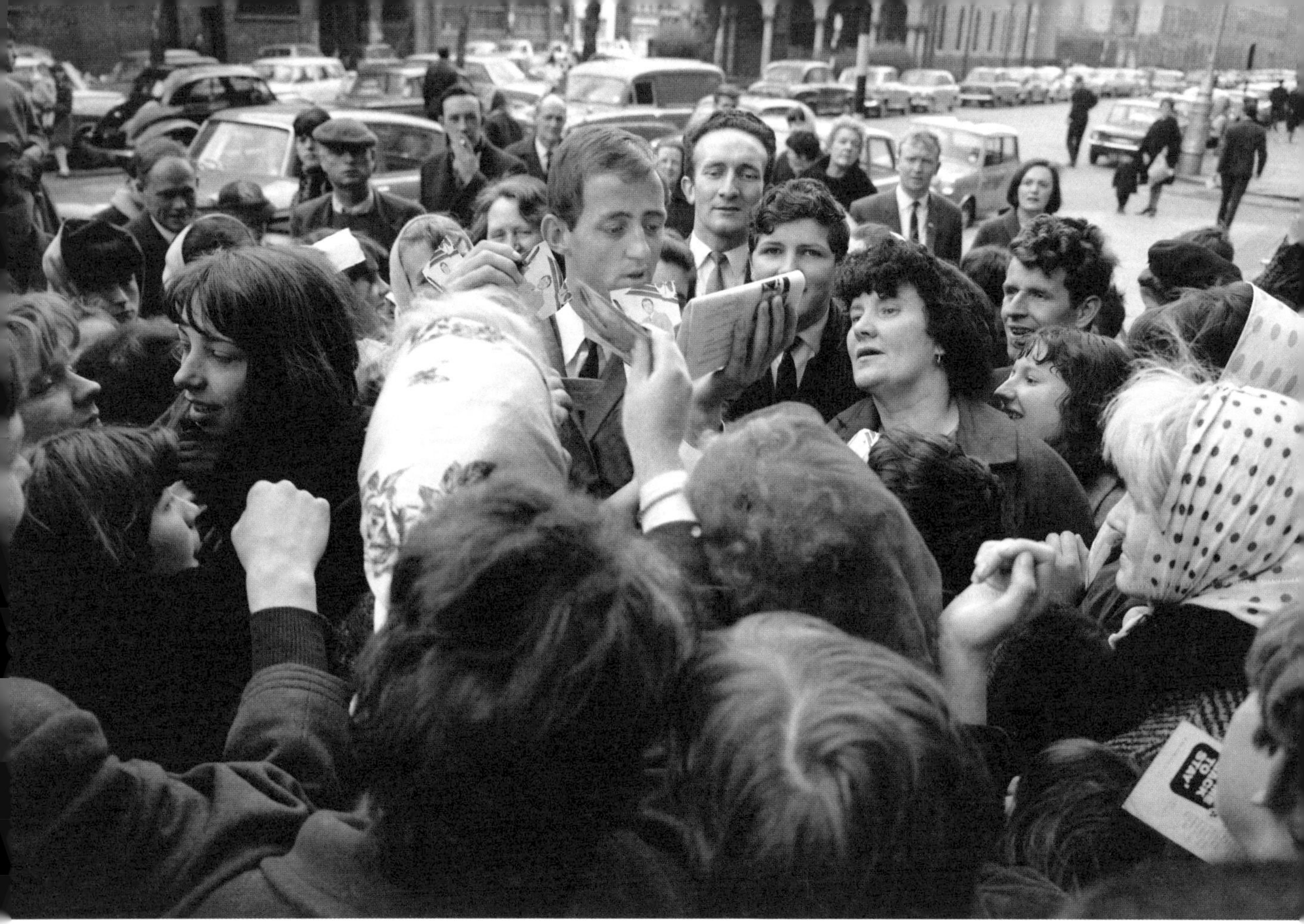

Dickie Rock is surrounded by fans looking for an autograph.

26 April 1966

T F O'Higgins, a candidate in the 1966 Presidential Election, casts his vote at Dalkey Town Hall, accompanied by his wife, and two of his sons, Shane (left), and Michael (right). O'Higgins came within 1% (or 10,000 votes) of defeating outgoing president Eamon de Valera.

1 June 1966

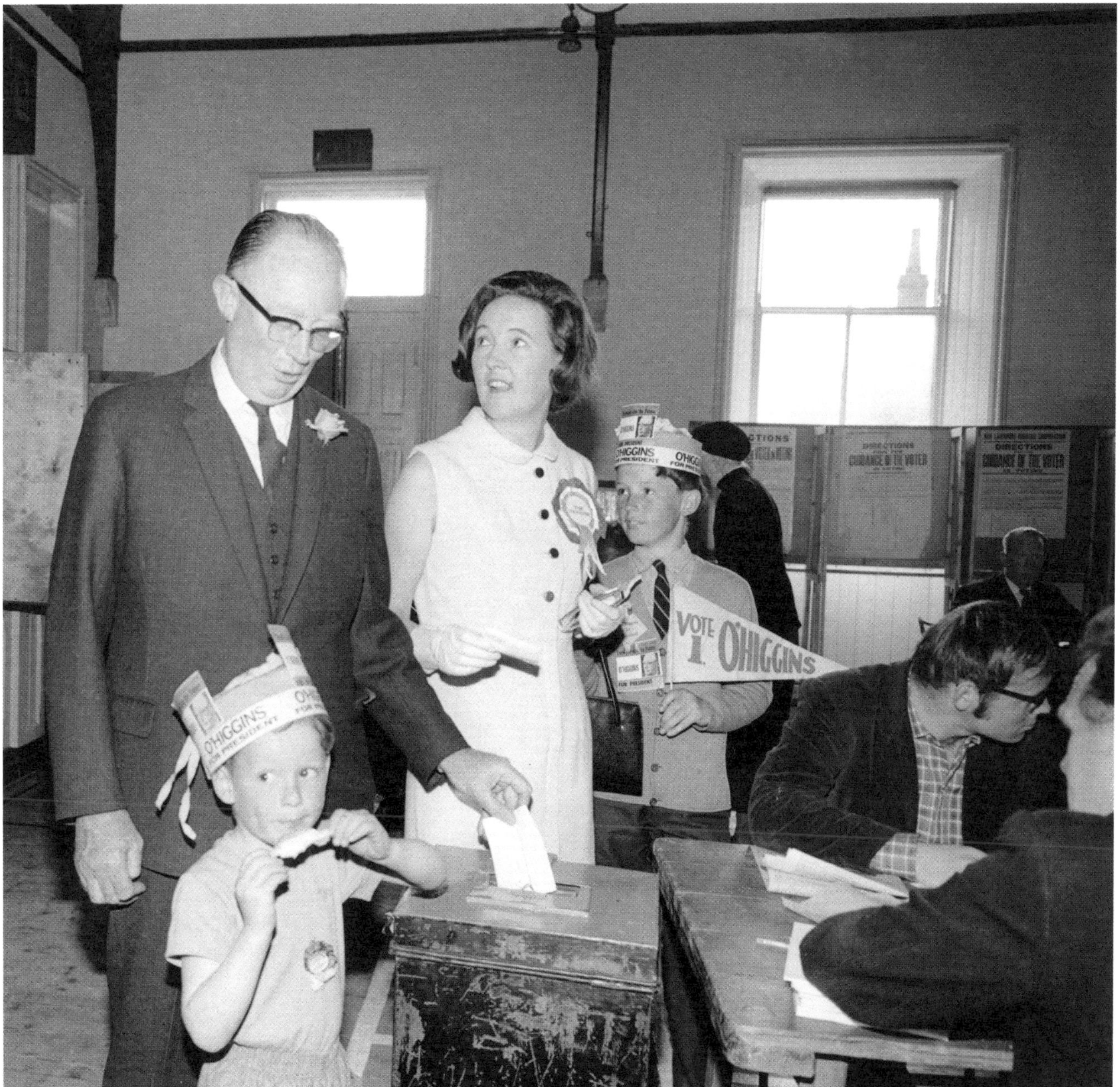
O'HIGGINS
FOR PRESIDENT
VOTE 1. O'HIGGINS
DIRECTIONS
GUIDANCE OF THE VOTER

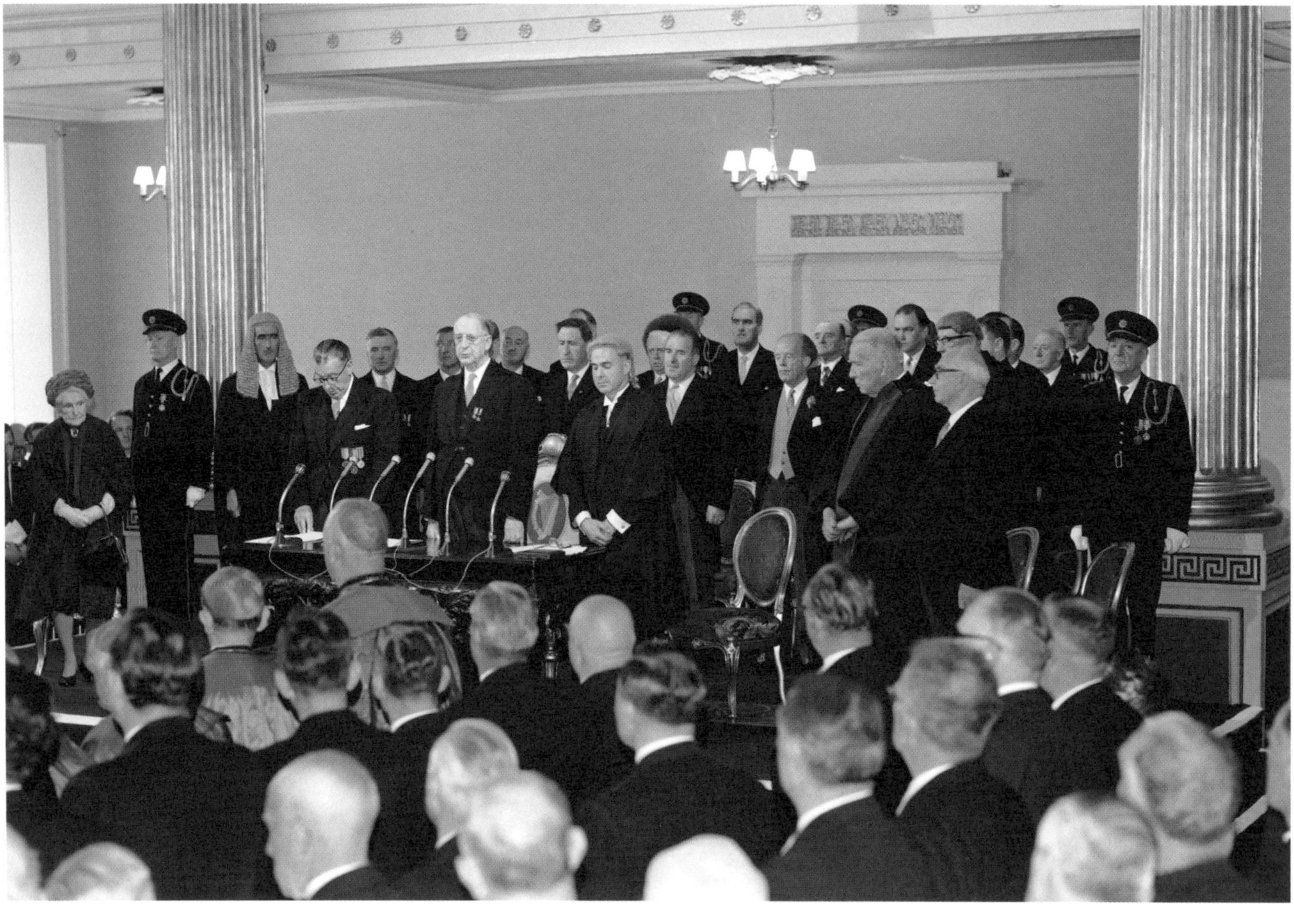

De Valera takes the oath of office administered by the Chief Justice, Cearbhaill Ó Dálaigh (right), in the presence of Taoiseach Sean Lemass (left) and members of the Government. First Lady Sinéad Bean de Valera is standing on extreme left of picture.

25 June 1966

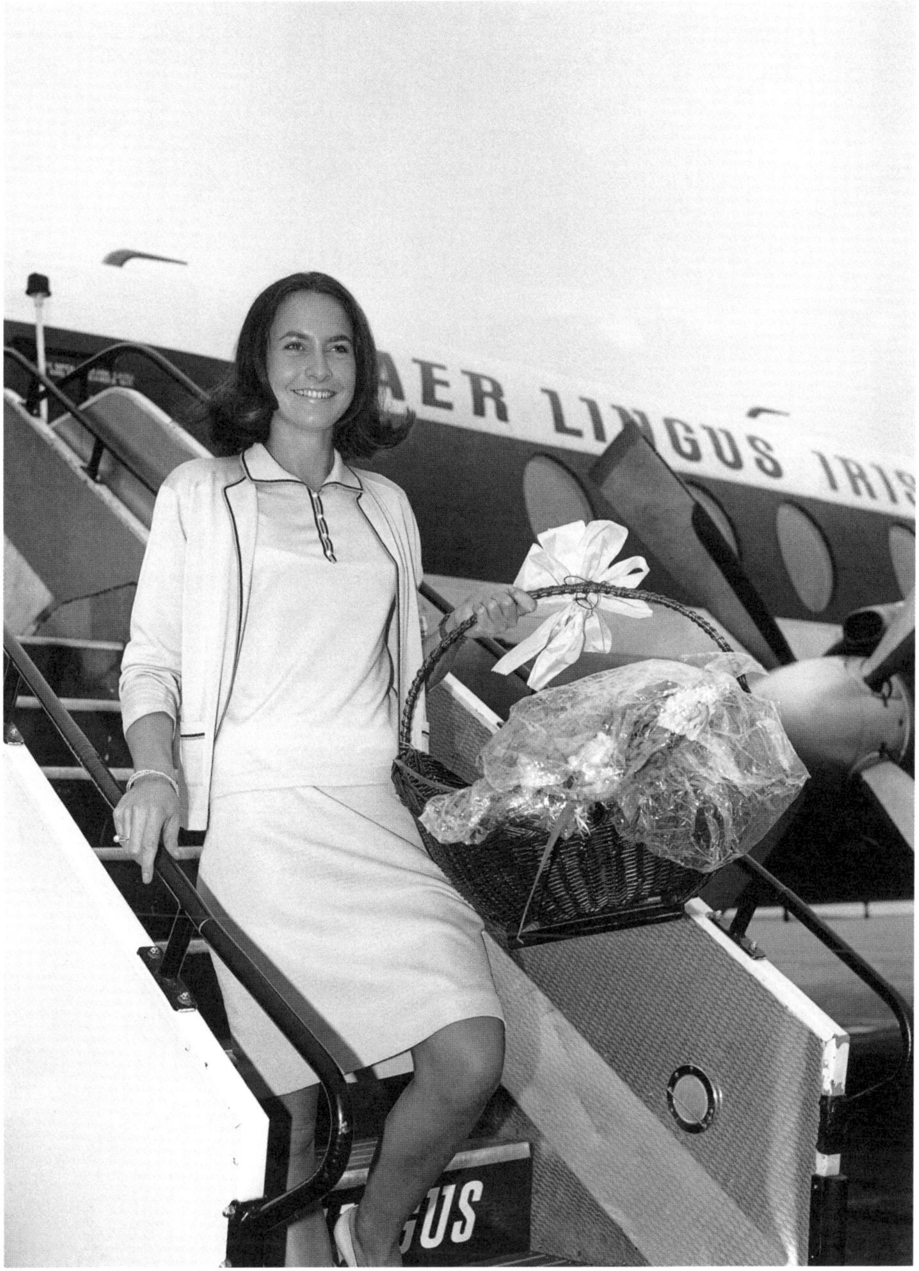

One of the best-known Irish models of the time, Grace O'Shaughnessy, returns from an assignment in Italy.

30 August 1966

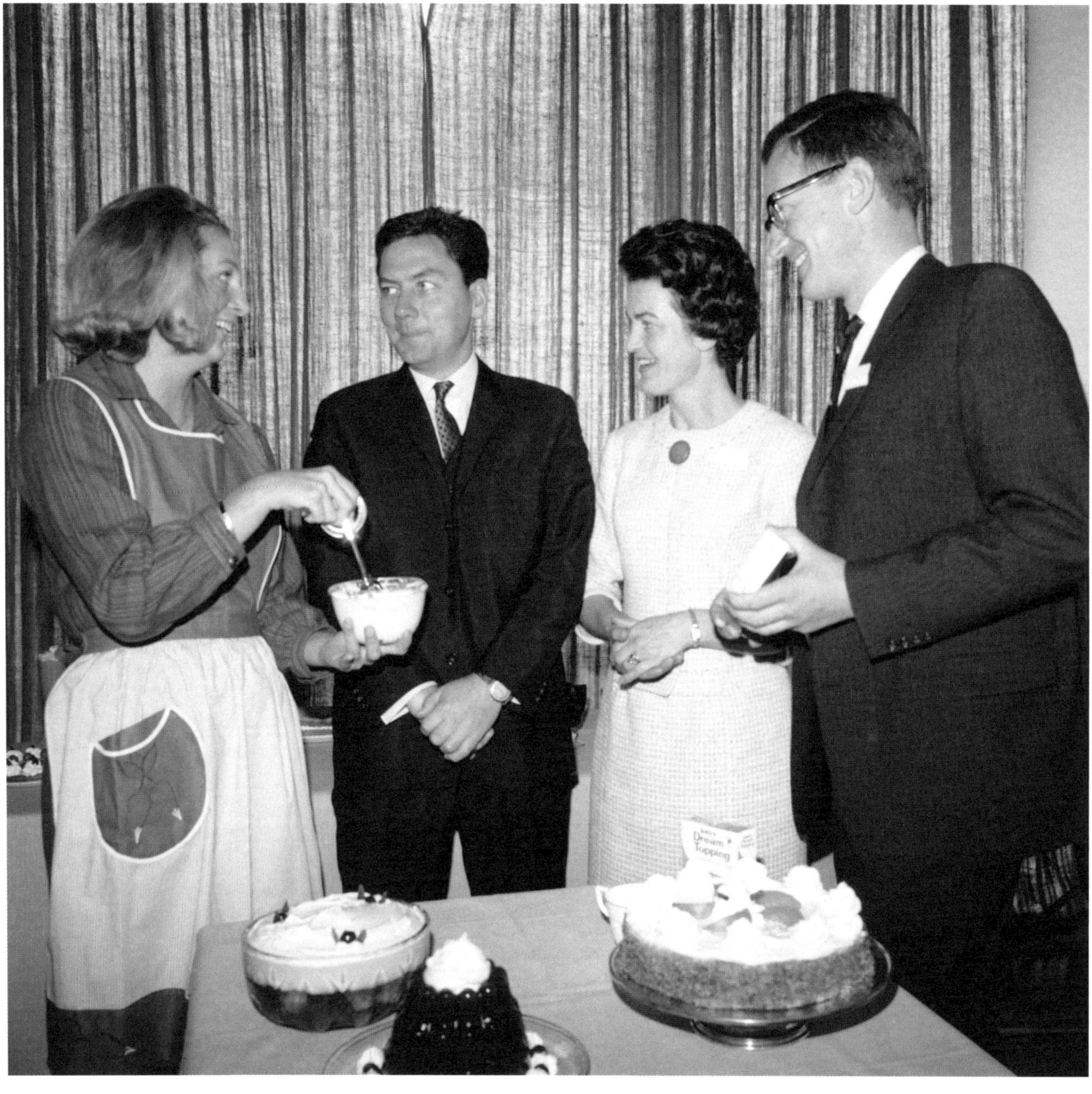
Dream
Topping

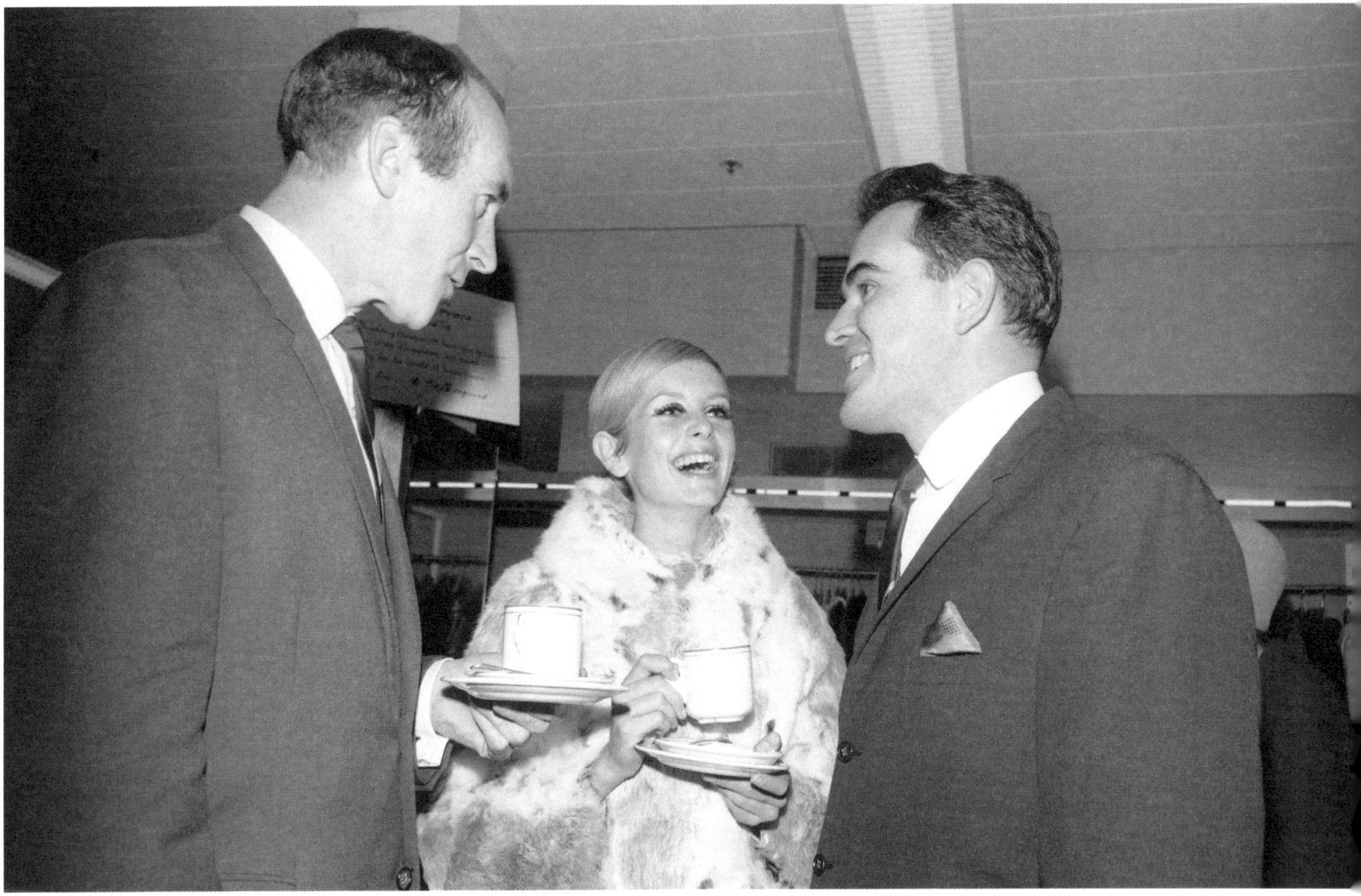

Internationally famous model Twiggy (Leslie Hornby) enjoys a cup of tea with Mr John Doody, (left) Manager of Arnotts, Henry Street, and Mr Vivian Dudgeon, Manager of Arnotts, Grafton Street, prior to the Arnotts Fashion Show.

12 October 1966

Miss Gillian Lodge, Home Economist, assures Gay Byrne that Birds' new product, 'Dream Topping' will be ideal for his jellies, trifles and any other desserts he cares to whip up! The topping was marketed as 'a great standby to have in the cupboard'. On Gay's right is Mrs Elizabeth Burdett, Demonstrator, and Mr Theo Harris, MD of Alfred Bird & Sons Ltd.

6 October 1966

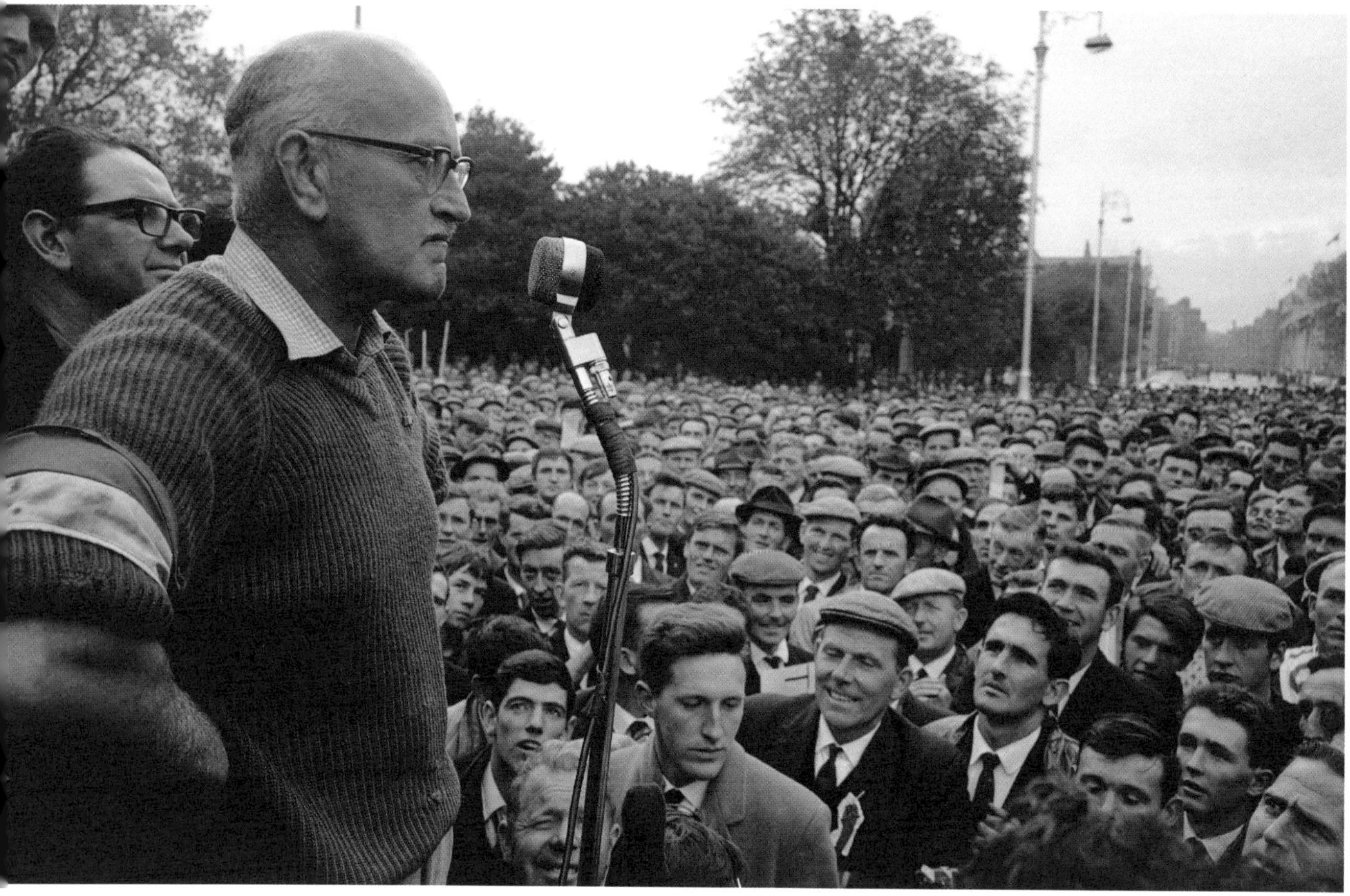

Rickard Deasy, President of the National Farmers Association, addresses a section of the huge crowd that took part in the protest marches that were a feature of the Farmers' Rights Campaign. Deasy and his supporters had walked the 217 miles from Bantry in west Cork to Dublin and staged a sit-down at the Department of Agriculture to draw attention to the economic plight of Irish farmers.

19 October 1966

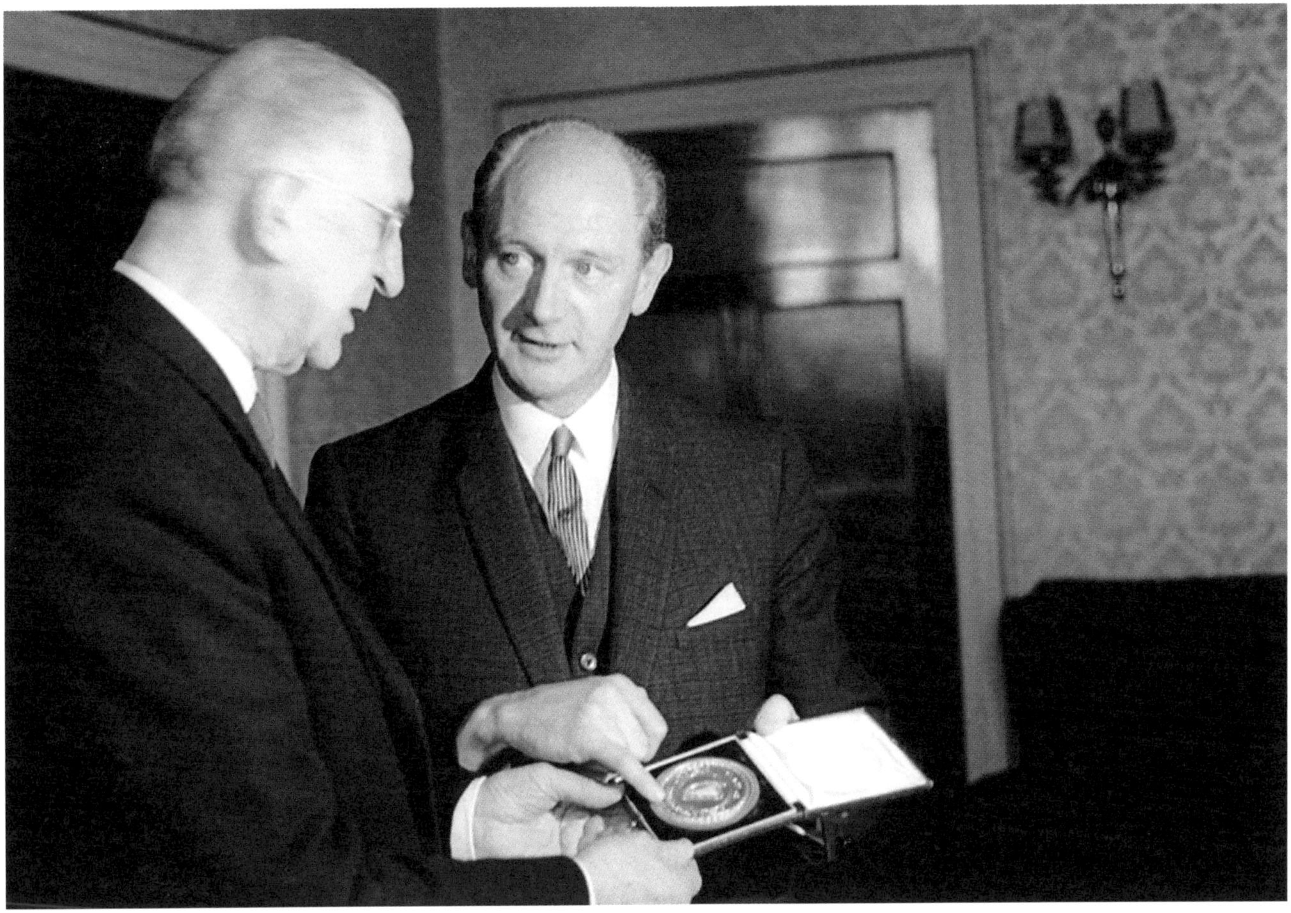

Jack Lynch receives his seal of office as the new Taoiseach from President de Valera.

10 November 1966

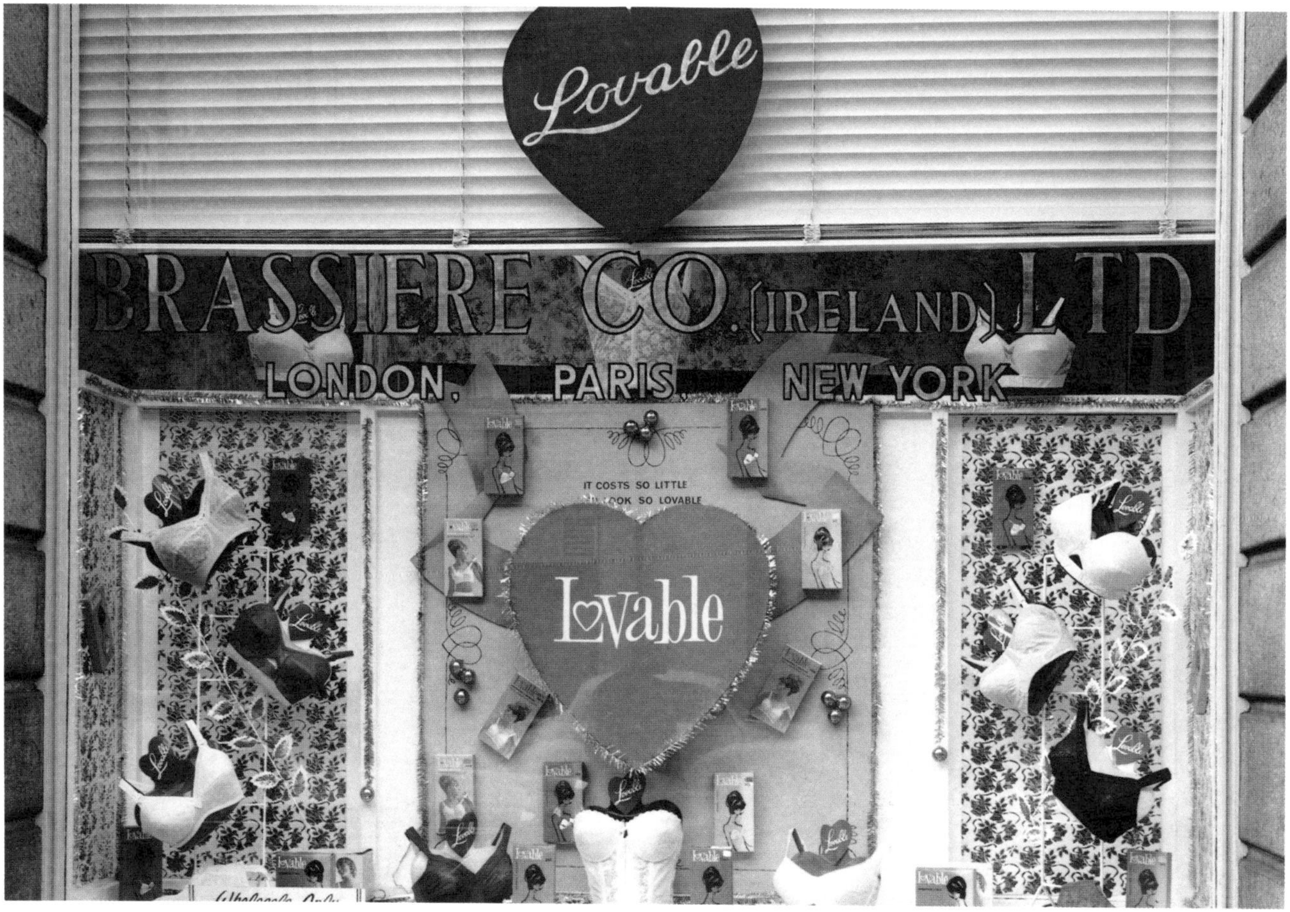

'It Costs So Little To Look So Lovable' proclaims the sign over the Lovable Bras display in the Brassiere Co. window.

18 November 1966

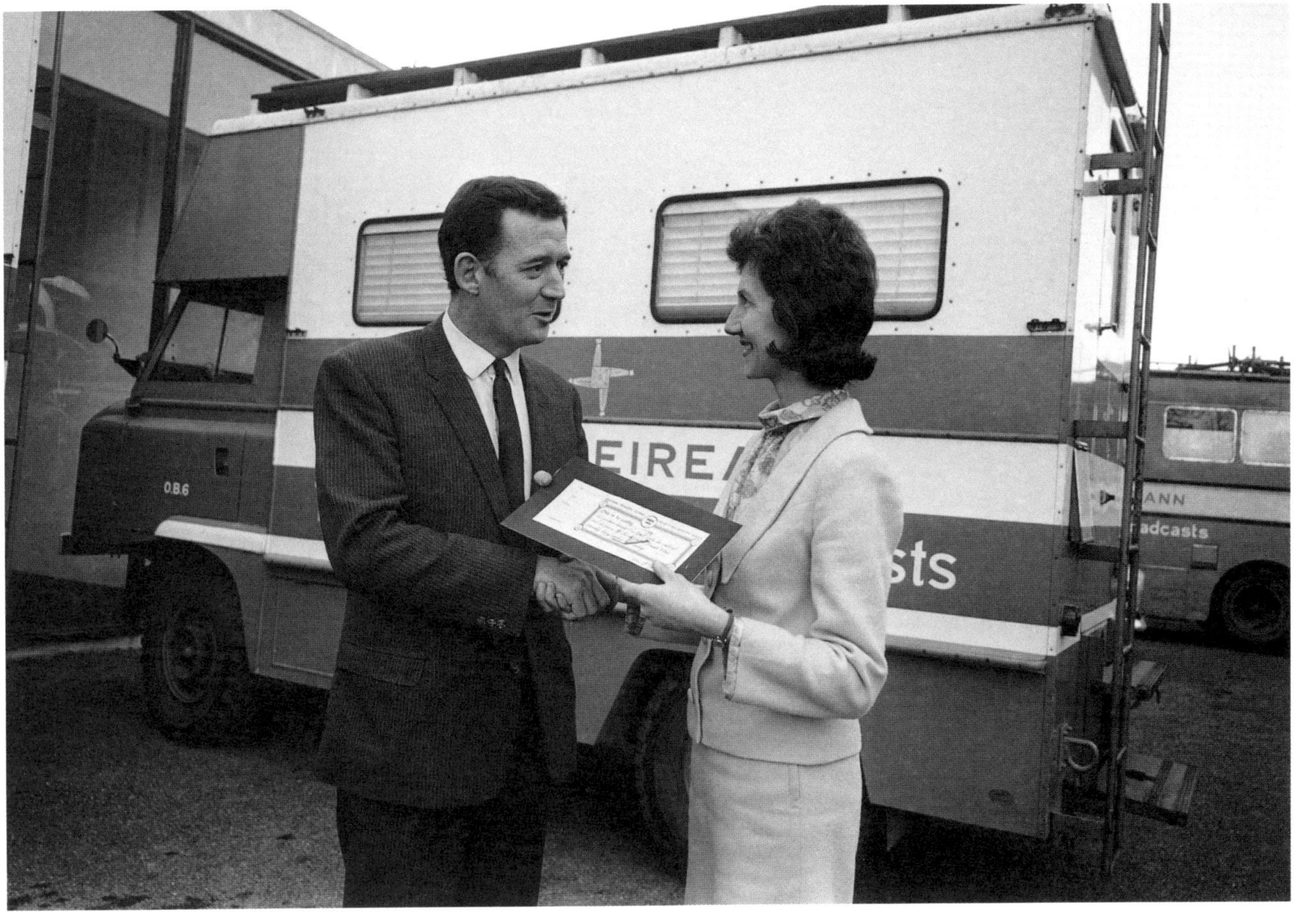

Popular TV and radio personality Bunny Carr buys the 'first brick' in the Central Remedial Clinic's novel fundraising drive.

17 February 1967

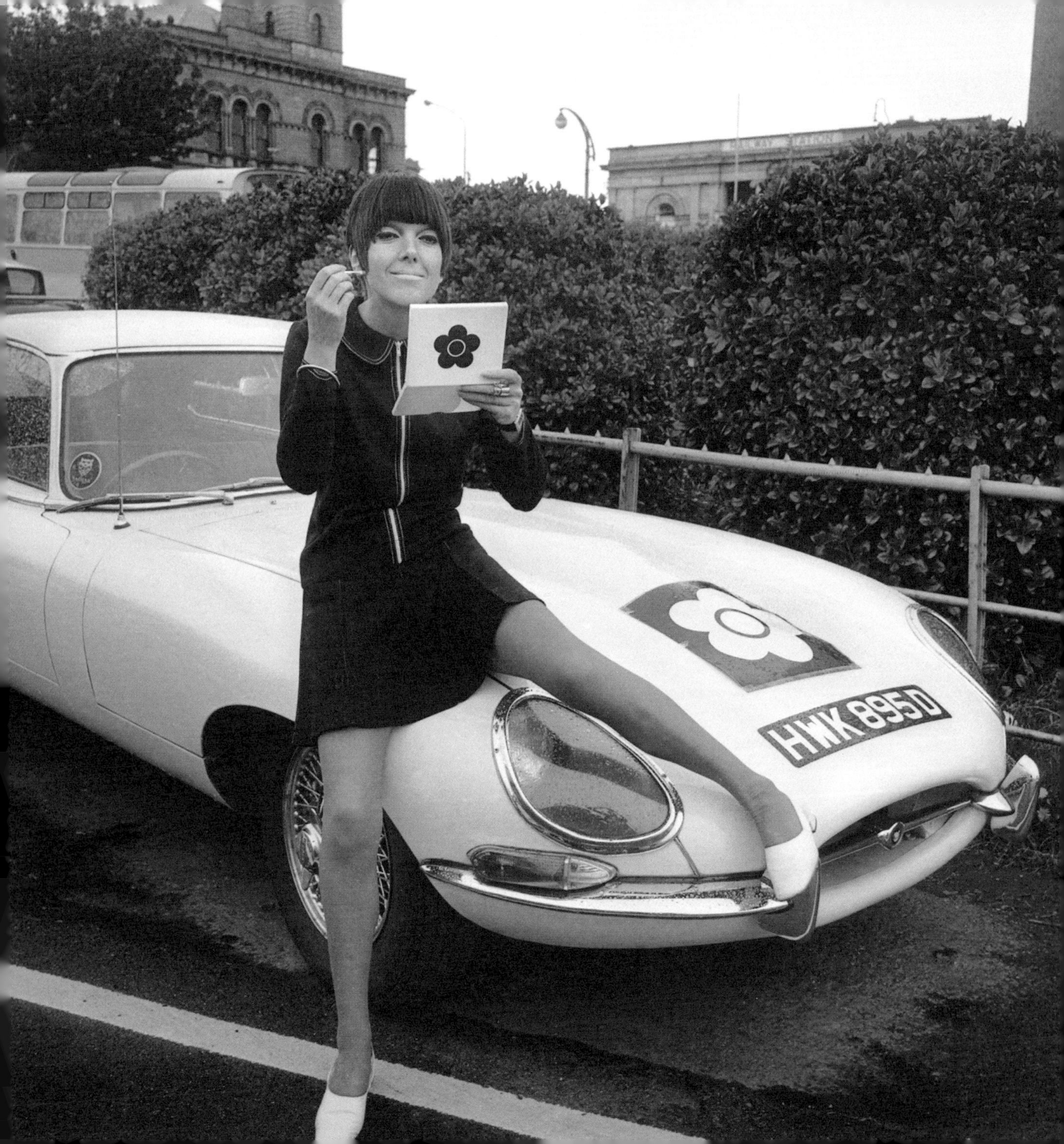
HWK 895D

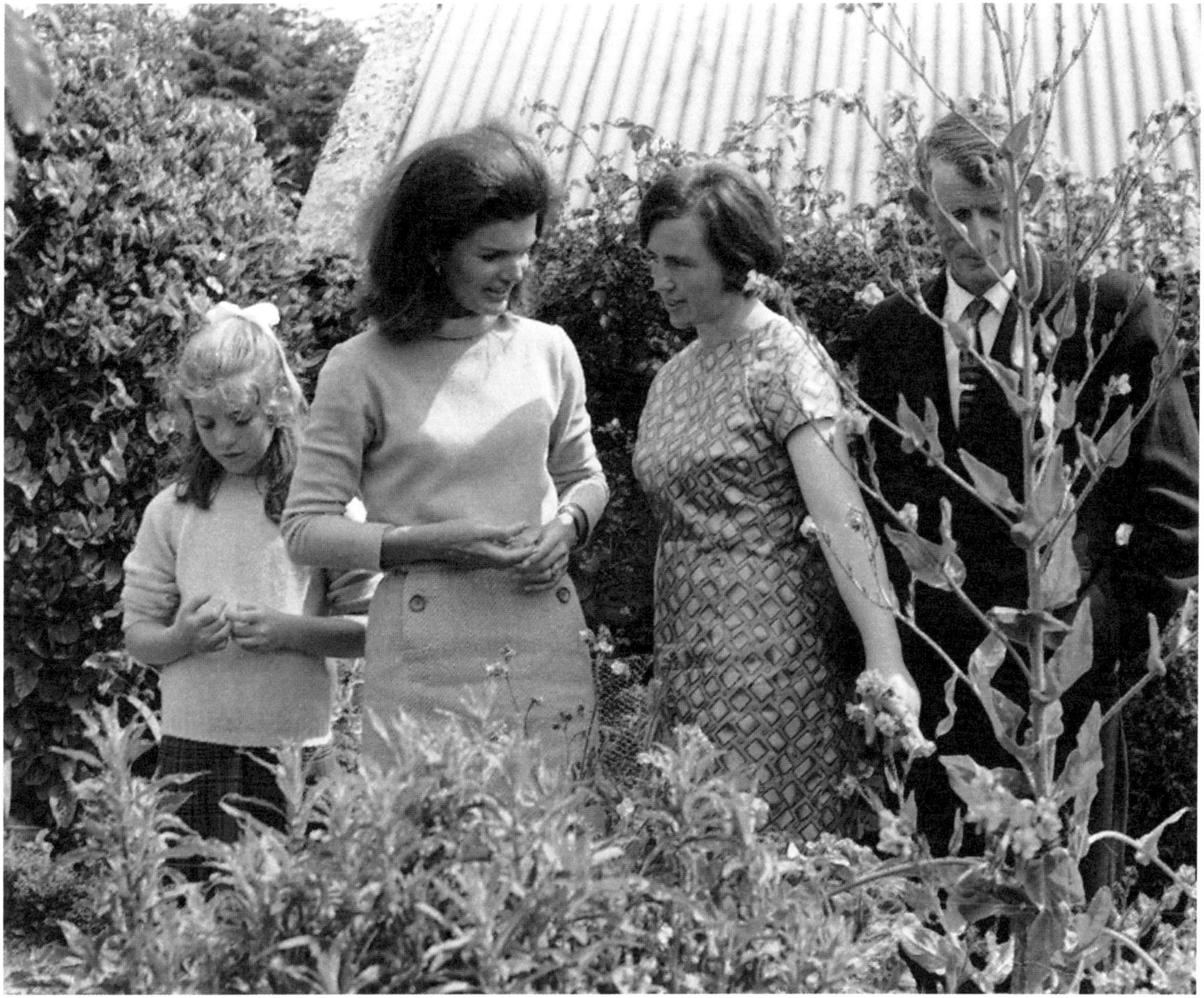

Fashion icon and designer Mary Quant brings her range of cosmetics to Ireland, complete with her trademark daisy motif. She is credited with the introduction of the mini-skirt and the hot pants.

24 April 1967

Jackie Kennedy and her daughter, Caroline, (left) visit her late husband's ancestral home place in Wexford.

28 June 1967

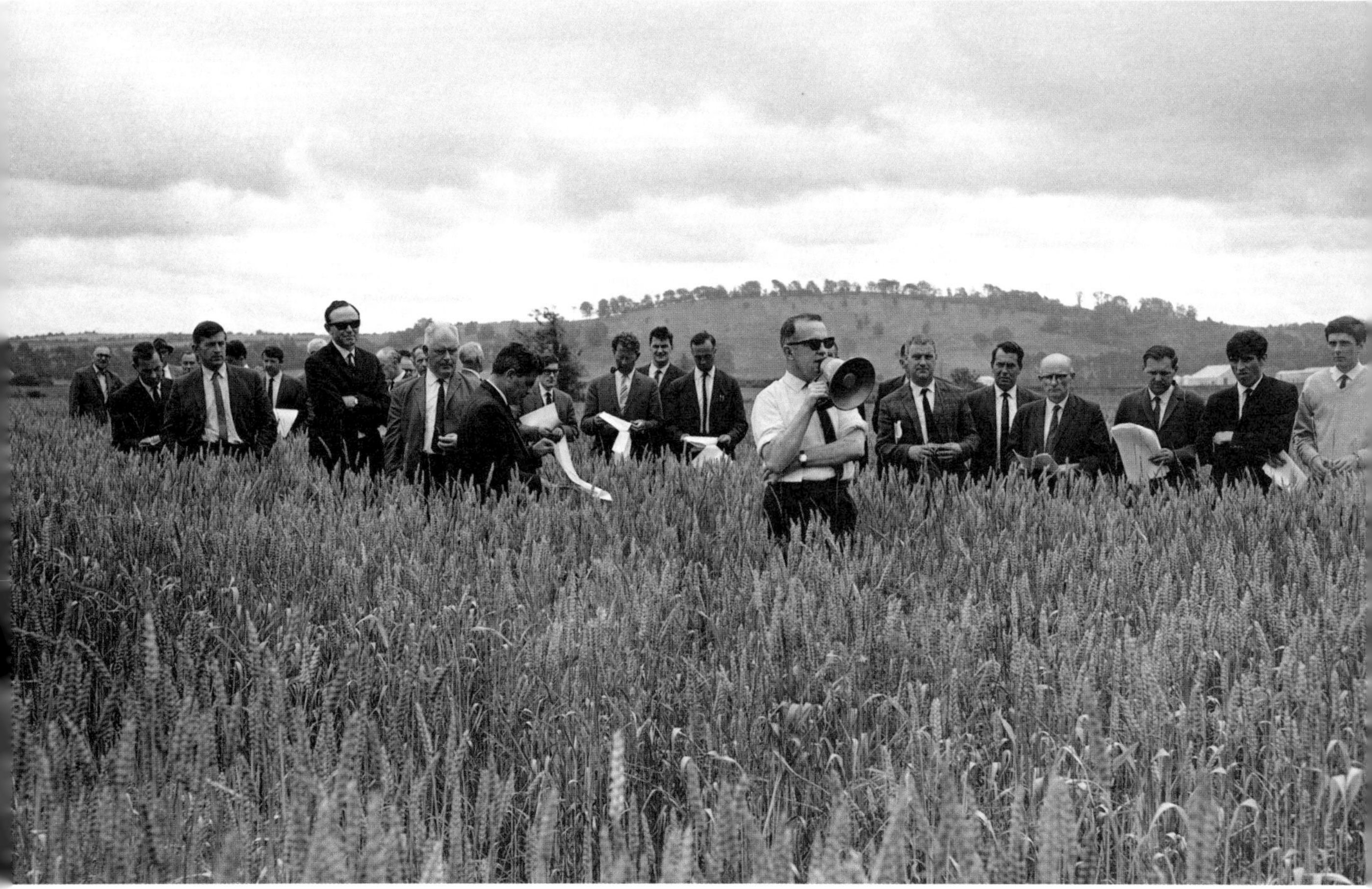

Wheatfield day at the University College farm, Lyons Estate, Celbridge, Co Kildare. Politicians, members of agricultural organizations, the grain trade and the flour industry inspect the wheat trials being carried out to test replacement wheat varieties and the impact of new fertilizers.

27 July 1967

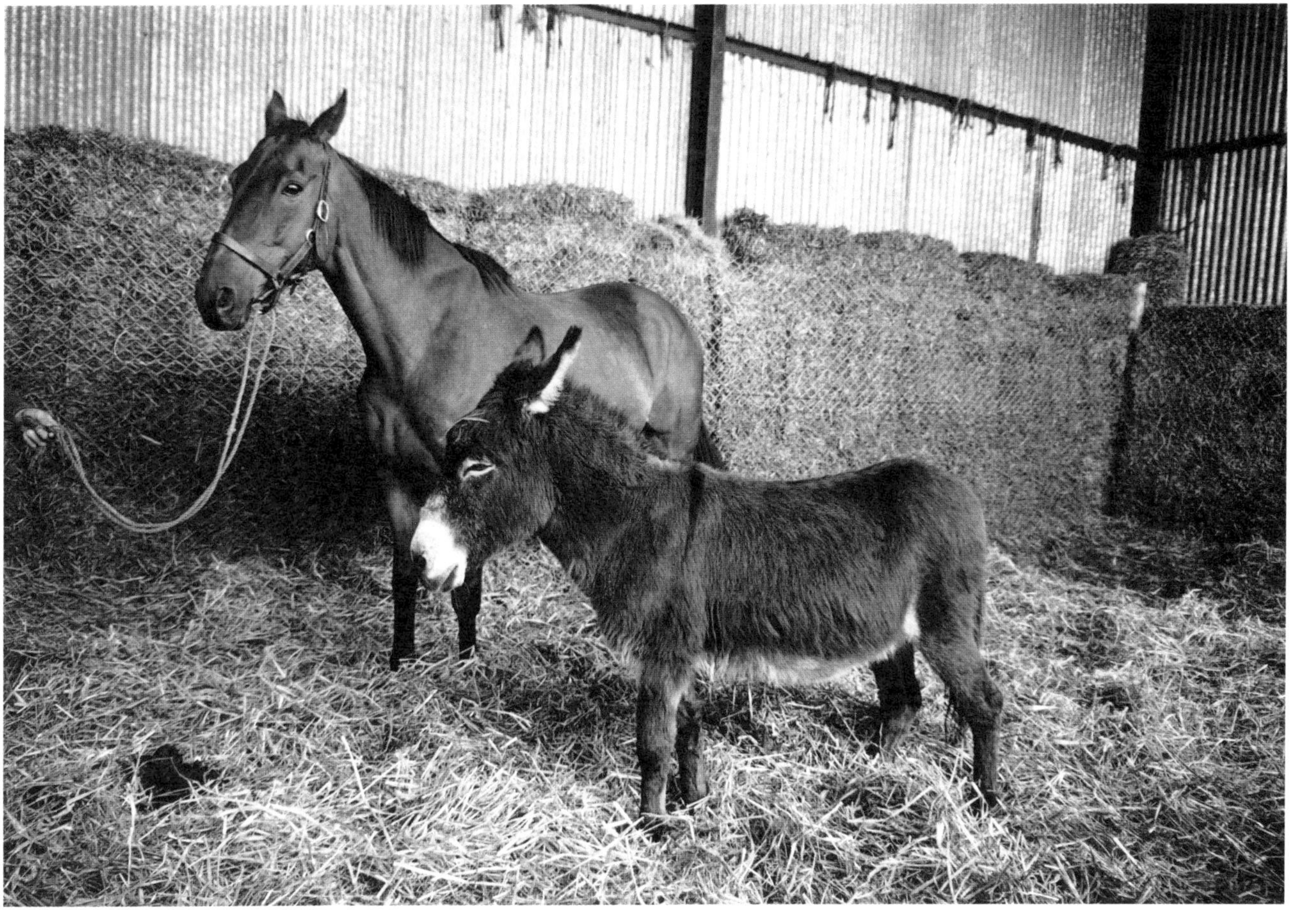

Legendary racehorse Arkle in retirement with a stable companion at Maynooth. The Tom Dreaper-trained bay won three Cheltenham Gold Cups (1964, 1965, 1966), the Irish Grand National and a host of other top prizes.

4 August 1967

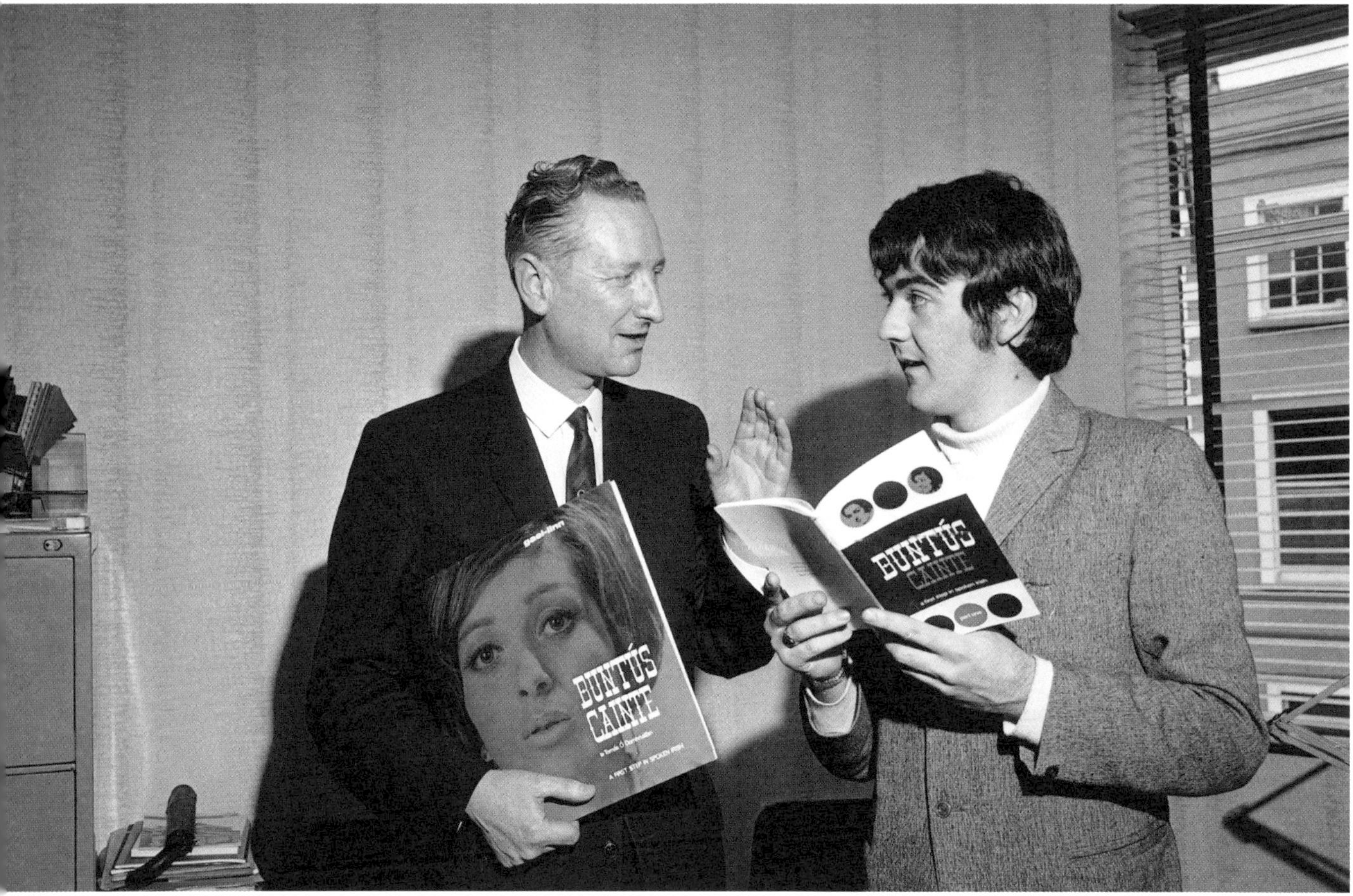

Singer Johnny McEvoy is presented with Gael Linn Buntús Cainte records and book, designed to teach Irish to those with very little knowledge of the language. The successful package was completed by a series of programmes on RTÉ. McEvoy had a No.1 hit in 1966 with 'Mursheen Durkin', followed by 'The Black Velvet Band'.

15 September 1967

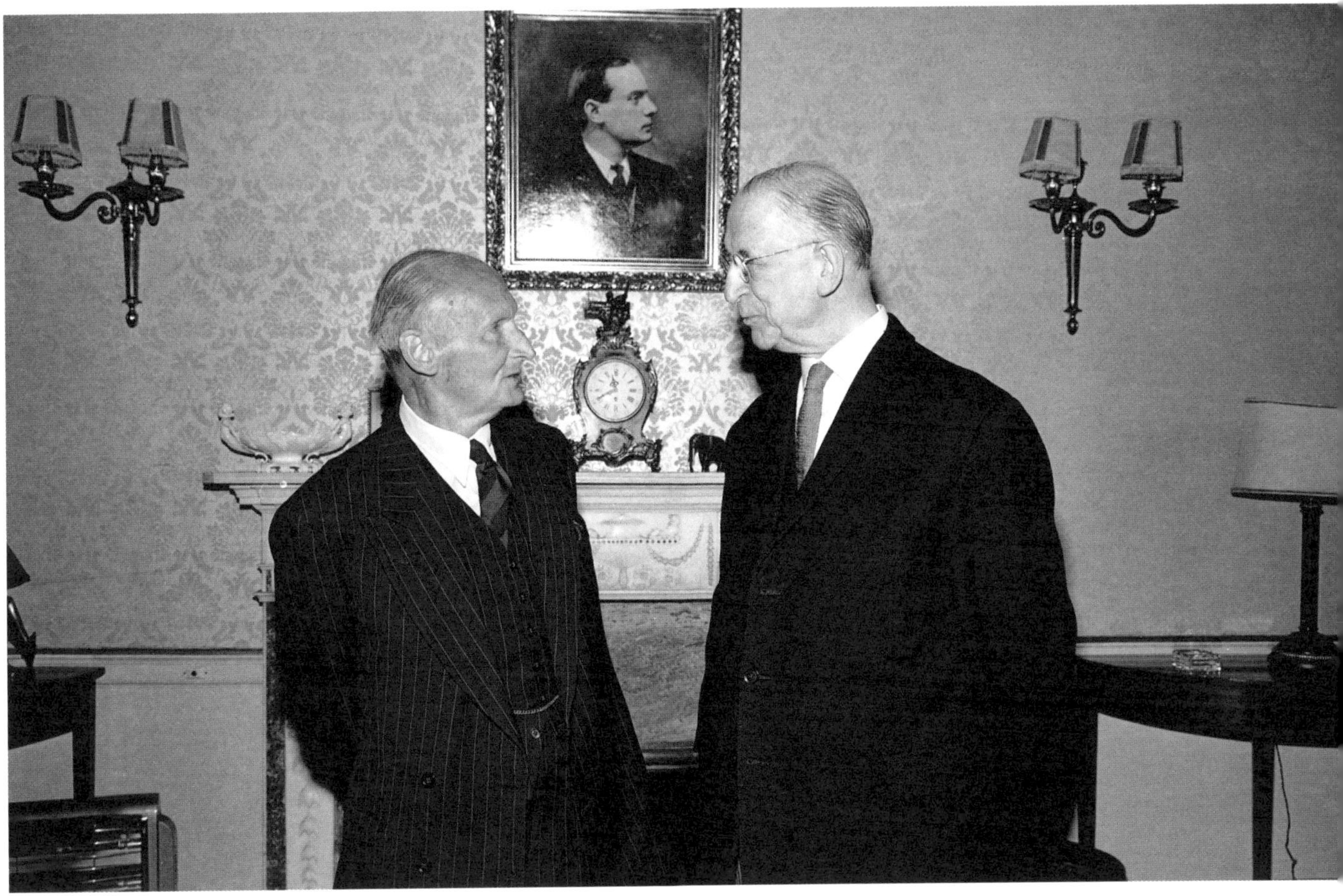

Field Marshal Viscount Bernard Montgomery chats with President de Valera at Áras an Uachtaráin, under a portrait of Patrick Pearse. During WW II 'Monty' was Commander of the 8th Army, before being given responsibility for planning the D-Day landings in Normandy. In the Irish War of Independence, he was in charge of the British 17th Infantry Brigade, stationed in Co Cork.

22 September 1967

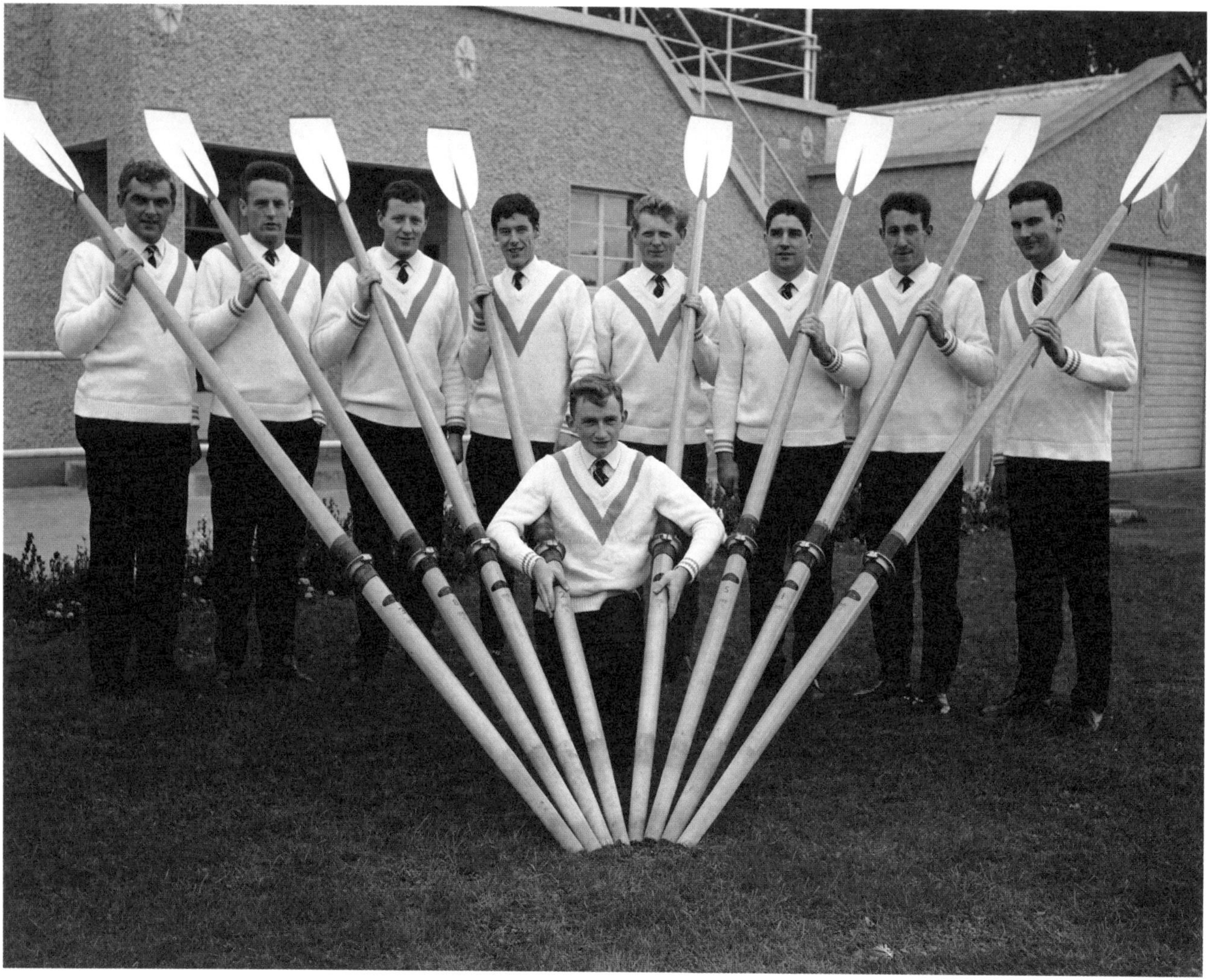

Members of the Garda Rowing Club resplendent in their Gaeltarra Éireann sweaters.

30 September 1967

Ann Foley, from Birmingham, Rose of Tralee 1967, leaves for a tour of the US. By coincidence, the Aer Lingus hostess pictured with her, Rosaline Kelleher, was the Dublin Rose in that year's competition.

12 October 1967

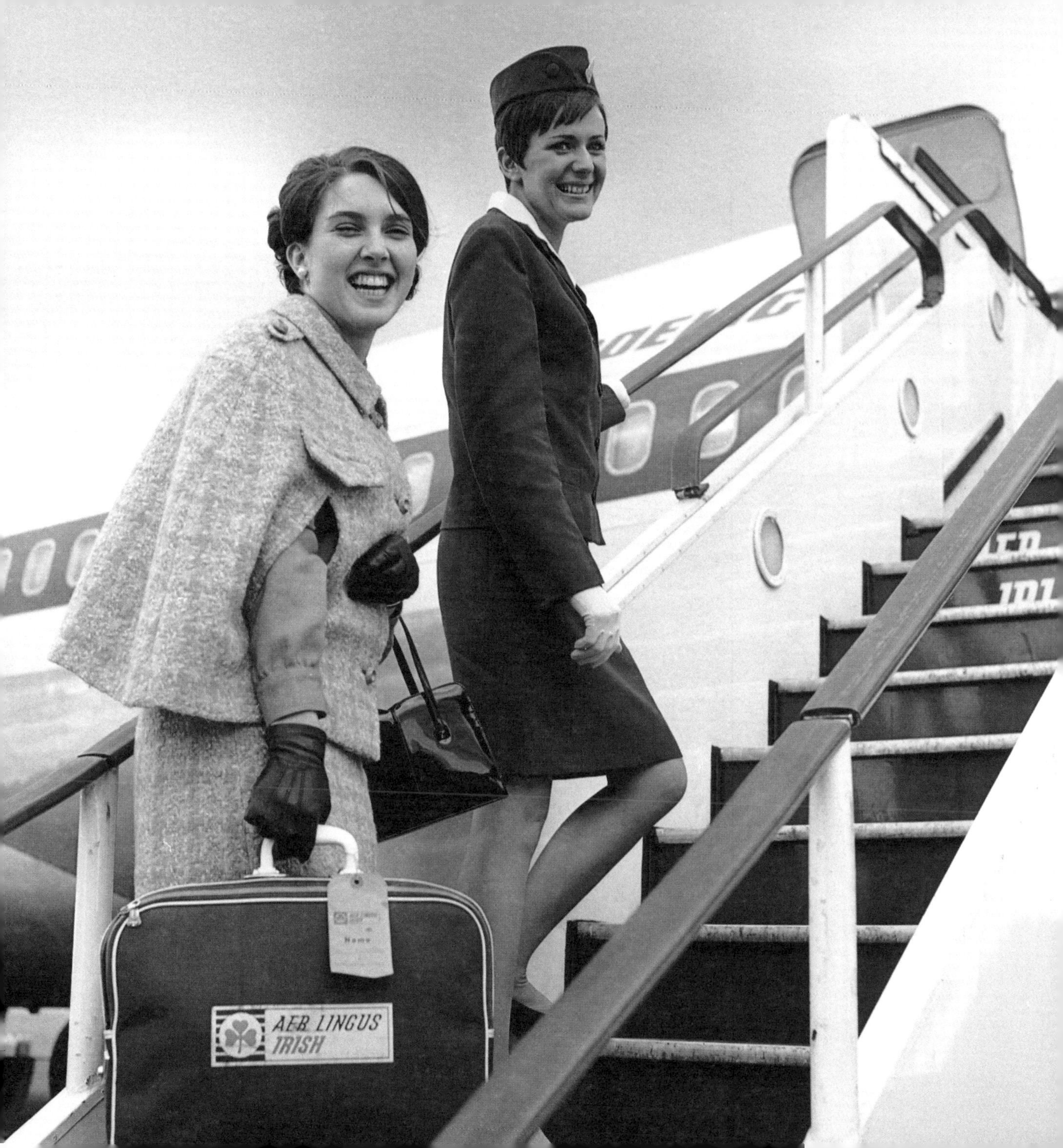
AER LINGUS
IRISH

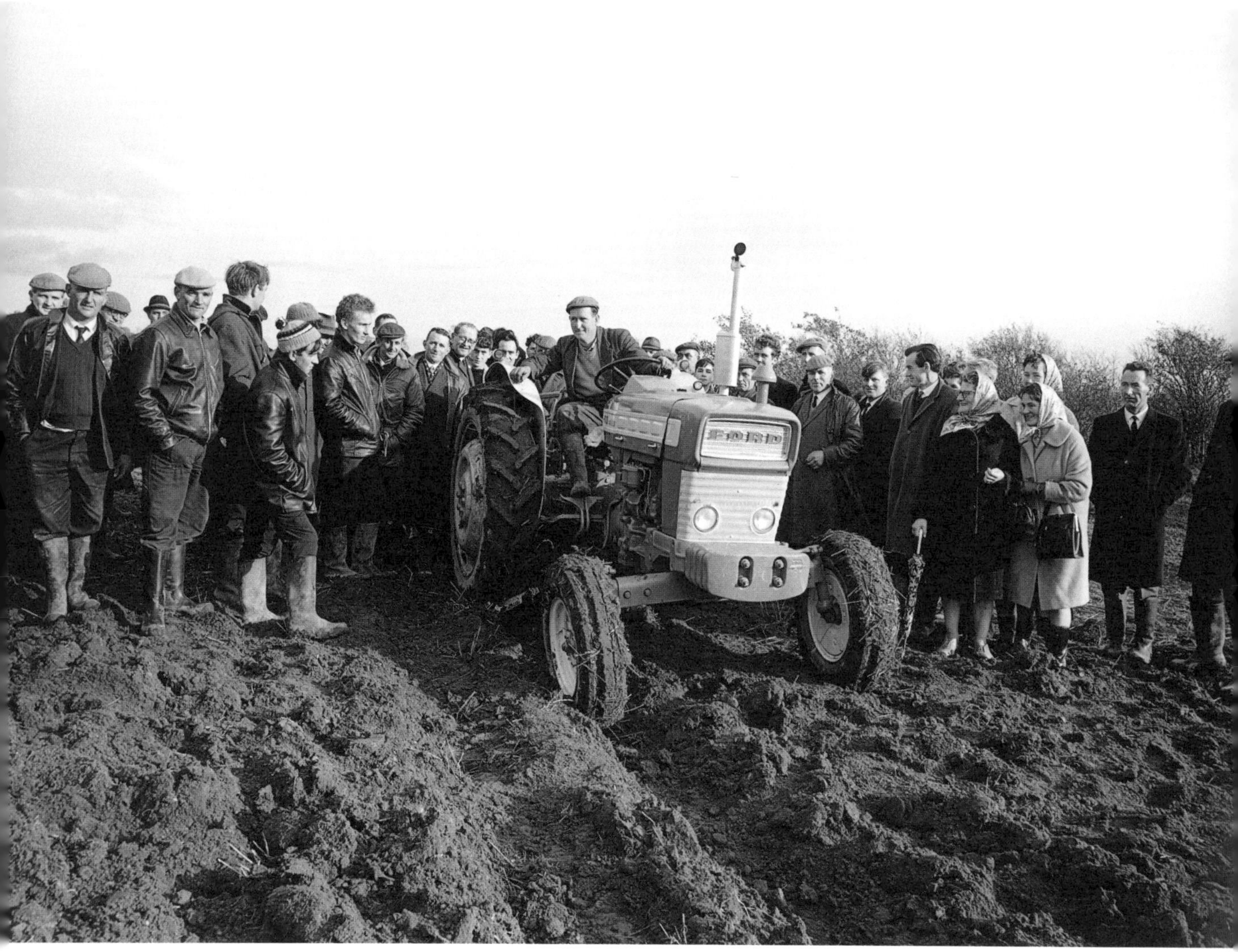

The National Ploughing Championships
at Tullow.

26 October 1967

'All for One, and One for All'. New Dáil Deputies Sean French (Cork) and Gerry Collins (Limerick) are welcomed to Leinster House by Neil Blaney TD.

26 October 1967

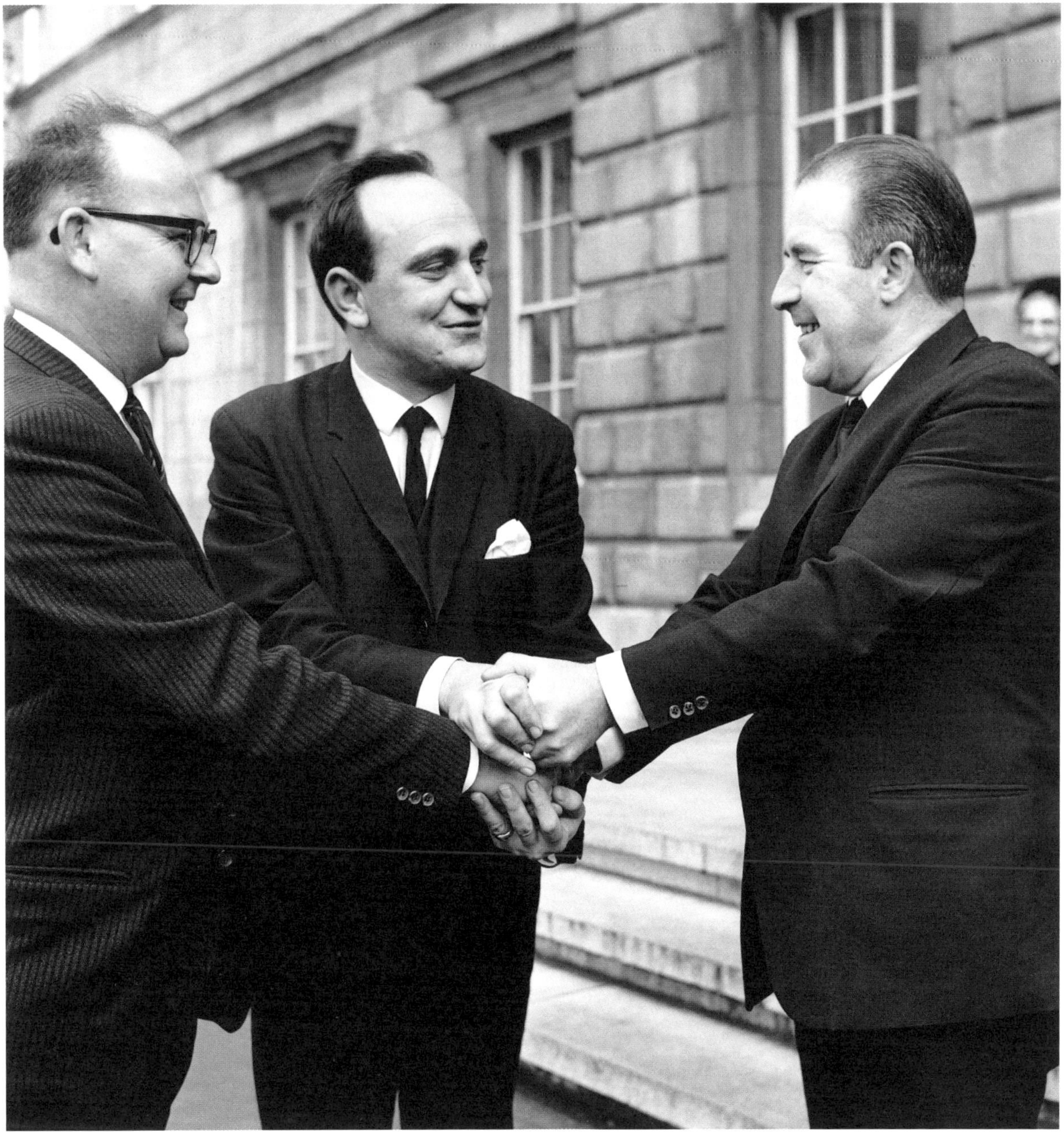

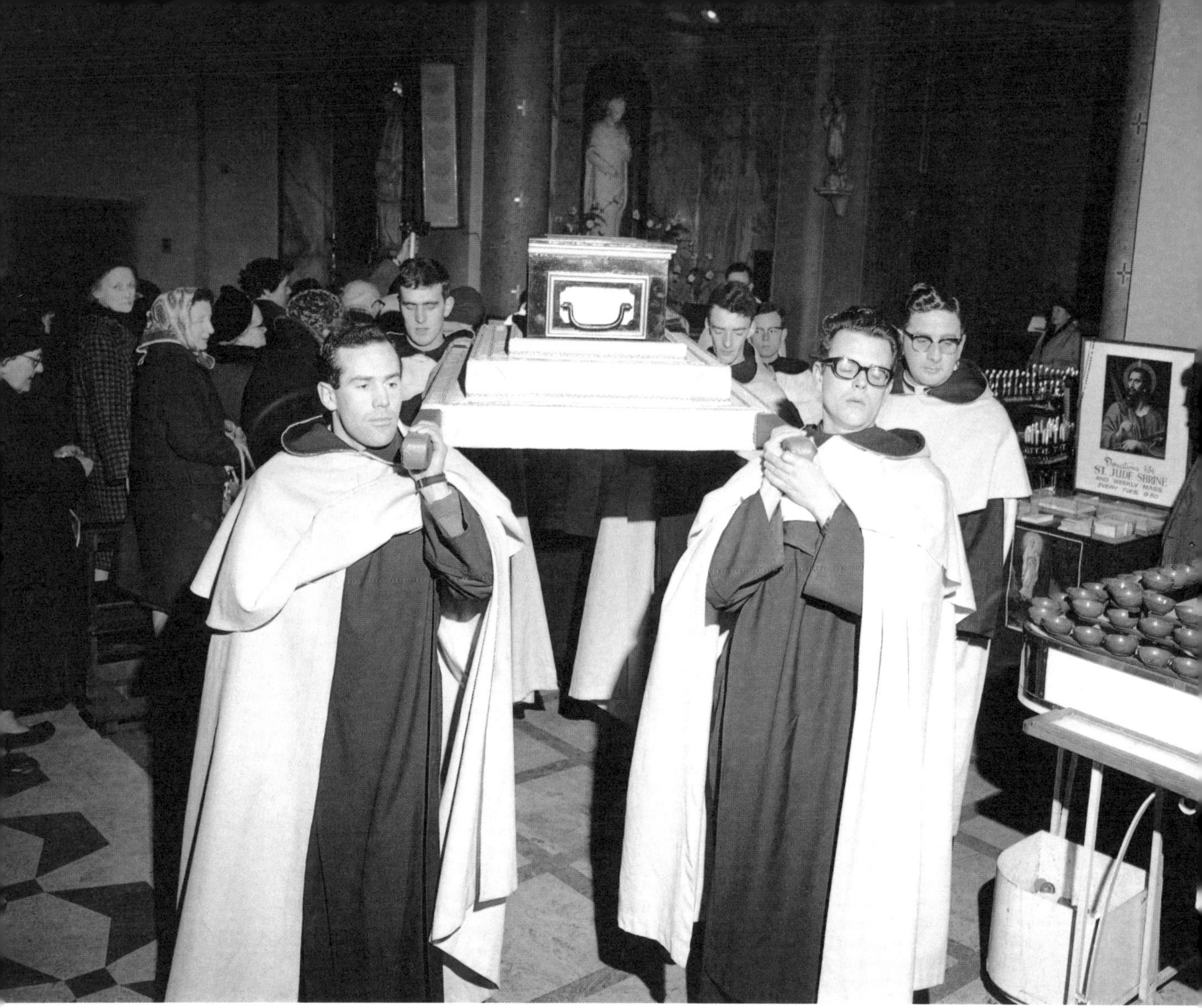

On St Valentine's Day, the remains of the saint, which are kept in the Carmelite Church in Whitefriar Street, Dublin, are taken from the shrine to the high altar where a special Mass is celebrated.

14 February 1968

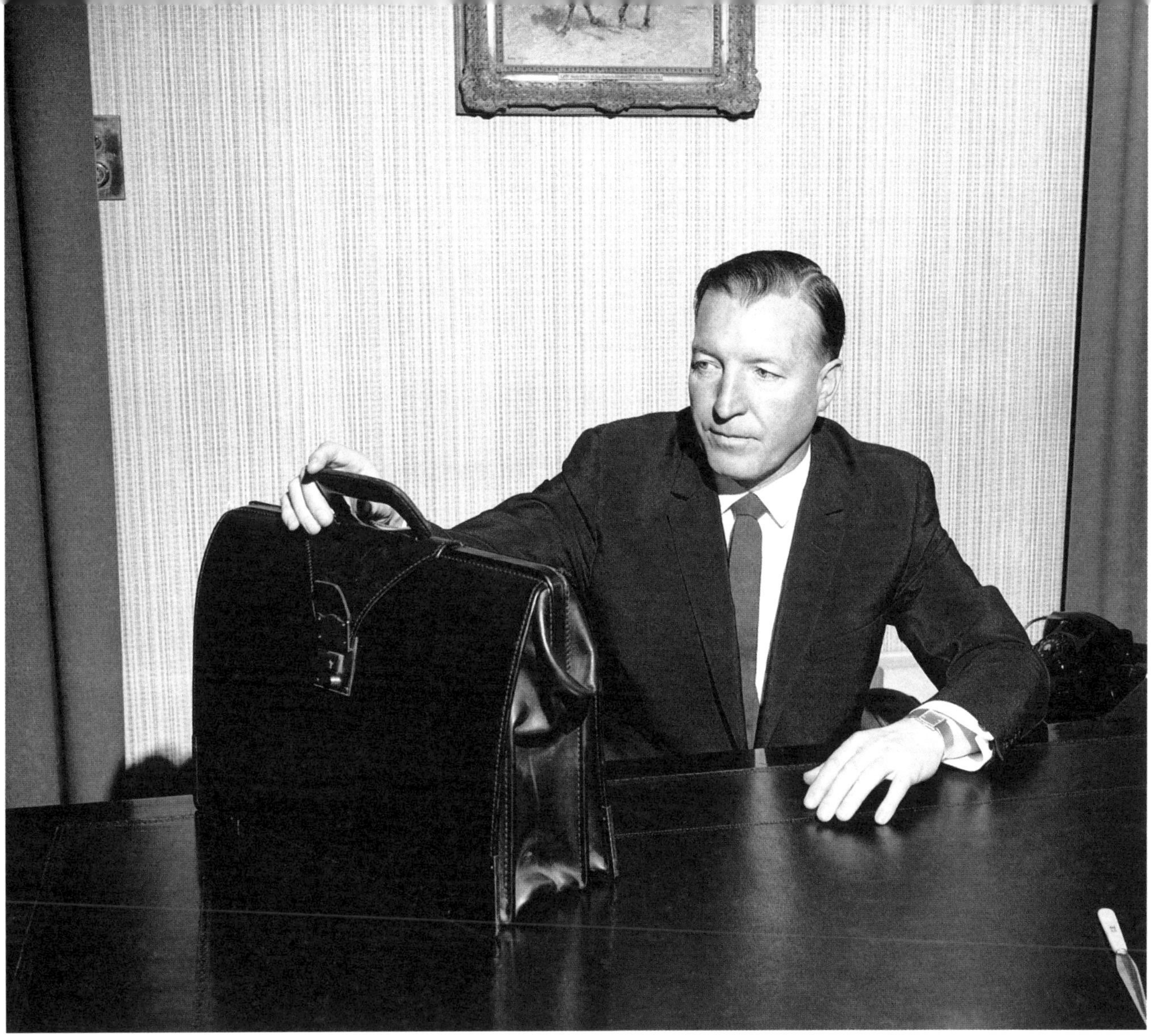

Minister for Finance, Charles Haughey, prepares to administer some belt-tightening measures on Budget Day.

3 April 1968

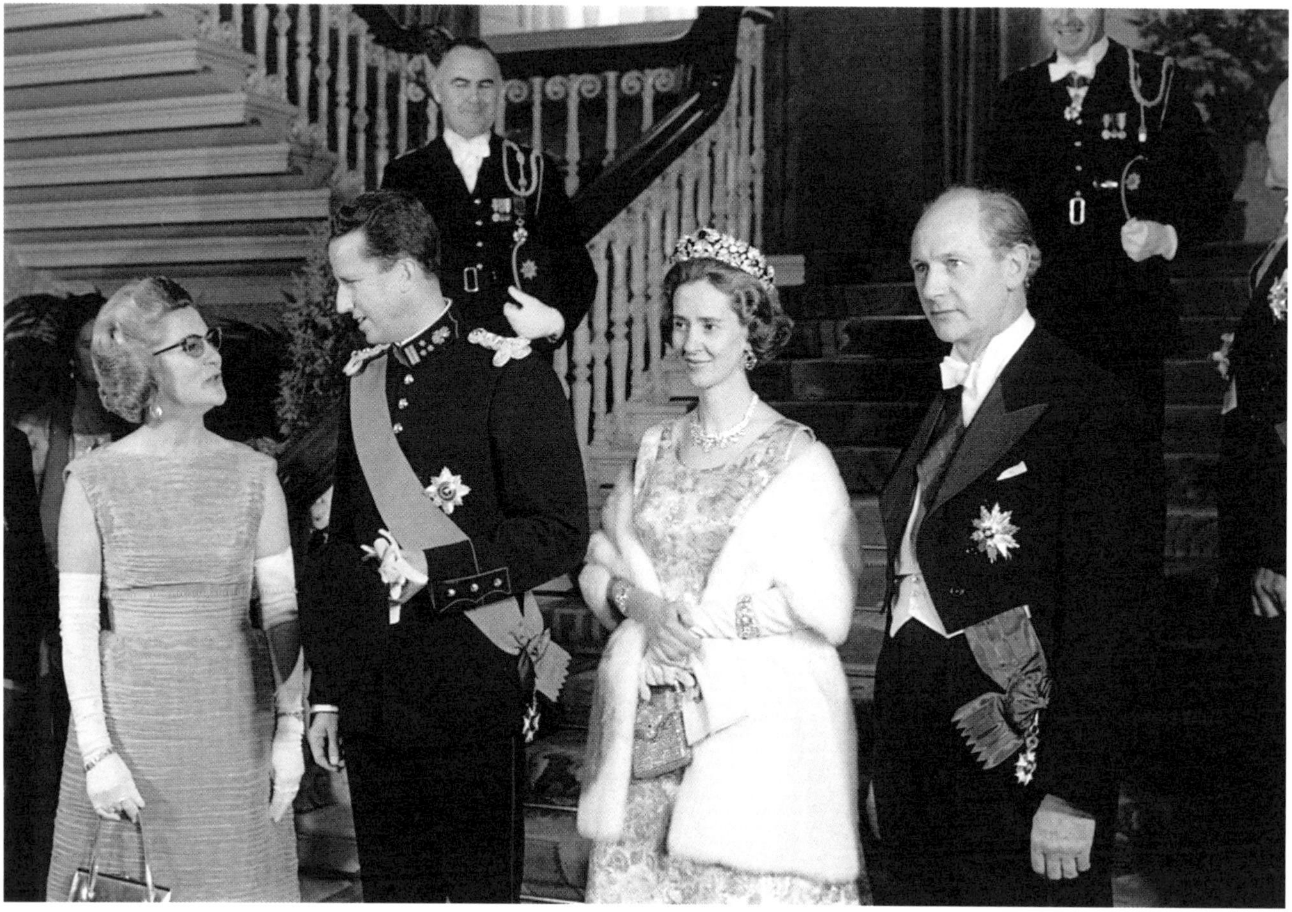

King Baudouin and Queen Fabiola of Belgium with Taoiseach Jack Lynch and Mrs Máirín Lynch at a function during their State visit.

14 May 1968

Having had a few lessons from All-Ireland winner Jack Lynch, King Baudouin takes a puck at the sliotar in the grounds of the Áras. Watching on are (l to r) Sean Ó Siocháin, GAA President, Minister Frank Aiken, President de Valera, and Taoiseach Lynch.

14 May 1968

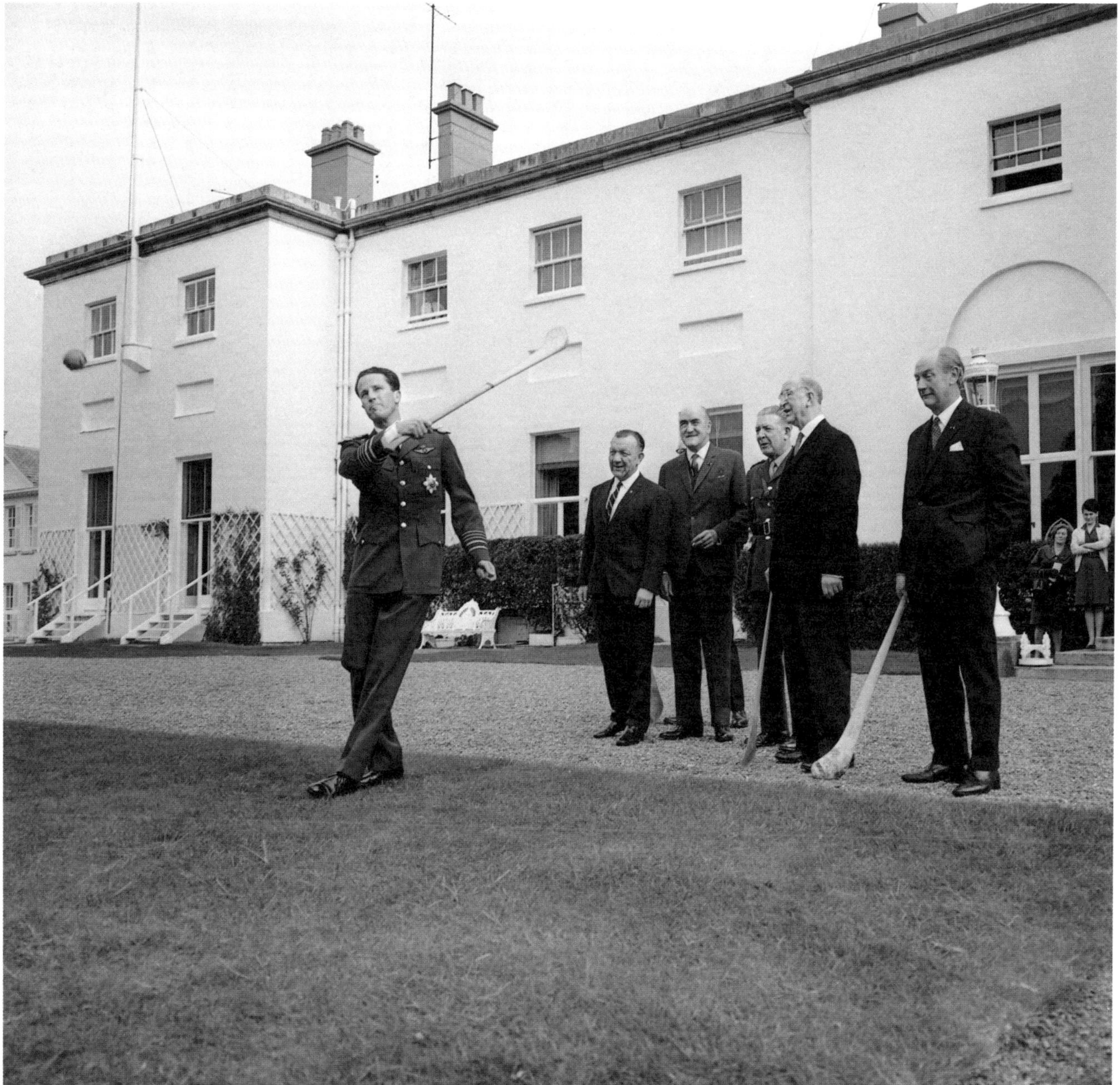

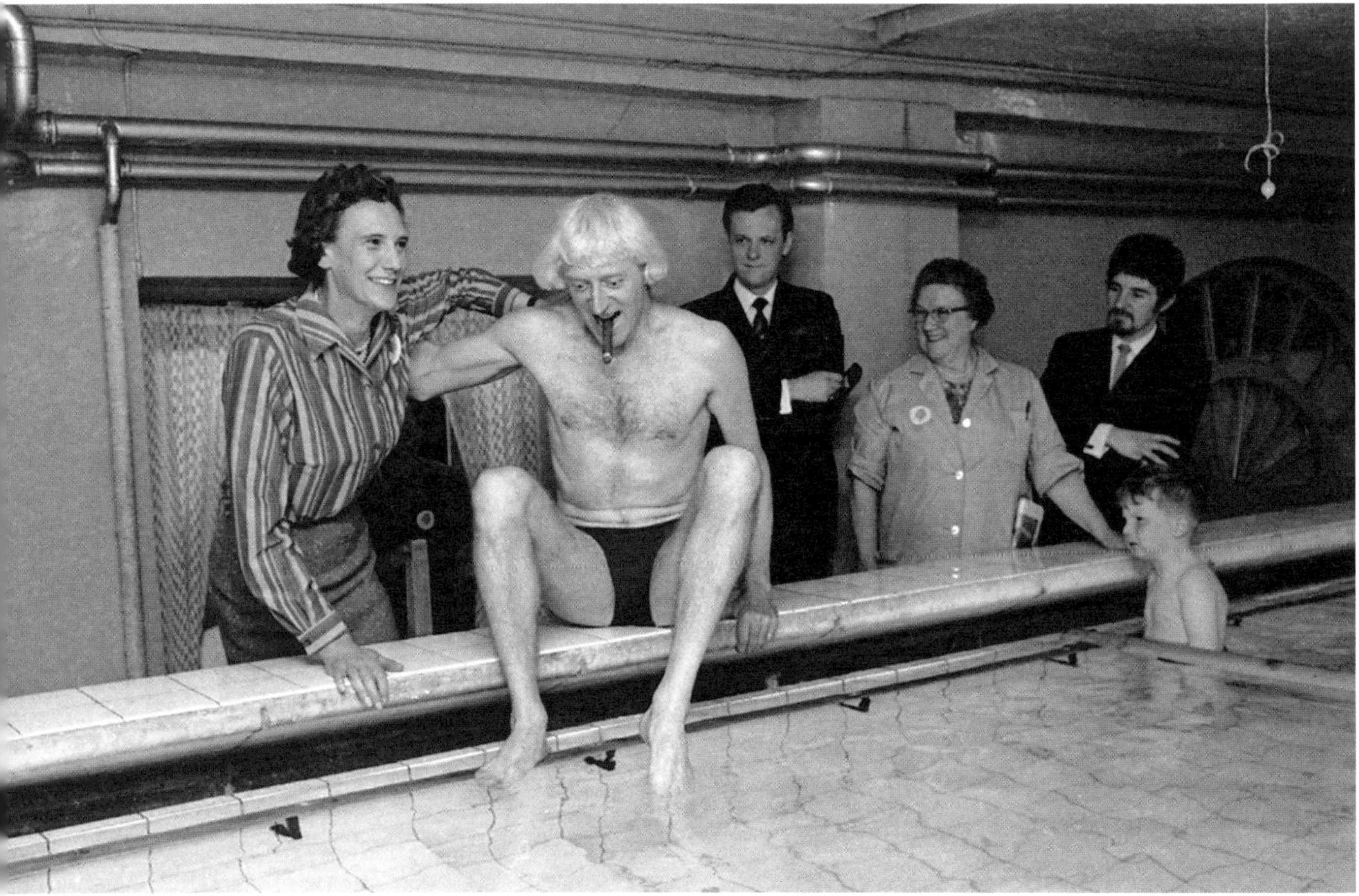

Lady Valerie Goulding (left) 'assists' Jimmy Savile, still chewing on his cigar, into the pool at the Central Remedial Clinic. The flamboyant DJ and TV personality was a great supporter of the clinic and led annual sponsored walks from Middle Abbey Street to Baldoyle.

1 May 1968

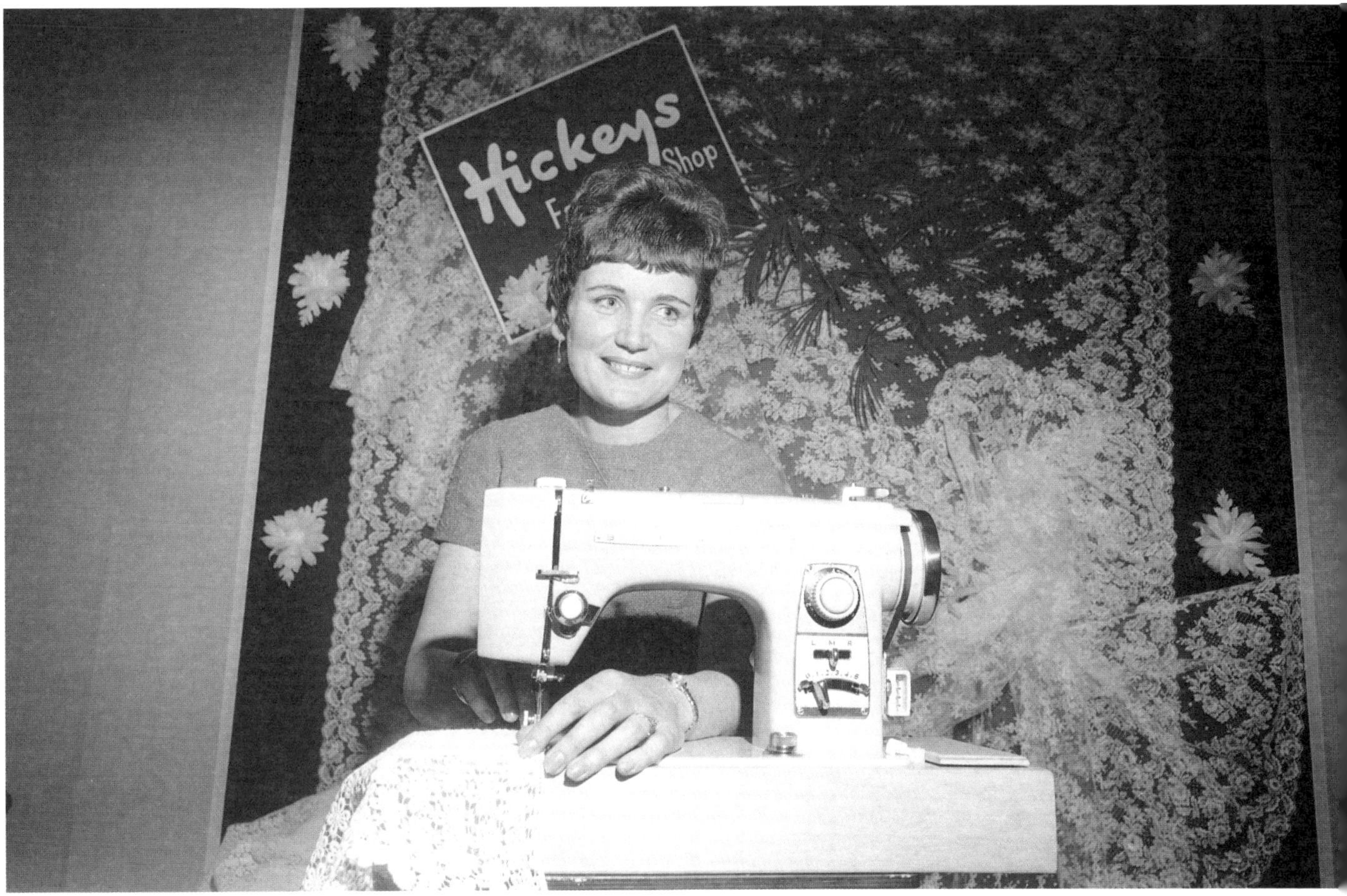

Miss Brigid Flynn, from Fenagh, Co Leitrim, tries out the new Brother sewing machine which she won as part of her prize for being Bride of the Year 1967.

17 May 1968

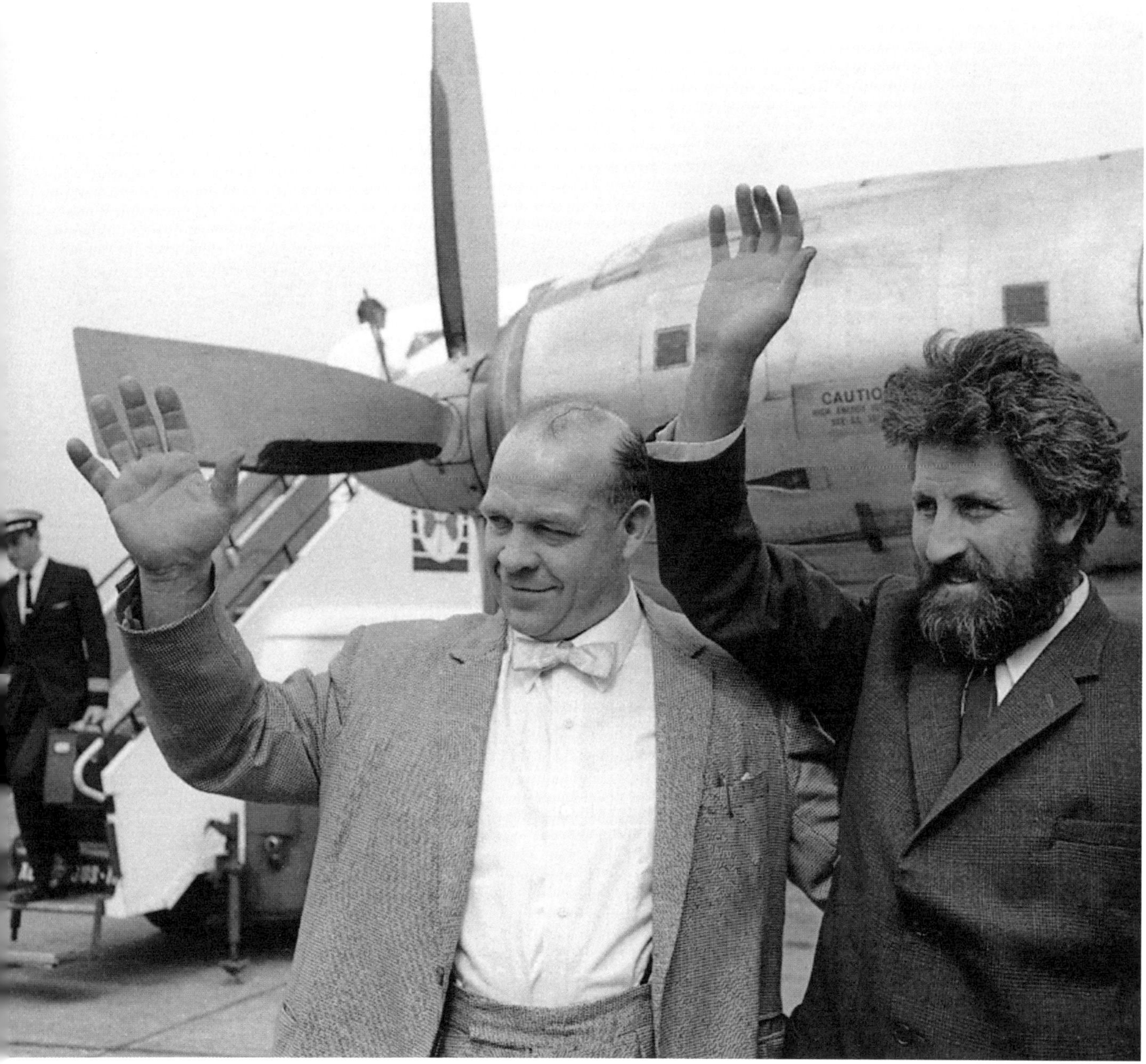

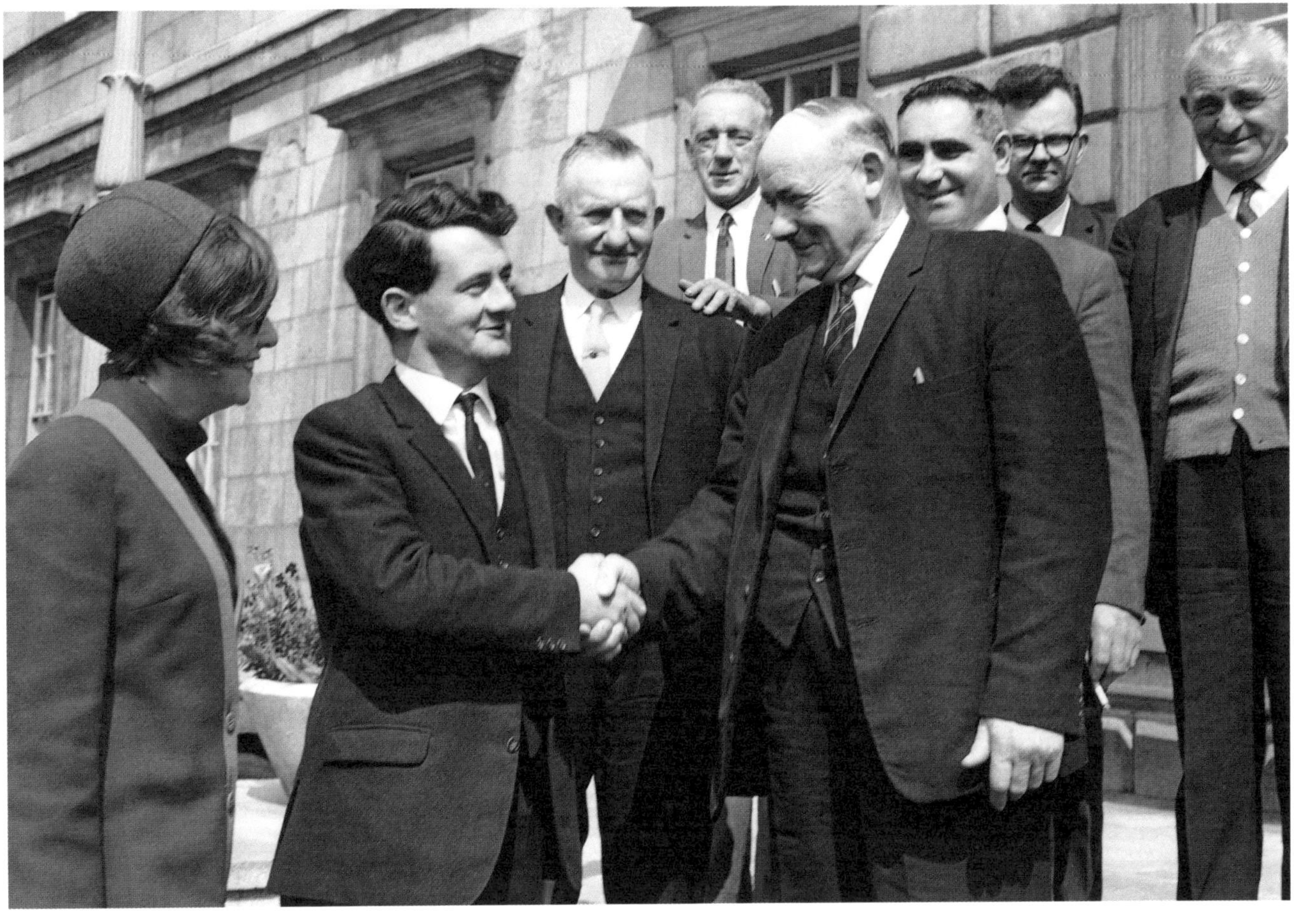

Newly elected Deputy Desmond O'Malley, and his wife, Pat, being welcomed at Dáil Éireann by Deputy Paddy Clohessy, Senator Patrick Ryan, and some friends from his East Limerick constituency.

28 May 1968

Mike Meaney, who broke the world record by spending 61 days buried alive in a coffin in Kilburn, with his promoter, legendary strongman Butty Sugrue from Kerry, who used to pull buses with his teeth.

25 May 1968

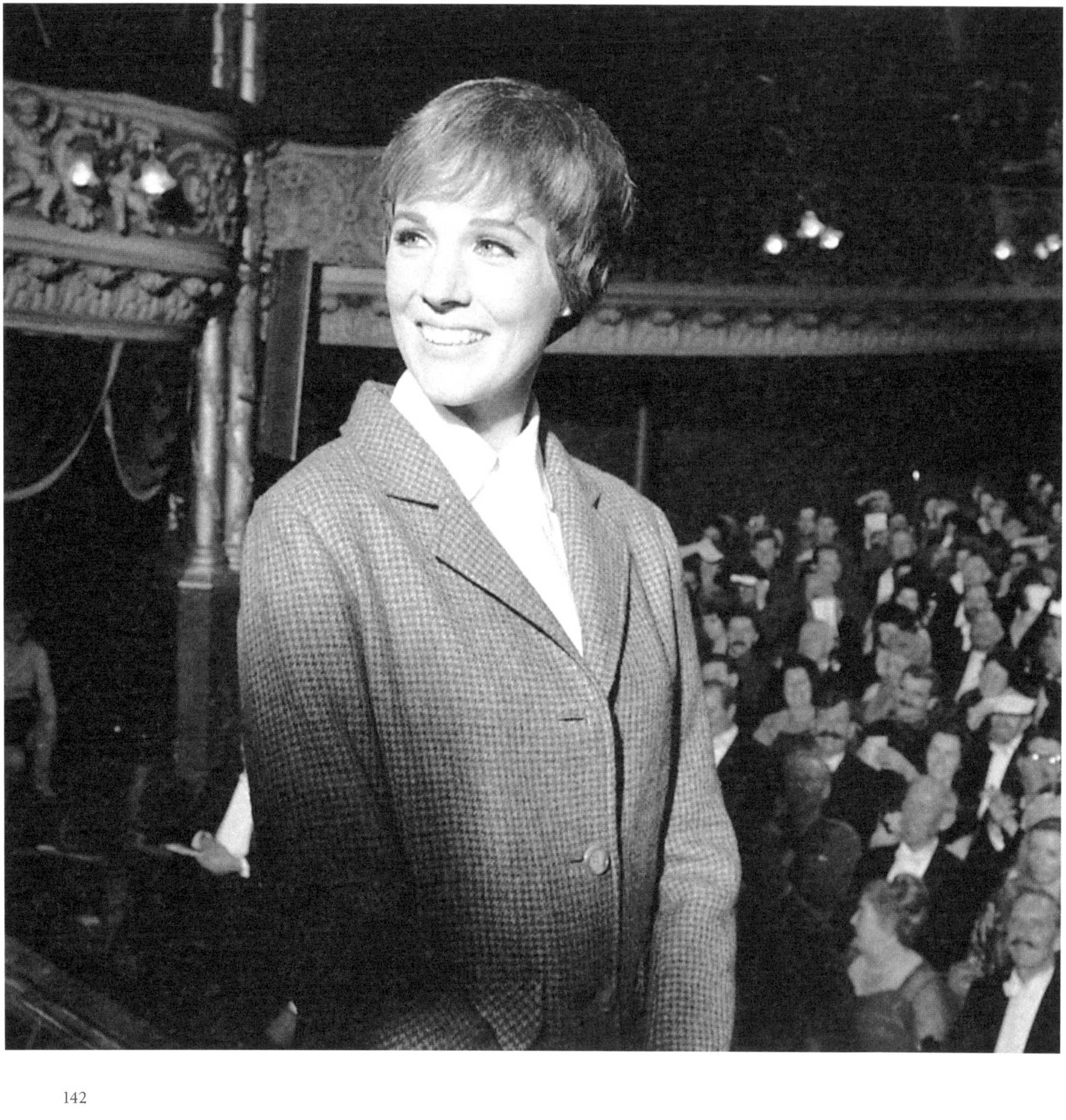

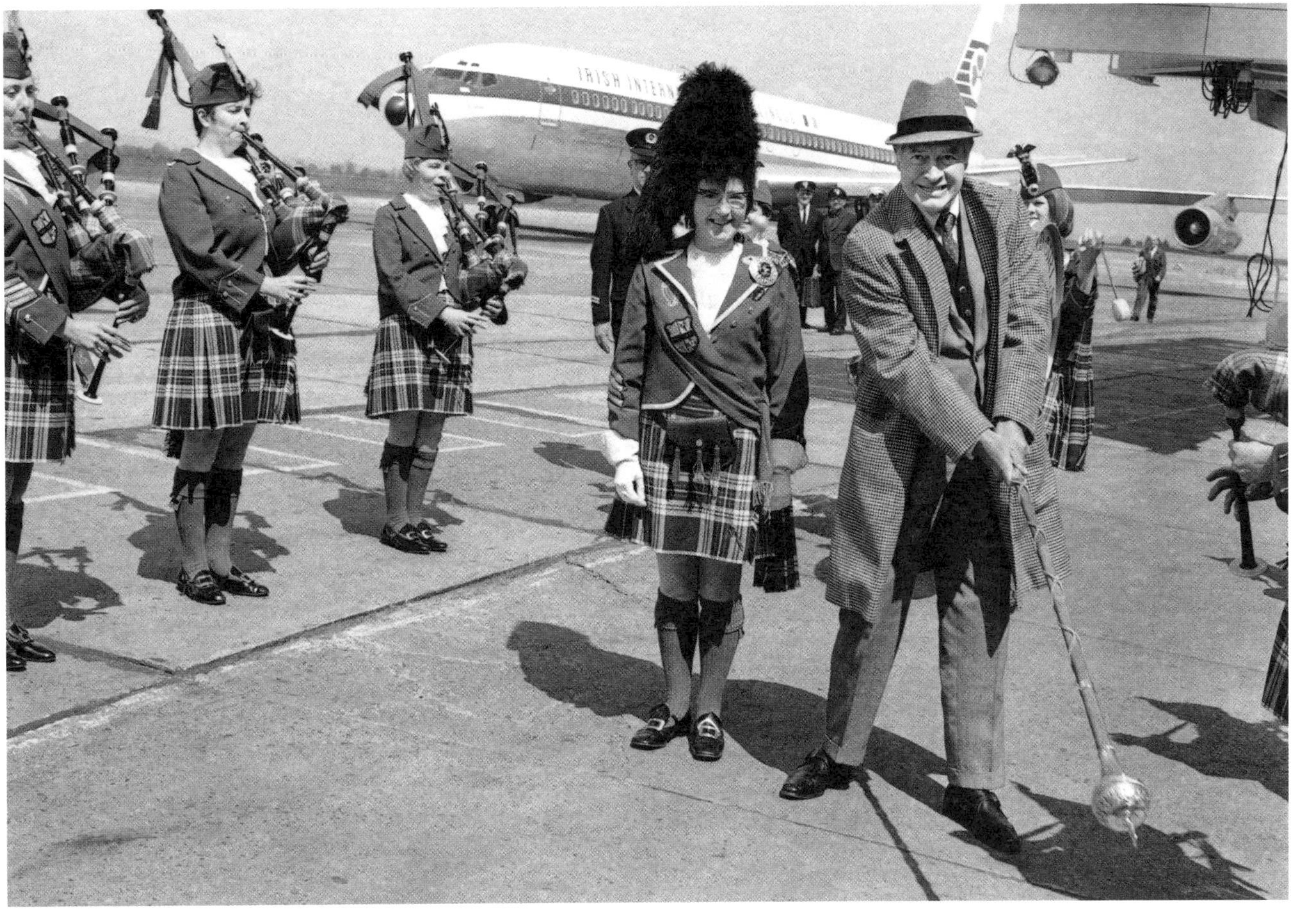

Bob Hope, arriving to attend the premier of his film 'Eight on the Run', amuses the Emerald Girls Pipe Band and their Drum Major, Marie Doran, by finding a new use for her mace.

1 August 1968

Julie Andrews pictured during filming of 'Darling Lili' at the Gaiety Theatre.

25 June 1968

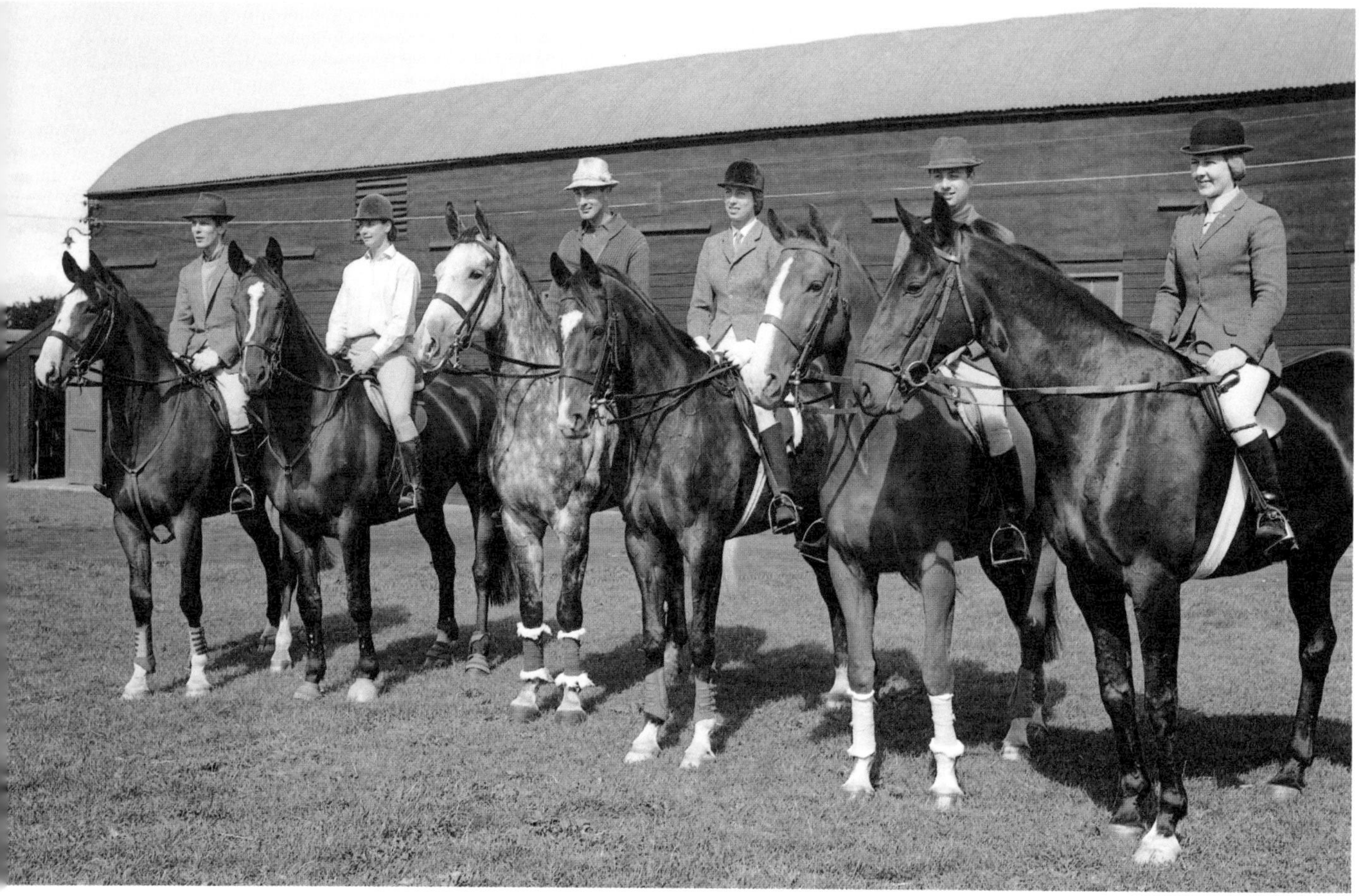

The Irish Olympic Equestrian Team which would compete in Mexico. (L to R) Mr John Fowler, 'March Hair'; Miss Juliet Jobling-Purser, 'Jenny'; Mr Alan Lillington, 'Biddlecome'; Mrs Diana Wilson, 'Chianto Rosso'; The Hon. Patrick Connolly Carew, 'Ping Pong'; Miss Penny Moreton, 'Loughlin'.

31 August 1968

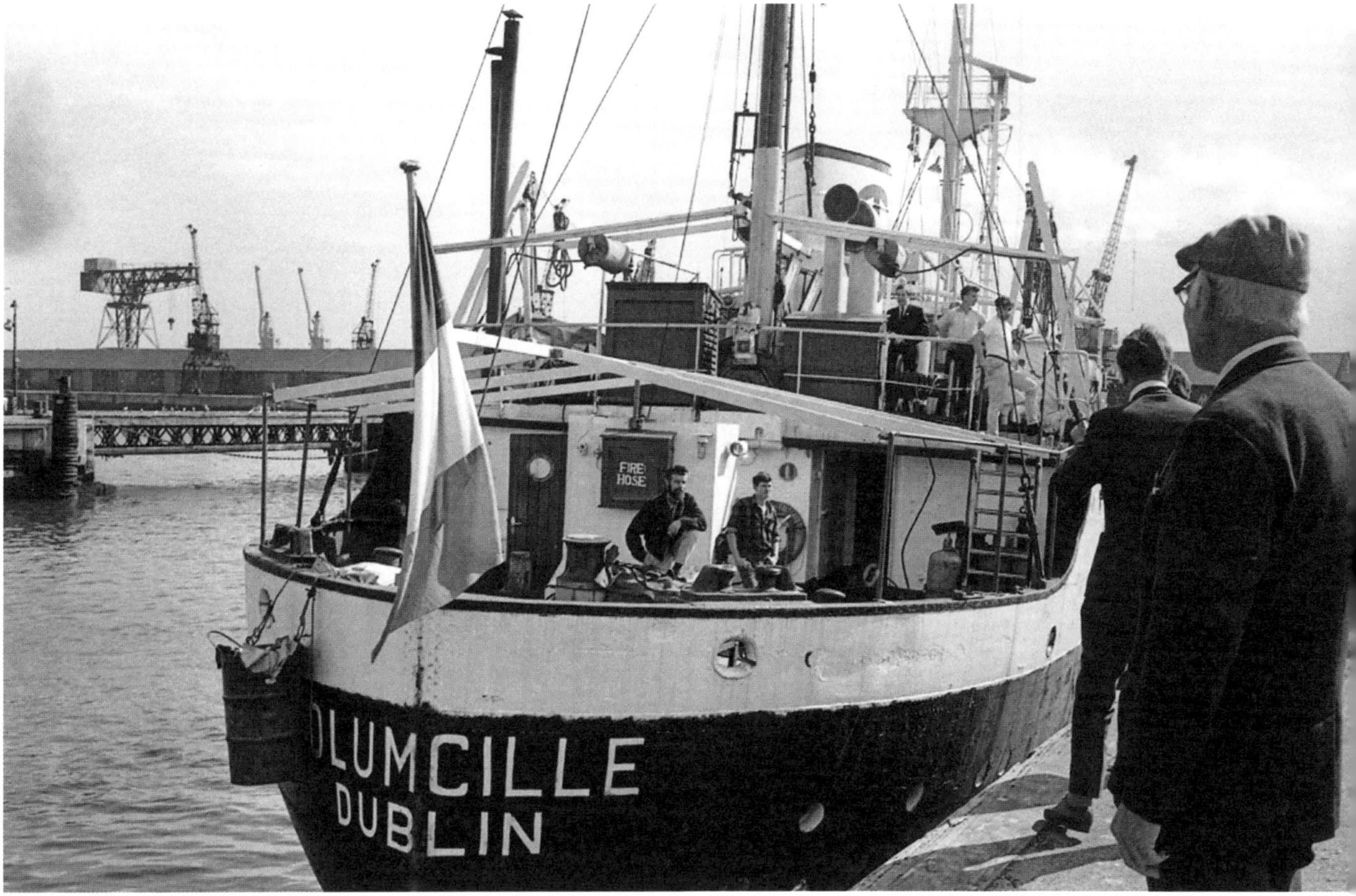

The MV Columcille sets sails for Biafra, carrying food, clothes and medicines. The Irish public had raised £100,000 for the newly-formed Africa Concern (now Concern). Three more ships followed in a two year period in which the charity raised more than £3.5m from the Irish public, a huge figure at that time.

6 September 1968

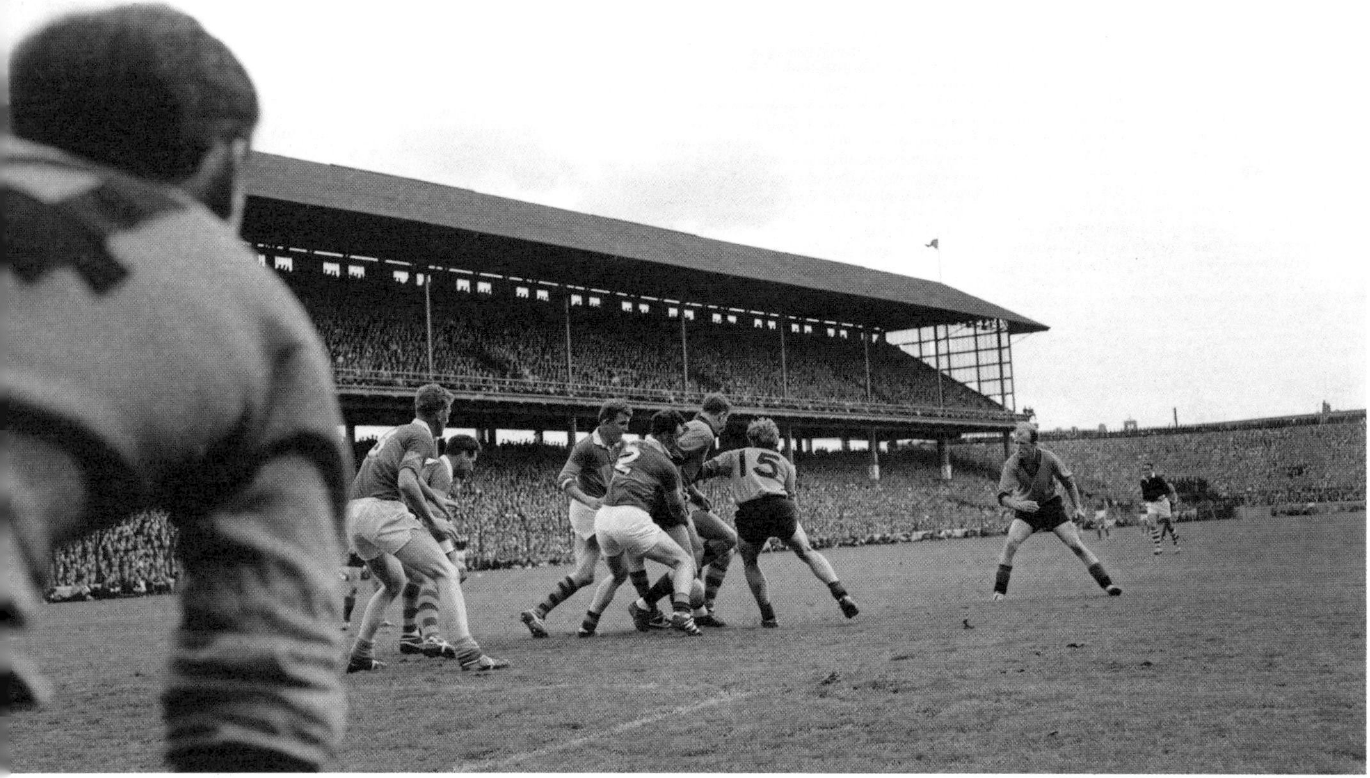

Action from the All-Ireland Senior Football Championship Final in Croke Park between Kerry and Down, which Down won 2-12 to Kerry's 1-13. Seán O'Neill and John Murphy were the goal scorers for Down, while Brendan Lynch's goal for Kerry came too late to make a difference.

22 September 1968

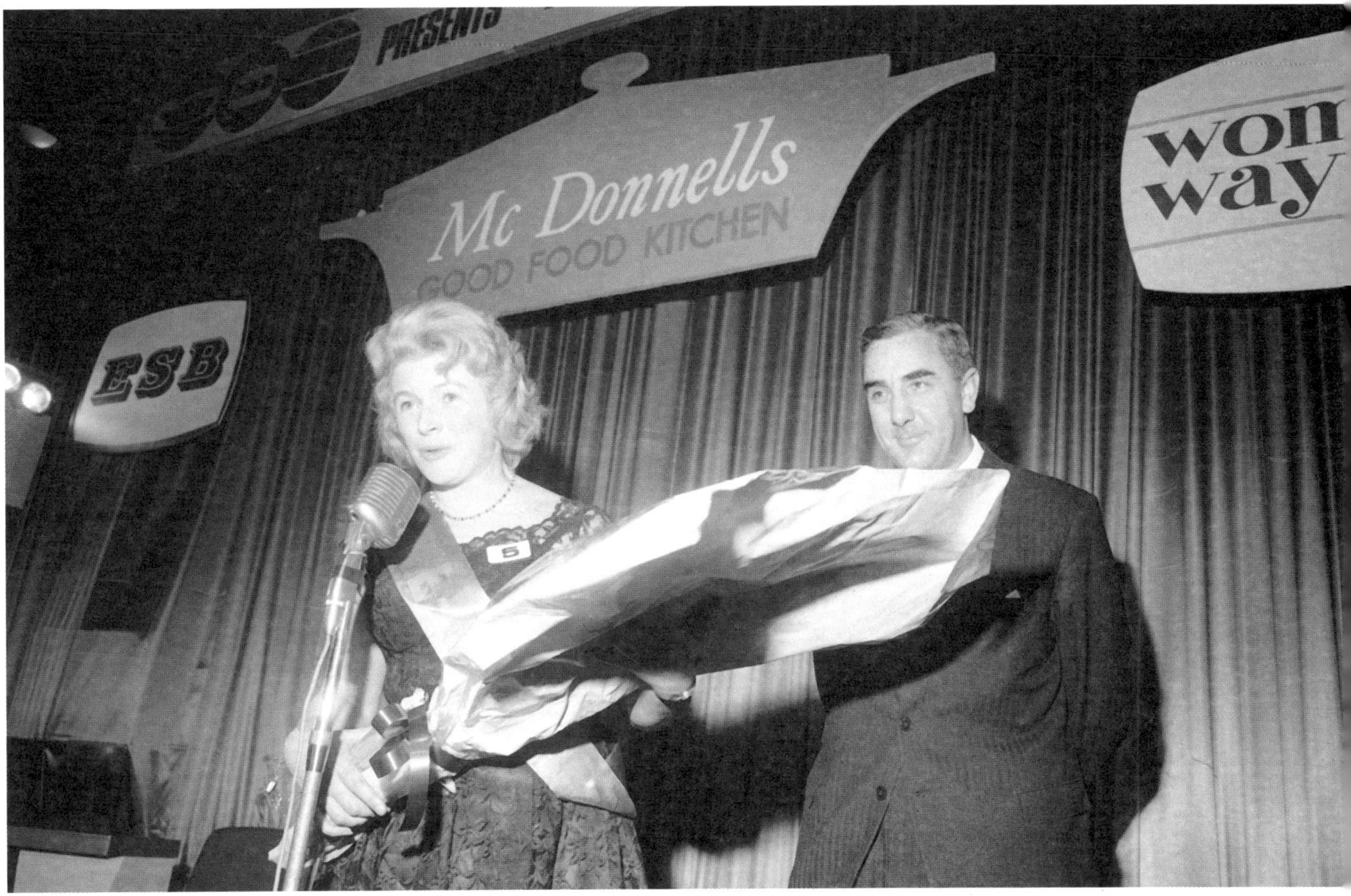

Mrs Sylvia Nagle, Killavullen, Mallow, Co Cork, after she had been chosen as Ireland's Housewife of the Year, in a competition sponsored by McDonnells, the ESB and Woman's Way.

4 November 1968

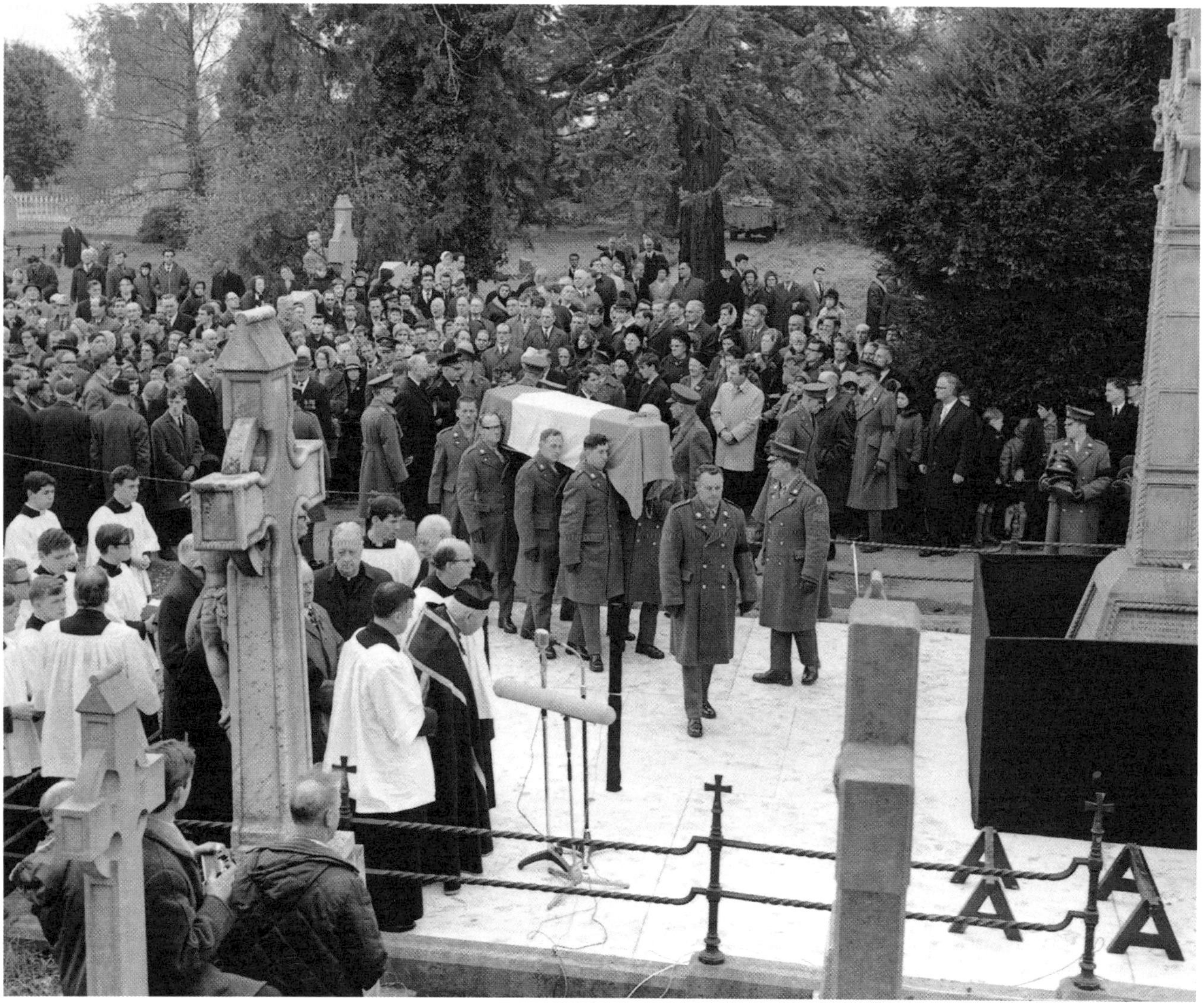

The funeral of Senator Miss Margaret Pearse, sister of Patrick and Willie Pearse, arrives at the family grave in Glasnevin cemetery.

9 November 1968

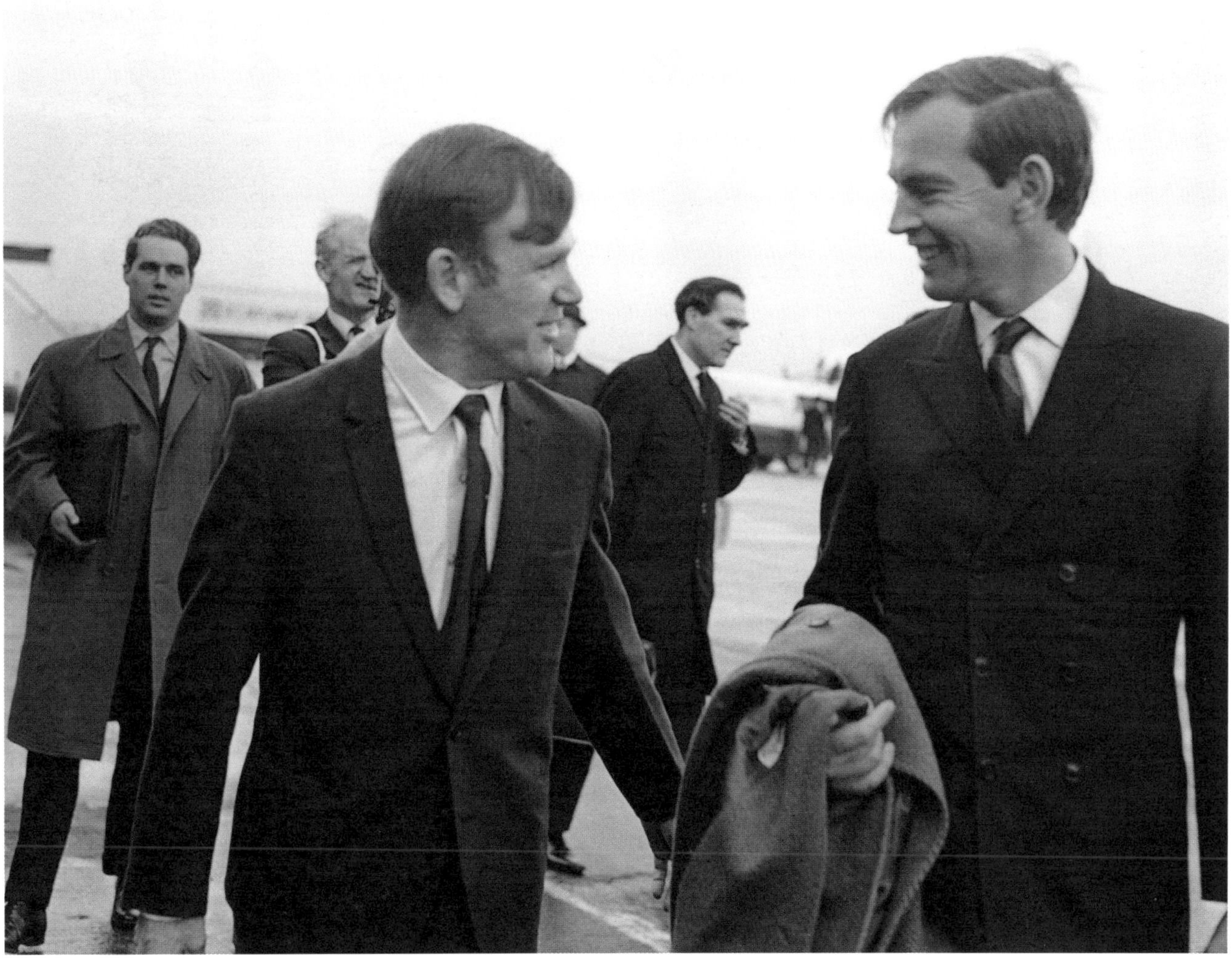

Heart transplant pioneer Dr Christian Barnard is greeted at Dublin airport by Dr John O'Connell, TD, who had arranged for him to give a lecture on Cardiac Transplantation at the Royal College of Surgeons.

11 November 1968

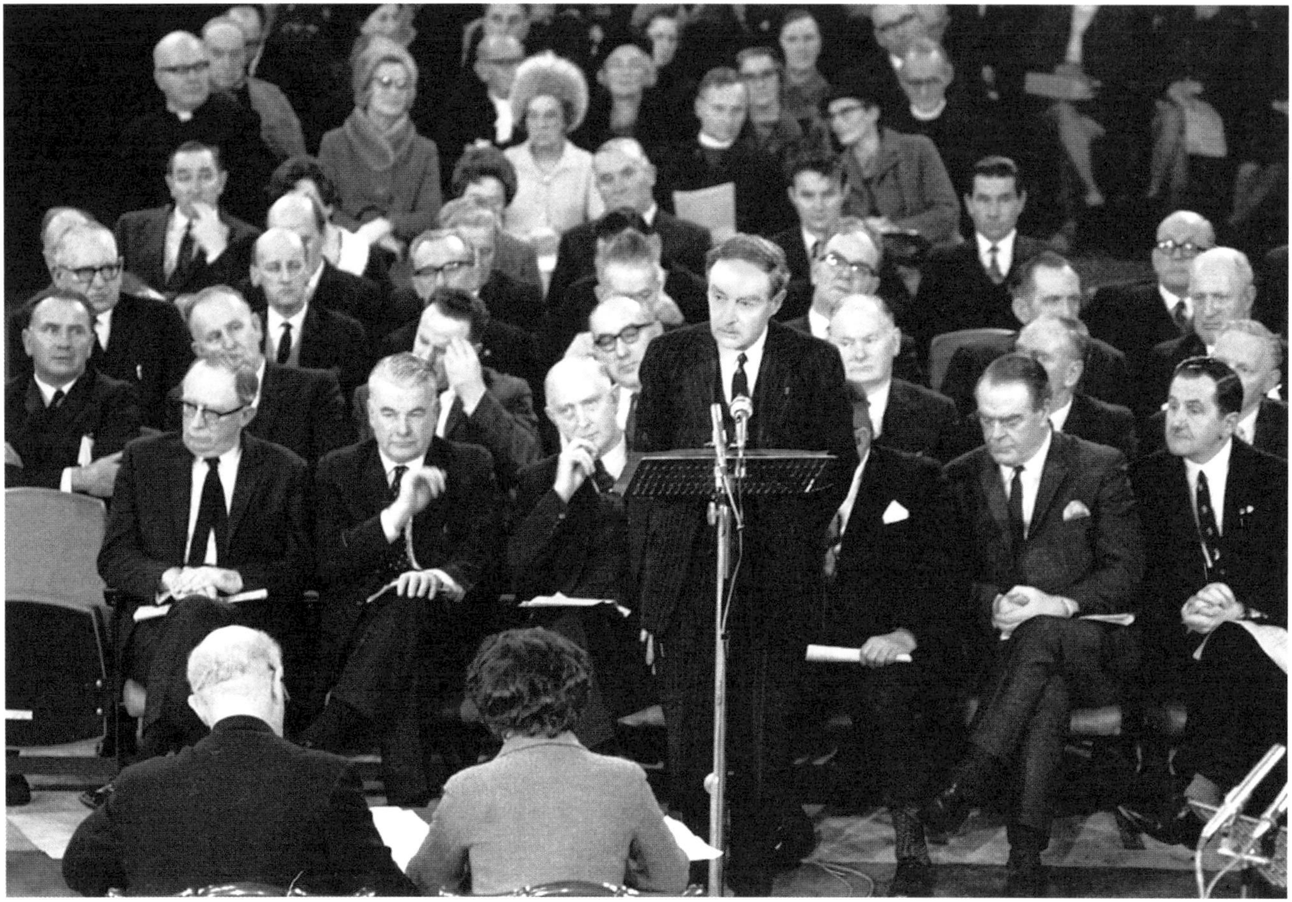

Fine Gael leader Liam Cosgrave addressing delegates at the gathering in the Mansion House to celebrate the 50th anniversary of the first Dáil.

21 January 1969

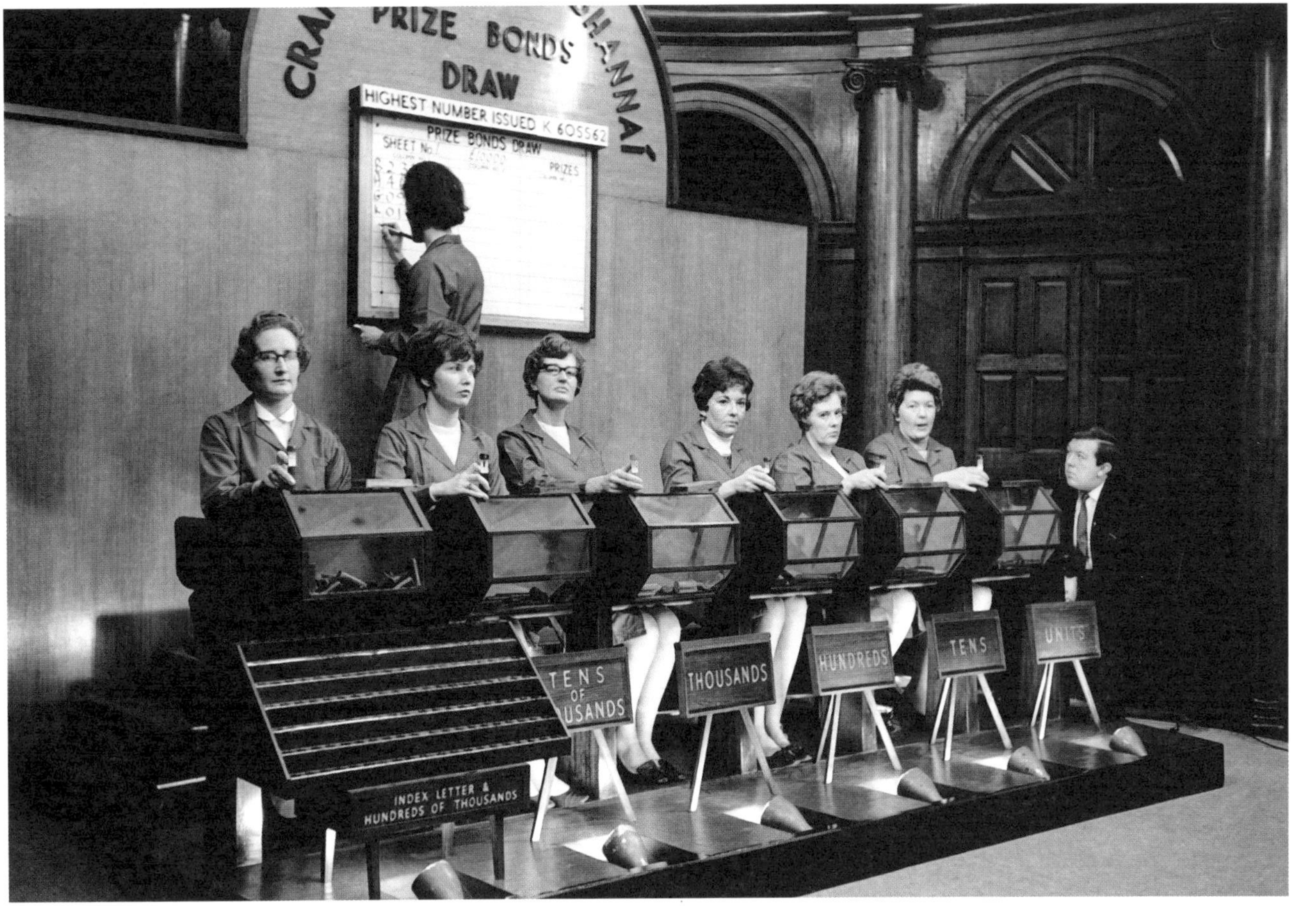

In pre-Lotto days, government-backed Prize Bonds were the only hope of a windfall on your investment, with your bond entered in a weekly draw for as long as you held it. Here the winning numbers are drawn at the Bank of Ireland. The scheme is still very popular.

3 March 1969

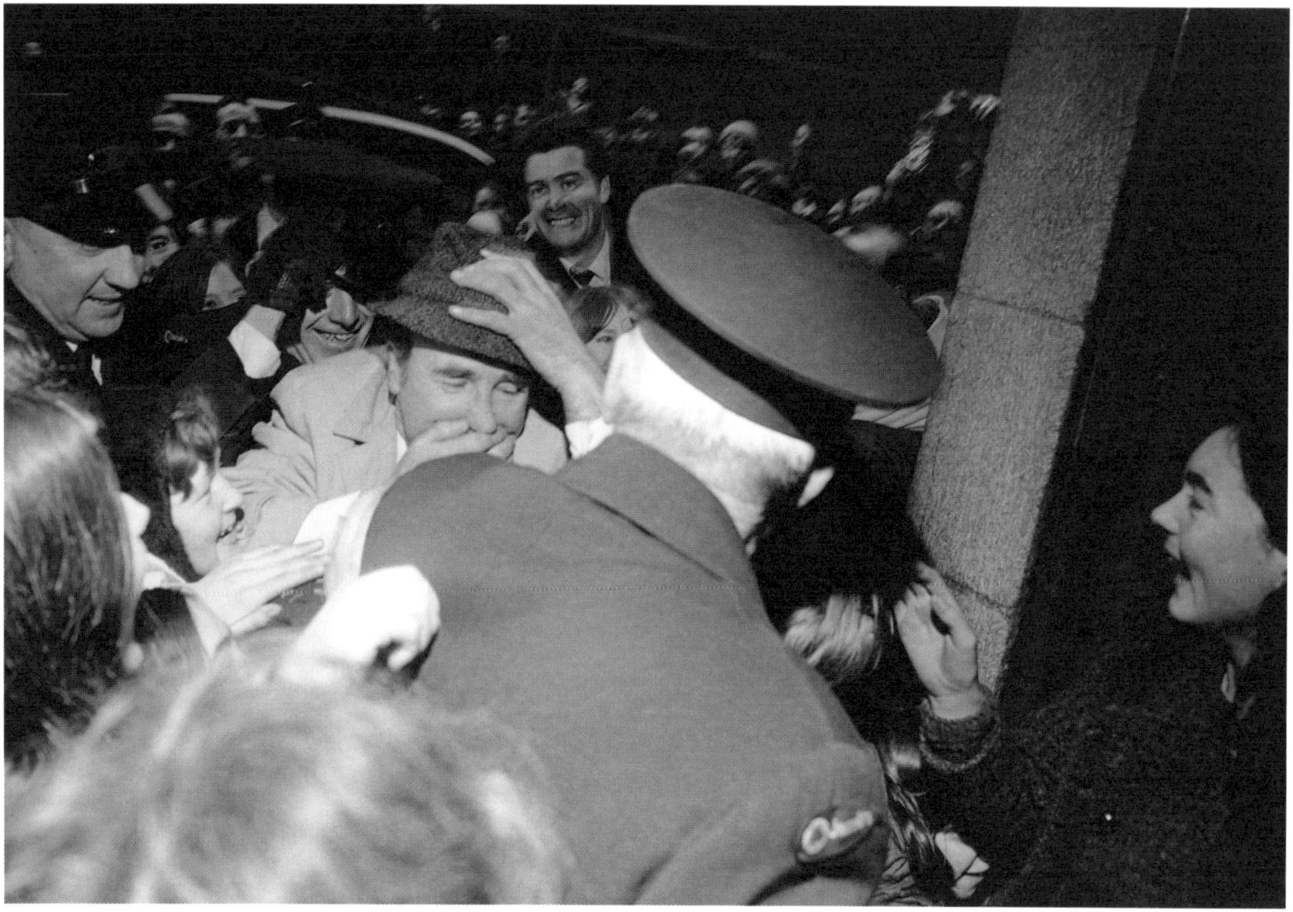

'Jim Figgerty', (holding hat) the man who put the figs in fig rolls, returns to Jacobs after a three-month absence and is mobbed by fans. Part of a hugely successful marketing campaign based on the question 'How do Jacobs get the figs in the fig roles?' Figgerty, and his sidekick, Habibi, (who asked the question in French) became part of the national consciousness.

19 March 1969

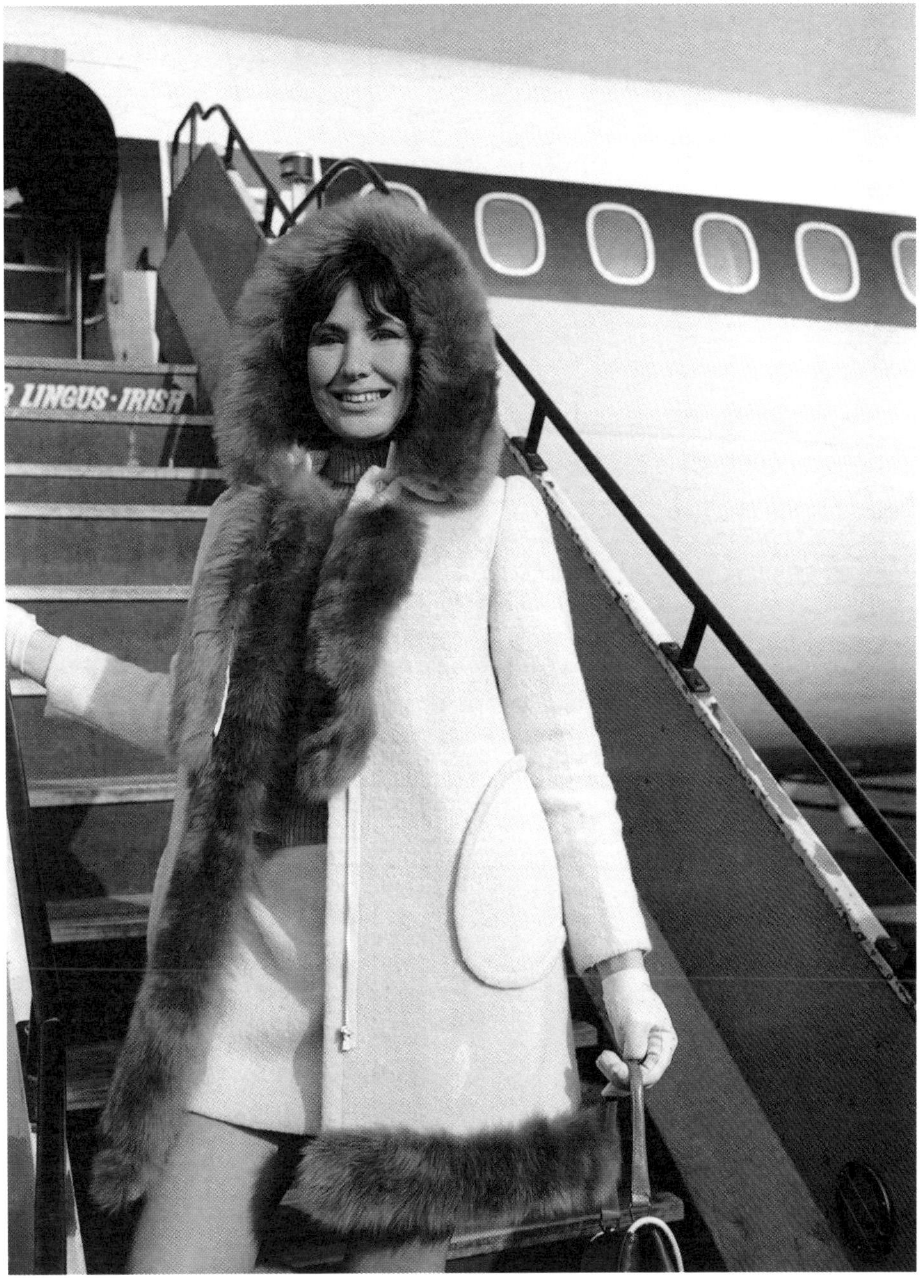

Muriel Day departs for Eurovision, Madrid. Her song, 'The Wages of Love' came seventh in a year when there were four winners: Spain, France, The Netherlands and the UK, with Lulu's 'Boom Bang-a-Bang'.

24 March 1969

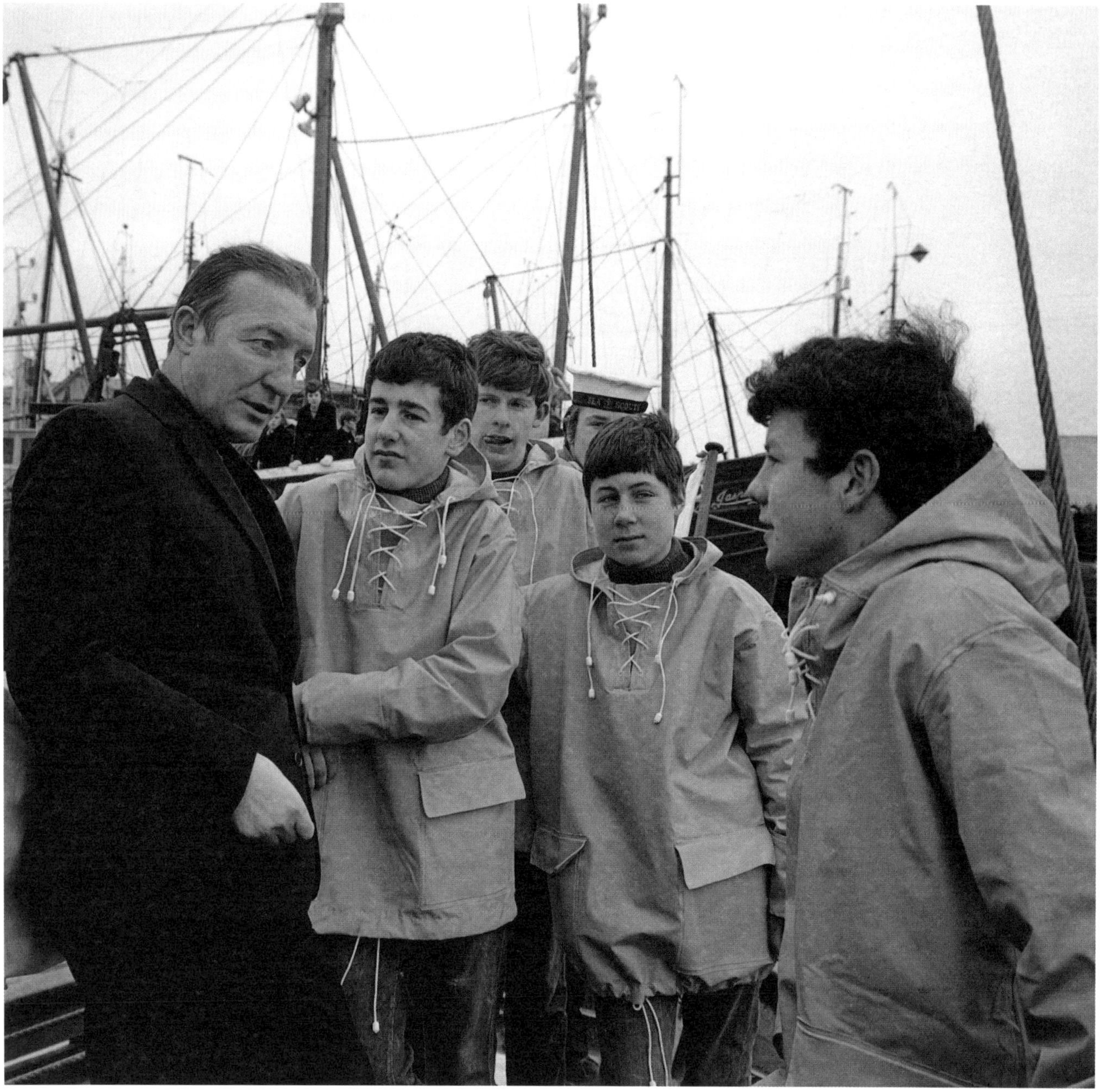

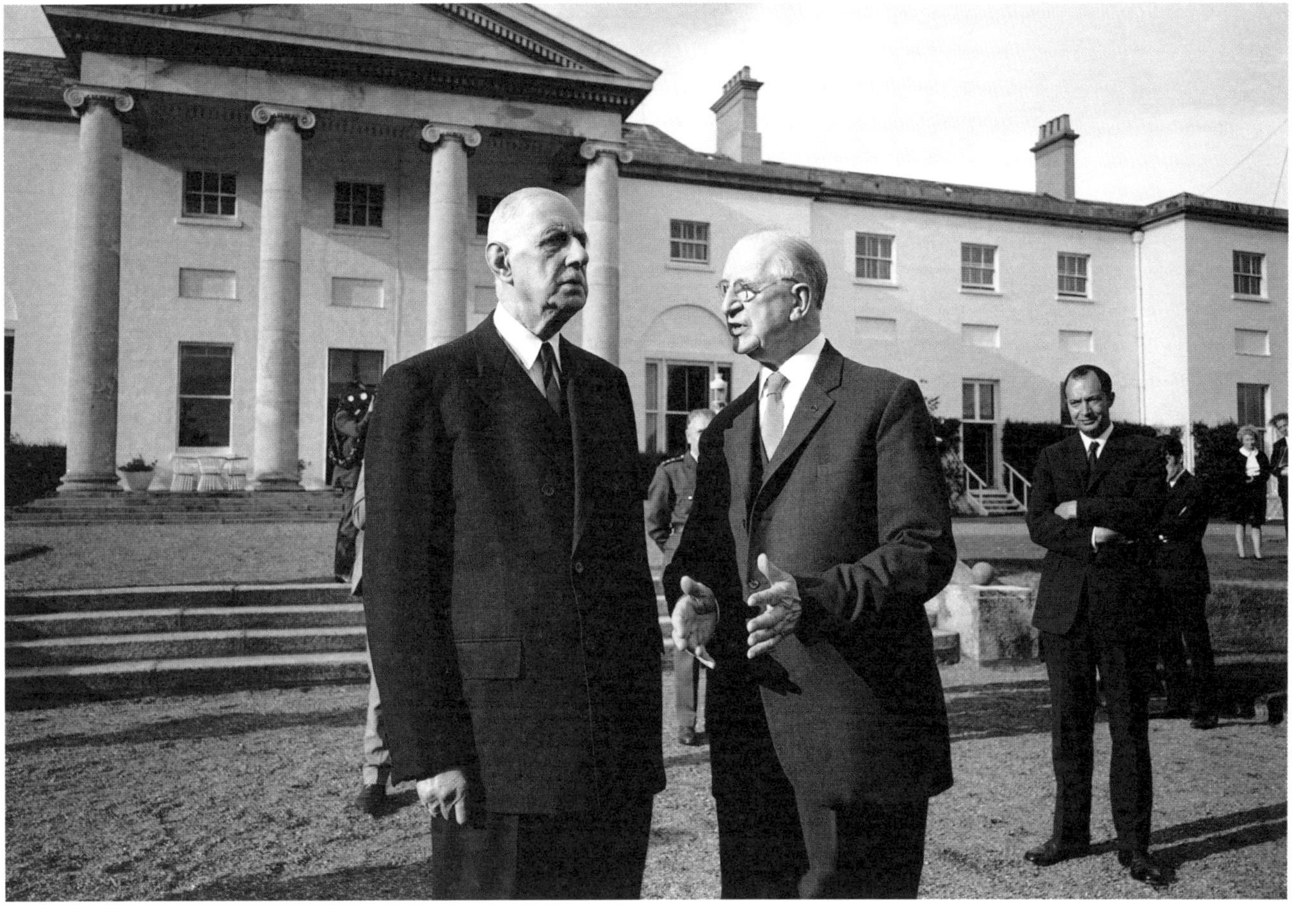

Very few visitors to the Áras could top De Valera, 'The Long Fellow' in height. But here, General de Gaulle manages to do it.

17 June 1969

Charles Haughey, himself a keen sailor, talks to young crew members at the commissioning of the Asgard as Ireland's first sail training vessel. The yacht originally belonged to Erskine Childers Snr. and was used in the 1914 Howth gun-running.

25 March 1969

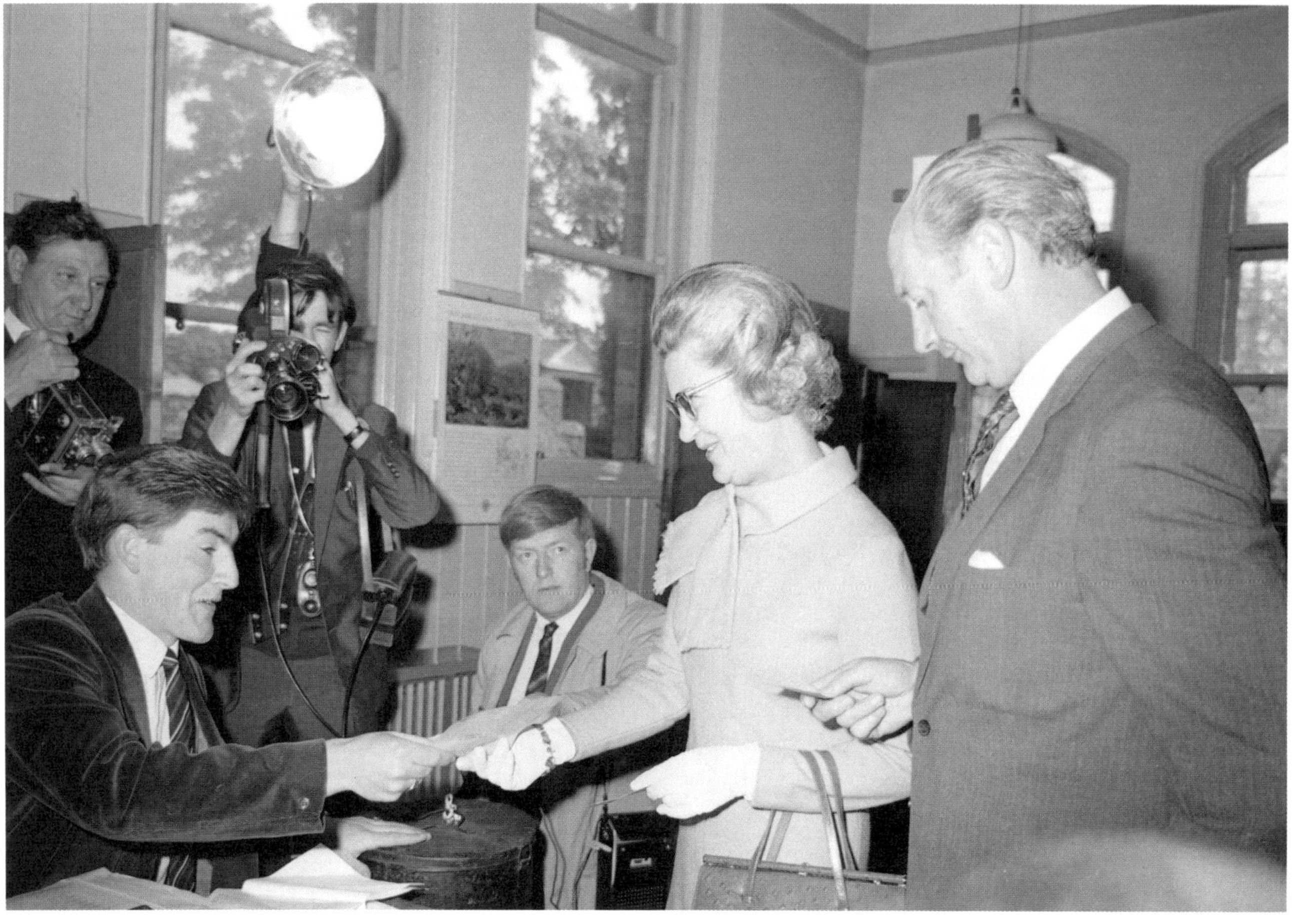

Taoiseach & Mrs Jack Lynch cast their votes
in Rathgar in the general election.

18 June 1969

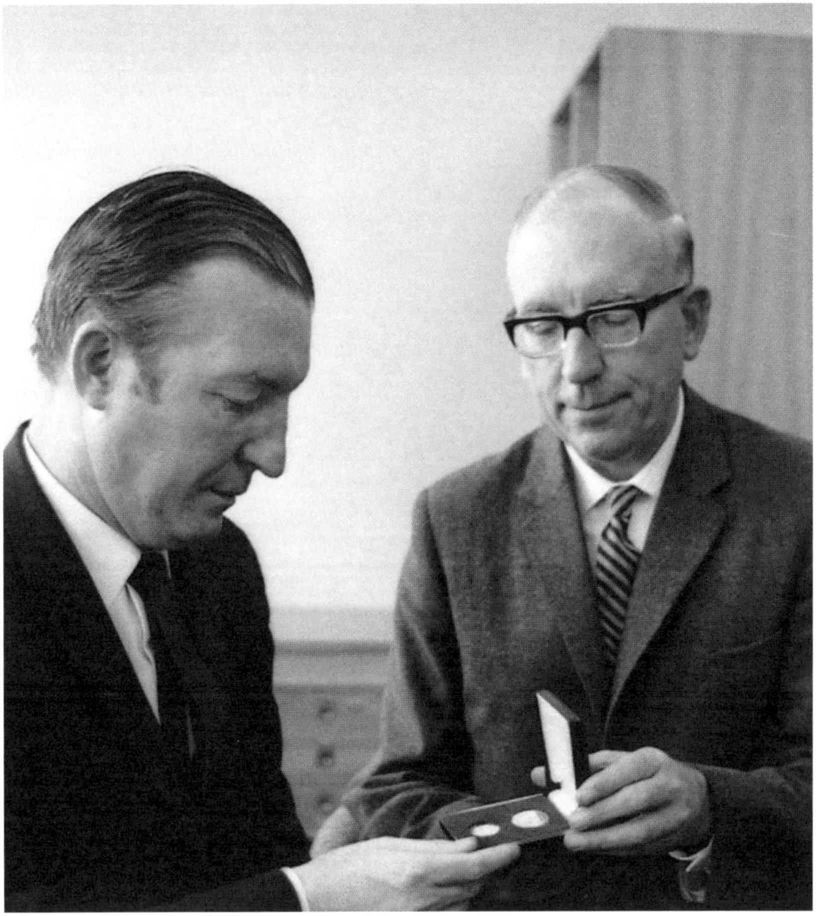

Minister for Finance Charles Haughey is formally presented with the first of Ireland's new decimal coins by Dr T K Whitaker, Governor of the Central Bank.

3 September 1969

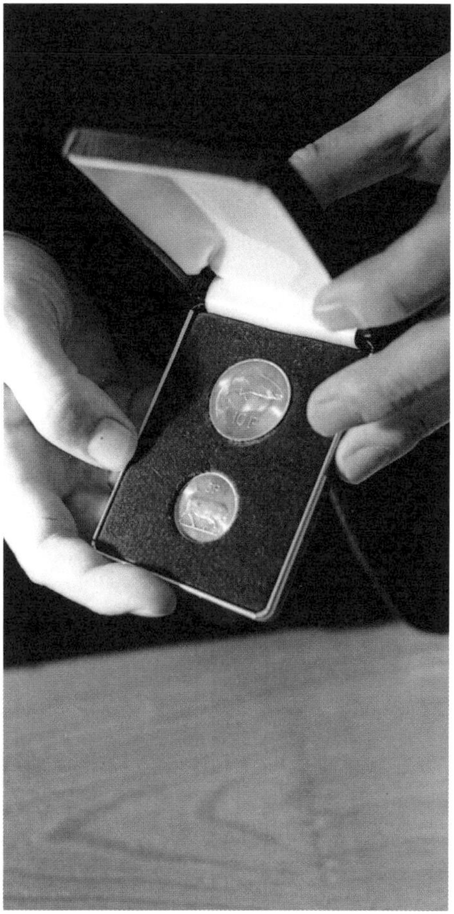

A close-up of the new 10p and 5p coins, which replaced the old 2 shilling and 1 shilling coins.

3 September 1969

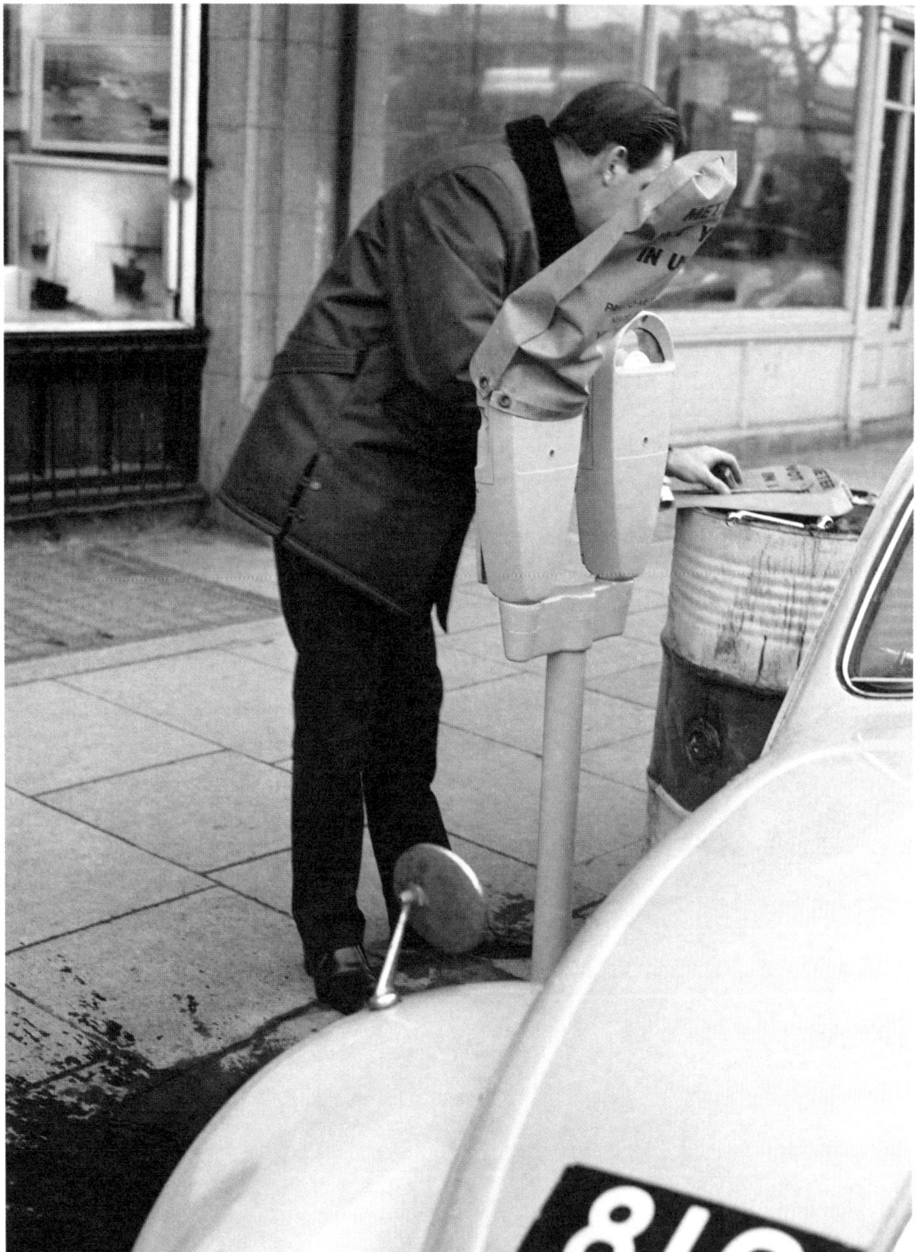

A sign of things to come: The first parking meters are installed in Dublin. They were due to come into operation in 1970.

4 December 1969

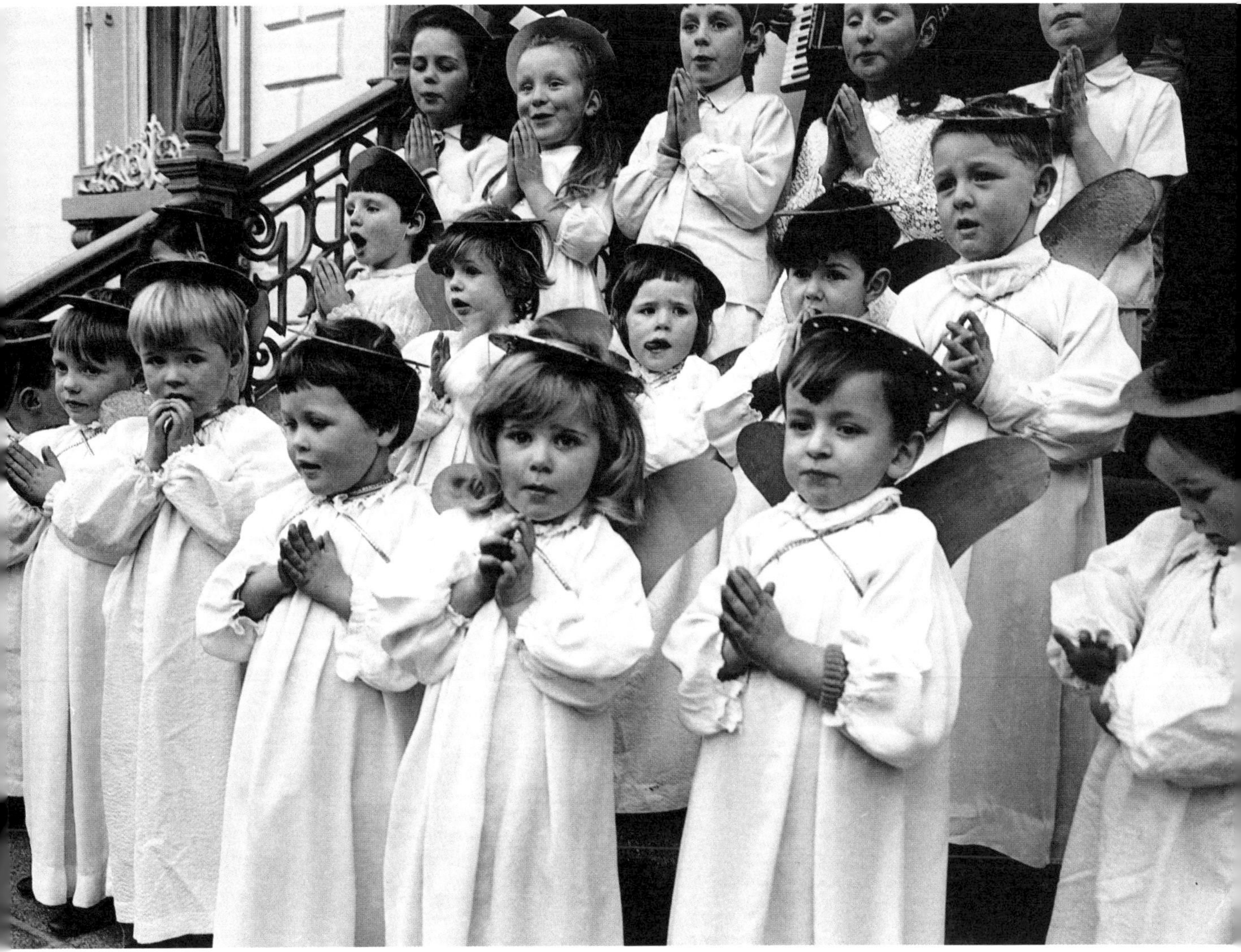

'Little Angels'- children from the Civics Institute of Ireland's nursery centres, sing at the opening of the crib at the Mansion House.

4 December 1969

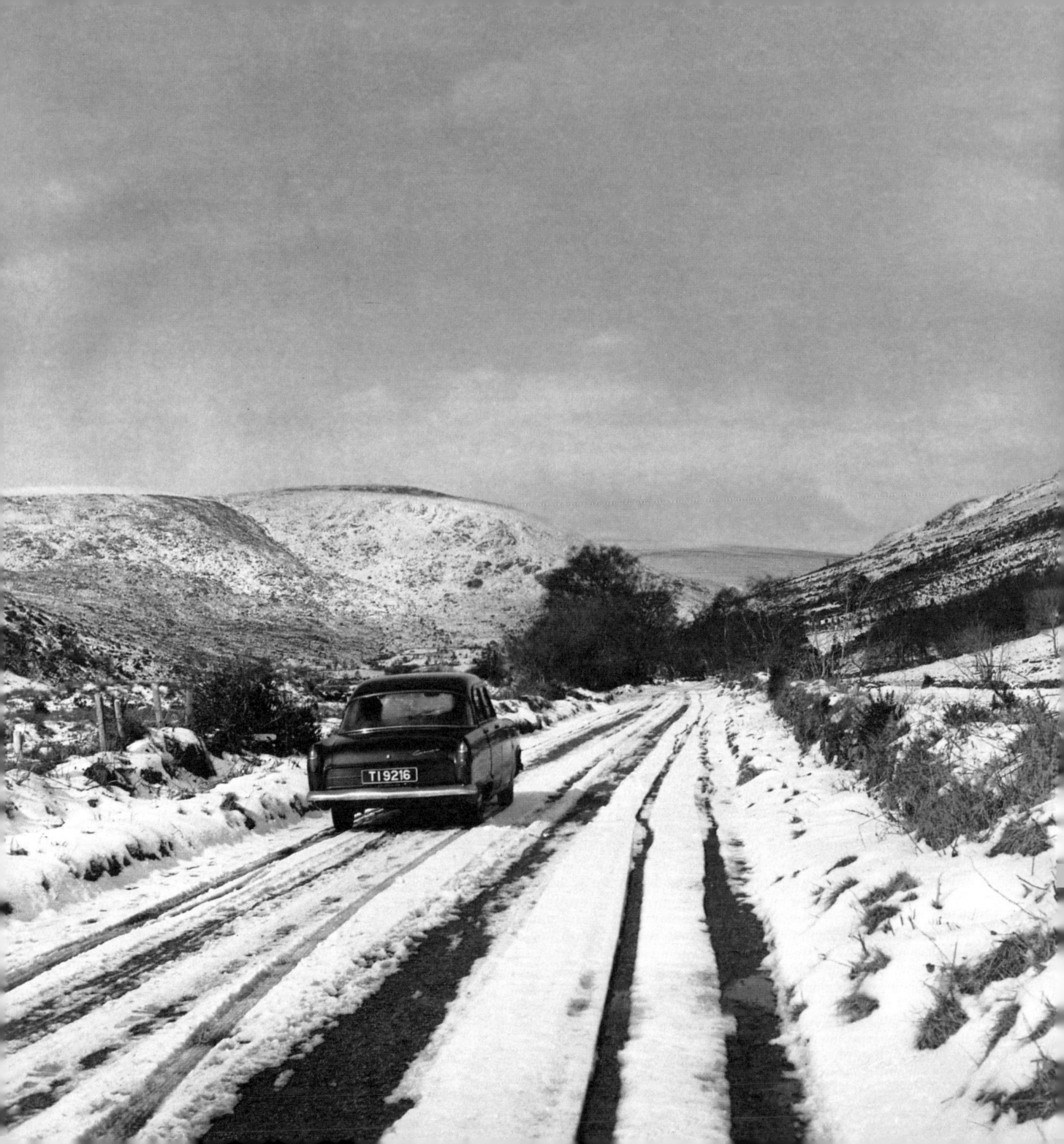
TI 9216